Intellectual Property Law in Greece

Intellectual Property Law in Greece

Second Edition

Dionysia Kallinikou
Lia I. Athanassiou
Christos Chrissanthis

This book was originally published as a monograph in the International Encyclopaedia of Laws/Intellectual Property Law.

Founding Editor: Roger Blanpain
General Editor: Frank Hendrickx
Volume Editor: Hendrik Vanhees

Wolters Kluwer

Published by:
Kluwer Law International B.V.
PO Box 316
2400 AH Alphen aan den Rijn
The Netherlands
E-mail: international-sales@wolterskluwer.com
Website: lrus.wolterskluwer.com

Sold and distributed in North, Central and South America by:
Wolters Kluwer Legal & Regulatory U.S.
7201 McKinney Circle
Frederick, MD 21704
United States of America
Email: customer.service@wolterskluwer.com

Sold and distributed in all other countries by:
Air Business Subscriptions
Rockwood House
Haywards Heath
West Sussex
RH16 3DH
United Kingdom
Email: international-customerservice@wolterskluwer.com

Printed on acid-free paper

ISBN 978-94-035-0530-5

e-Book: ISBN 978-94-035-0531-2
web-PDF: ISBN 978-94-035-0532-9

Printed in the United Kingdom.

The Authors

Dionysia Kallinikou is an Emeritus Professor of Civil and Copyright Law of the Faculty of Law-University of Athens. She holds a first degree in Law from the University of Athens, an LLM in Droit des Affaires from the University of Paris II, and a PhD in Doctorat d' Etat en Droit from the University of Paris V (1981). Her professional practice and academic interests emphasize in the field of copyright and family law. She is President of the Greek Group of ALAI and Project Leader of EU Twinning Projects in the field of intellectual property law and civil enforcement.

Lia I. Athanassiou is a Professor of Commercial Law at the Law Faculty of the University of Athens and a barrister-at-law entitled to plead before the Supreme Court. She holds a Master of Laws from the University of Athens, two LLM degrees, in Commercial Law from the University *Aix-Marseille III*) and in General Private Law from the University of *Paris II-Panthéon-Assas*, and a PhD from the University of *Paris I-Panthèon-Sorbonne,* as well as authorization by the University of *Paris I-Sorbonne* to supervise University research. She is also a visiting scholar – *Harvard Law School* (2007–2008), Fulbright Scholar (2007–2008); member of the Hellenic Competition Commission (2003–2008); and has served as member of Legislative Committees on various commercial law issues. She has published extensively on matters of Commercial, Competition, Company, European, and Shipping law. Furthermore, she has consistently participated and served as a member of the organizing committee in numerous international and national Conferences and Congresses.

The Authors

Christos Chrissanthis is an Assistant Professor of Commercial Law with the University of Athens, Faculty of Law, and a fully practising attorney-at-law at Athens, Greece. He holds a first degree in Law with honours from the University of Athens (1991), an LLM from the University of London (1992), and a PhD in Law with honours from the University of Athens (1996). His professional practice and academic interests emphasize in the fields of intellectual property, companies' acquisitions, and insurance law. He has also studied accounting, marketing, and negotiation strategies. He is a member of INTA, MARQUES, and AIDA.

Table of Contents

Table of Contents

List of Abbreviations

AP	Areios Pagos (Supreme Court of Greece)
Arm.	Armenopoulos (a Greek law journal)
ArxN	Arxeio Nomologias – Jurisprudence Archive (a Greek law journal)
CA	Court of Appeal
ChrID	ChronikaIdiotikou Dikaiou – Private Law Chronicles (a Greek law journal)
CP	Court of Peace
Ddik	Dioikitiki Diki – Administrative Trial (a Greek law journal)
DEE	Dikaio Epichiriseon & Etairion – Business and Company Law (a Greek law journal)
DIKI	Trial (a Greek law journal)
DIMEE	Dikaio Meson Enimerosis kai Epikoinonias – Media and Communication Law (a Greek law journal)
EEmpD	Epitheorisi Emporikou Dikaiou – Commercial Law Review (a Greek law journal)
EEN	Efimeris Ellinon Nomikon – Greek Jurists Journal (a Greek law journal)
EllDni	Elliniki Dikaiosyni – Greek Justice (a Greek law journal)
EPC	European Patent Convention
EpiskED	Episkopisi Emporikou Dikaiou – Commercial Law Appraisal (a Greek law journal)
GCC	Greek Civil Code
Int'l Tax & Bus. Law	International Tax and Business Lawyer (an American law journal)
IUS	(a Greek law journal)
KrEp	Kritiki Epitheorisi – Critical Review (a Greek law journal)

List of Abbreviations

L.	Law
MD	Ministerial Decision
MMCFI	Multi-Member Court of First Instance
Ndik	Neon Dikaion – New Law (a Greek law journal)
NoV	Nomiko Vima – Law Tribune (a Greek law journal)
OG	Official Gazette of the Hellenic Republic
RIDA	Revue Internationale du Droit d'Auteur
SMCFI	Single-Member Court of First Instance
Themis	(a Greek law journal)

General Introduction[1]

§1. General Background

I. Geography

1. Located in south-eastern Europe, on the Balkan Peninsula, Greece[2] is one of the oldest countries in the world, whose civilization has set the foundations for the western way of thinking. Although Greece is a rather small country,[3] it possesses a tremendous coastline of about 13,676 km, including the mainland as well as the Greek islands, whose number reaches that of 6,000, along with numerous uninhabited islets.[4] The northern part of the Greek mainland borders with Albania, Bulgaria, and the former Yugoslav Republic of Macedonia (FYROM), the western part is surrounded by the Ionian Sea, the southern by the Mediterranean Sea, and the eastern by the Aegean Sea and Turkey. Greece is divided into nine distinct regions: Thrace, Macedonia, Epirus, Thessaly, Central Greece, Peloponnesus, the Ionian Islands, the Aegean Islands, and Crete. The capital of Greece is Athens.

II. Cultural Composition

2. Greece has always been a homogeneous country in terms of cultural composition, which is mainly reflected in its culture, language, population, and religious beliefs. It is believed that the first Greek-speaking population inhabited the Greek mainland around 1900 B.C. Modern Greek language and culture have maintained many elements of their predecessors.

3. From the beginning of Greek history to the present, wars and foreign dominations have played a key role in shaping the Greek culture, politics, and economic development, the most important being the Ottoman domination (*Tourkokratia*), which lasted for nearly 400 years (1453–1821) and had a huge impact in the present

1. The authors wish to thank and acknowledge Mr George Panitsas, attorney-at-law LLM, for his valuable contribution in the Introduction Section.
2. Official name: Hellenic Republic. In Greek the country is called 'Ellada' or 'Hellas'.
3. Greece is the ninety-seventh largest country in the world.
4. Official Website of Greek Tourism Organization (EOT), available at http://www.visitgreece.gr/en/geography.

cultural composition of the country. Throughout this long period of foreign occupation, Greece managed to preserve its solid cultural background, language, religion, and traditions. In 1922–1923, following the Convention Concerning the Exchange of Greek and Turkish Populations signed on 30 January 1923 in Lausanne, many Greeks who lived in Asia Minor were evacuated or relocated to Greece. The Greeks of Asia Minor had a very strong influence on the economy and culture of the Greek State.

4. The official language is Greek and is spoken by around 98% of the population. This language (Modern Greek) is based on Ancient Greek, which no longer exists as a spoken language.[5]

5. The prevailing religion is that of the Eastern Orthodox Church of Christ. Western Thrace is inhabited by the Muslim minority of Greece, who number 140,000, and they are the only minority in the country who are officially recognized by the Greek State. The Muslim minority enjoys special privileges from the Greek State and comprise mostly of people of Turkish origin.

6. Since 1990, Greece has received many immigrants, mostly from the Balkans and the countries of the former Soviet Union. Further, thanks to its strategic location, Greece is often seen as the perfect gateway to the rest of Europe. It is to be noted that illegal immigration, coming mostly from Asia and Africa, has been an escalating problem for Greece over the past two decades.

7. As far as education in Greece is concerned, according to the Greek Constitution, all Greeks must complete nine years of compulsory education (Article 16(3) Constitution). Education is free on all levels, at State educational institutions. In general, Greeks tend to pursue university degrees, in their own country as well as abroad.

III. Political System

8. Greece is a parliamentary republic. The present Constitution of Greece came into force in 1975. It has been amended three times, i.e., in 1986, 2001, and 2008. Inspired by Montesquieu's principle of 'the separation of powers',[6] the Constitution provides for the separation of the State's powers among three branches: the legislative, the executive, and the judicial (Article 26).

9. The legislative power is exercised by the Parliament and the President of the Republic. The Parliament consists of 300 members, elected through direct, universal, and secret ballot. The citizens with the right to vote must be at least 18 years

5. However, Ancient Greek is a basic material subject in the educational system of Greece.
6. 'La séparation des pouvoirs' *Baron de Montesquieu*, '*De l'esprit des lois*', 1748. *Montesquieu* was inspired by the British constitutional system where there was separation of powers among the monarch, the parliament and the courts of law.

old. The Members of Parliament are elected for a period of four consecutive years, with the possibility to be re-elected. The President of the Republic is elected by the Parliament through personal nominal vote, for a term of five years, while re-election of the same person as President is permitted only once. The President regulates the function of the institutions of the Republic. Bills and law proposals are debated and voted by the Parliament. The President of the Republic promulgates and publishes the laws passed by the Parliament within one month of the vote. During this time limit, the President may send back a bill or law passed by the Parliament, stating his reasons for not sanctioning the law. If the law is passed again by the absolute majority of the total number of the Members of the Parliament, then the President of the Republic is bound to promulgate and publish it.

10. The executive power is vested in the hands of the President of the Republic and the Government. The Government, constituted by the Cabinet, which is composed of the Prime Minister and the Ministers, defines and directs the general policy of the country in compliance with the provisions of the Constitution and the laws (Article 82(1) Constitution). The Prime Minister safeguards the unity of the Government and directs its actions. According to Article 37 of the Constitution, the President of the Republic appoints as Prime Minister the leader of the party that has the absolute majority of seats in the Parliament. The other members of the Government are recommended by the Prime Minister and appointed by the President. The Government must enjoy the confidence of the Parliament and is obliged to request a vote of confidence by the latter. The Parliament may decide to withdraw its confidence from the Government or from one of its members.

11. The judicial power is exercised by three categories of courts with civil, criminal, and administrative jurisdictions. The civil and criminal courts include the Courts of Peace, the Courts of First Instance, the Courts of Appeal, and the Supreme Court (Areios Pagos), which operates as a cassation court. The administrative courts deal with matters of administrative nature, i.e., disputes between the Greek State and the citizens. The Council of State has the highest jurisdiction with regard to these matters. There is also the Court of Auditors (*Elegtiko Synedrio*), whose main mission is to audit the financial transactions of the State and those of public sector entities. Judges enjoy functional and personal independence.

12. The Greek legal system is based on Civil/Roman Law, where only the legislation is accepted as a source of law, as opposed to Common Law countries which recognize two sources of law: the legislation as well as the jurisprudence. Greek courts are bound not to apply laws whose content is contrary to the Constitution, according to Article 93(4) of the Constitution.

13. The Constitution provides, in Article 28(1), that the international conventions, which are sanctioned by law, are an integral part of domestic law and superior to any contrary provision of national law. This provision is of vast importance, especially when it comes to intellectual property law, as Greece has been a Contracting State to many international intellectual property conventions. In the same vein, we should remind our readers that, since Greece is a member of the European Union (EU), European law naturally takes precedence over any form of Greek law, including the Constitution.[7]

IV. Population Statistics

14. According to the official 2011 census performed by the Greek Statistical Authority,[8] the population of Greece reached 10,815,197 persons in 2011. The Eurostat, in its turn, counted 11,309,885 people inhabiting Greece on 1 January 2011.[9] During the last fifty years the population of Greece has increased by approximately 27% (8,331,700 in 1960). A significant part of the population are inhabitants of Athens and the wider region of Attica (3,074,160), whereas the rest of Greece, especially the rural locations, is sparsely populated.

15. Greece faces a serious decrease in fertility and mortality rate and a higher life expectancy of the population, which is a common demographic phenomenon in the majority of European countries ('Aging Europe').[10] According to the World Bank, the annual growth rate during the period 2008–2012 was 0.2%.[11]

§2. Historical Background

16. The science of history itself was primarily conceived in Ancient Greece by the famous Greek historian Herodotus, who pioneered the technique of narrative history and became known as the 'father of history'.

17. The Greek civilization emerged around 1900 B.C. and influenced Western civilization like no other. One of the most important periods of Greek history was the 'Classical Period', which is placed between 510 B.C. and the death of Alexander the Great (323 B.C.). Athens, during this period, was one of the most important City–States in Greece, where democracy was born, and a centre of science, art, and philosophy. Another important period of Greek history is between the years 330 and 1453 when Greece was part of the Roman Empire, also referred to by historians as the Byzantine Empire. The capital of the Byzantine Empire was Constantinople, known today as Istanbul. In this introductory chapter, we will not proceed to

7. Case C-11/70- *Internationale Handelsgesellschaft MBH v. Einfuhr- und Vorratsstellefür Getreide und Futtermittel of 17 Dec. 1970.* Also Case C-6/64 – *Costa v. E.N.E.L. of 15 Jul. 1964.*
8. *Greek Statistical Authority Press Release of 23 Aug. 2013* (in Greek) available at http://www.statistics.gr/portal/page/portal/ESYE/BUCKET/General/nws_SAM01_GR.PDF.
9. At http://epp.eurostat.ec.europa.eu/tgm/table.do?tab=table&init=1&plugin=1&language=en&pcode=tps00001.
10. According to the European Commission in 2060, one third of Europe's population will be aged 65 or over, http://ec.europa.eu/economy_finance/articles/structural_reforms/2012-05-15_ageing_report_en.htm.
11. At http://data.worldbank.org/indicator/SP.POP.GROW.

further reference regarding the Ancient Greek Civilization or the Byzantine Empire, but we will mainly focus on the development of the Modern Greek State.

18. In 1453 the Ottoman Turks conquered Constantinople, and the Byzantine Empire collapsed. After the fall of Constantinople, all the land that comprised the Modern Greek State became part of the Ottoman Empire. In 1821 the Greeks rose up against the Ottoman Empire, and in 1829 the Great Powers (France, Britain, and Russia) recognized the claims of the Greek rebels, while in 1832, under the Treaty of Istanbul, Greece was recognized as a fully independent kingdom, which consisted of Peloponnesus and a part of Central Greece. The first governor of Greece was Ioannis Kapodistrias (1828), who was assassinated in 1831. In 1832 the Great Powers chose Otto of Wittelsbach, a Bavarian noble, as the King of Greece. Otto reigned for thirty years. In 1863 Otto was forced, due to a military rebellion, to resign and leave the country. After Otto was forced to leave, the Great Powers appointed George, a Danish prince, as King of Greece, and due to the fact that King George was pro-British, Britain ceded the Ionian Islands to Greece. In 1896 the first Olympic Games of the modern era were staged in Athens.

19. After the Balkan Wars of 1912–1913, Crete, the Aegean Islands, Epirus, and Macedonia were annexed to the Kingdom of Greece. After World War I, Smyrna, located in Asia Minor, and its hinterlands, which were all inhabited by Greek nationals, were occupied by the Greek troops. During the Greco-Turkish war of 1919–1922, Greek nationals were forced to leave Asia Minor. During World War II Greece refused to submit to Italy, and later on to Germany. Greek troops were able to repel the Italian army but were not able to stop the German troops, and the latter occupied Greece, until October 1944. In 1947 the Dodecanese Islands were united with Greece. After the end of the war Greece entered into a civil war until 1949, between the Governmental forces of Greece, supported by the UK and the US, and the military branch of the Greek communist party (Democratic Army of Greece), supported by the Soviet Union. The civil war concluded with the victory of the Governmental army, and Greece joined NATO. The period 1949–1967 was extremely turbulent as the wounds of the civil war were not fully healed, and the relationships between the King of Greece and some of the political leaders were tense. The continuing political crisis of that period peaked on 21 April 1967, when a group of colonels seized power in a coup d'état and established a military junta.

20. After the fall of the military junta in 1974, Konstantinos Karamanlis returned from exile to establish a Government that would organize national elections. In 1974 a referendum took place, which resulted in the abolition of monarchy. Karamanlis founded the political party New Democracy (ND) and won the majority of the seats in the Parliament, in the elections of 1975 and of 1977. On January 1981, Greece became a member of the European Community (the predecessor of the EU), and in October 1981 the political party PASOK, which was founded and led by Andreas Papandreou, won the national elections. PASOK again won the national elections in June 1985. In the elections of 1989 coalition Governments were formed, and on February 1990 ND, led by Konstantinos Mitsotakis, won the elections. Due to internal disagreements this Government collapsed, and in the elections of September 1993 PASOK won the majority of the seats in the Parliament. After the death of Andreas Papandreou, Kostantinos Simitis succeeded him as leader of PASOK and won the elections in 1996 and in 2000. In the elections of March 2004, as well as in those of September 2007, Kostas Karamanlis[12] led ND to victory. On June 2012 Antonis Samaras won the elections and coalition Governments were formed (ND, PASOK, Democratic Left and ND, PASOK). Today Greece is governed by a coalition Government of SYRIZA (Alexis Tsipras) and ANEL.

§3. Introduction to Intellectual Property Law

I. The Concept of Intellectual Property Law

21. Intellectual property (IP) law is the set of rules regulating the legal rights that stem from any kind of intellectual activity in the industrial, scientific, literary, and artistic fields.[13]

22. IP law is divided into two main branches: copyright and industrial property. Copyright includes rights relating to literary, artistic, and scientific works (author's rights), as well as performances of performing artists, phonograms, and broadcasts, which are usually called 'related rights'. Industrial property includes patents, industrial designs, trademarks, and other distinctive signs, as well as protection against unfair competition.[14]

23. IP law grants exclusive rights to the creator which consist in:

- Exclusive property rights: the holder of the IP right becomes the legitimate owner of his creation, having the exclusive right to manage and economically exploit the latter, either directly or indirectly. In addition, the holder of the IP right has the power to prevent any third party from using/exploiting his intellectual creation.
- Moral right: in the case of copyright and patents the holder of the IP right has the right of attribution and the right to the integrity of his work.[15]

12. Nephew of Konstantinos Karamanlis.
13. According to Art. 2(viii) of the Convention Establishing the World Intellectual Property Organization (WIPO) (14 Jul. 1967), '*intellectual property shall include rights relating to: literary, artistic and scientific works, performances of performing artists, phonograms and broadcasts, inventions in all fields of human endeavor, scientific discoveries, industrial designs, trademarks, service marks and commercial names and designations, protection against unfair competition, and all other rights resulting from intellectual activity in the industrial, scientific, literary or artistic fields*'. Further, *see WIPO Intellectual property Handbook*, 3, http://www.wipo.int/export/sites/www/about-ip/en/iprm/pdf/ch1.pdf.
14. *See* Art. 10*bis* (2) of Paris Convention for the Protection of Industrial Property.
15. Regarding copyright, according to Art. 6*bis* of the Berne Convention the author's moral right is the '*right to claim authorship of the work and to object to any distortion, mutilation or other modification of, or other derogatory action in relation to, the said work, which would be prejudicial to his honor or reputation*'.

24. Copyright provides exclusive rights to the creator of an original intellectual creation and covers the form, in which the ideas are expressed, and not the ideas themselves. As already mentioned above, the works protected by copyright are divided into two categories: the author's rights and the related rights that *can be described as the 'carriers' of the authors' rights.*[16] Computer programs and databases are also included in the scope of copyright protection.[17]

25. Patents are granted upon application, by a Governmental authority, and provide that only the holder of the IP right can economically exploit the patented invention.[18] Further, utility models are another type of IP rights similar to patents, yet characterized by a lesser degree of protection.

26. A trademark is a sign[19] used as a distinctive element of goods and services. Once a trademark is registered, the holder of the IP right is granted the exclusive right to use the specific trademark for the classes of products or services that he has registered. Hence, the owner of a trademark is granted a monopoly[20] over the use of the trademark for as long as registration lasts.[21] Besides trademarks, there are also other distinctive signs, such as company names, distinctive titles, and other distinctive marks.

27. A silicon or microchip, legally known as topography of a semiconductor product, is an article that performs an electronic function. The law defines a topography of a semiconductor product as *a series of related images, however fixed or encoded, (i) representing the three-dimensional pattern of the layers of which a semiconductor product is composed and (ii) in which series every image includes the pattern or part of the pattern of a surface of the semiconductor product at any stage of its manufacture.*[22]

28. Unfair competition is a set of rules that comprise mainly of torts as well as criminal offences that harm a business due to a wrongful, deceptive, or immoral practice of a competitor. Unfair competition legal regimes preserve that competitors will operate in a fair way. From our point of view, the rules of unfair competition provide protection to intellectual creations, which are not protected by an IP right.[23]

16. C. Colston, *Principles of Intellectual Property Law*, 28 (Cavendish Publishing London-Sydney 1999).
17. *See* Arts 4 and 5 of WIPO Copyright Treaty that was adopted in Geneva on 20 Dec. 1996.
18. The term 'patent' is also used to describe the administrative act that grants the patent right.
19. It can be a logo, a phrase or a slogan, a name, a word or even a single letter, a number, a design or a symbol, etc.
20. *See* footnote 25.
21. C. Colston, *supra* n. 16, at 5.
22. Article 2(b). PD 45/1991.
23. *WIPO Intellectual property Handbook*, 131, http://www.wipo.int/export/sites/www/about-ip/en/iprm/pdf/ch2.pdf.

II. Justification of IP Law

29. In order to appreciate the importance of IP law, one must first examine the various functions of IP rights, not only from the legal point of view but also from the socio-economic standpoint.

30. First and foremost, as stated above, IP protection is provided through proprietary rights. In other words, the creator becomes the owner of his creation, which means that no one has a legitimate right to 'use' his creation without his permission. But why would the ownership of such 'property' be so important to the creator? Why would the law be so sympathetic towards the creator and so eager to protect his rights? One can defend the creator's interests simply by relating to his efforts: why not protect and reward, both financially and morally, a person who has used his brains and invested his time and even his money to create a novelty, and therefore hopes, with good reason, to obtain financial benefits as well as recognition in return, both of which, of course, would be ruined if everyone could claim his creation as their own.

31. Needless to say, by ensuring such protection for the creator, IP law gives strong incentives and encourages the bringing of new products and ideas to the market, which can contribute to the technological, scientific, or cultural progress or economic growth. Hence, IP law serves the society as a whole, not only the creator himself.

32. A strong legal framework regarding IP law is, therefore, imperative for a country in order to attract important investments. Multinational enterprises would not jeopardize their investments by entering into a market where they wouldn't be able to protect their legitimate interests in their products, services, and ideas.

33. Every type of IP right has a unique purpose and scope of protection; copyright gives incentives for creativity and protects the author's reputation while patents encourage invention and innovation. Trademark law protects not only the consumer, by allowing him to distinguish the origin and quality of a product or service, but also the reputation and brand name of an enterprise and the business itself, i.e., the producer, who, in fact, commercializes the above creations/inventions.[24]

34. In the light of the above, we should not lose sight of the interests of the other parties of the market, such as the consumers, whose choices of consumption are mainly determined by two criteria: quality and good prices. Nevertheless, when it comes to the protection of the consumers, there is a great deal of doubt as to exactly how important and effective IP law really is. First of all IP rights create a

24. J.E. Somorjai, *The Evolution of a Common Market: Limits Imposed on the Protection of National Intellectual Property Rights in the European Economic Community*, 9 Int'l Tax & Bus. L. 431 6–7 (1992), http://scholarship.law.berkeley.edu/bjil/vol9/iss2/4.

monopoly;[25] only the holder of the IP right and him alone can use a trademark for a specific product or service, or can economically exploit a patent or a copyrighted work, etc. However, monopolies are not compatible with the concept of a free market economy, which falls into the scope of protection of competition/antitrust law. Moreover, monopolies are not in the consumers' best interests either, as they tend to keep prices high by controlling the supply and put restrictions on the further development and improvement of a product or service. Arguably, the consumers are adequately protected from long-term monopolies since the IP rights are only conferred for a certain period of time and not indefinitely. IP law manages to draw *delicate balances* among the legitimate interests of creators/inventors, competitors, consumers, and the public.[26]

35. To conclude, the idea of an effective protection of intellectual creations without the need of special legal provisions to those ends is simply not plausible. The protection provided under the Greek tort law (Articles 914 et seq. GCC) is not sufficient for that matter.[27] At the same time, it is very difficult to determine the degree of damage that the infringer may have caused to the creator, in order to claim the appropriate amount of compensation.

III. History of IP Law

36. The protection of intellectual creations dates back to practices that were first employed in Ancient Greece; in the colony of Sybaris, located in Italy, chefs were granted year-long monopolies for creating particular dishes.[28] During the Medieval times, States provided monopoly privileges to individuals in order to produce particular goods and services. The first organized legal system of IP protection began in England: the Statute of Monopolies, enacted in 1624, granted monopoly privileges to authors and inventors for fourteen years, while the Statute of Anne (1710) is considered to be the first statute of modern copyright protection.[29]

37. As far as the Greek legal order is concerned,[30] the first IP provisions stretch back to the old penal code (1834), which included provisions for illegal reprinting, etc.[31] IP law in Greece was further developed in the following texts:

25. The term 'monopoly', as it is used in this context, should not be confused with the term 'monopoly' under competition/antitrust law. IP rights are monopolistic rights, in the sense that they provide an exclusive right over their exploitation to their holder, *see* N. Rokas, *Industrial Property*, 5 (Athens 2011 (in Greek)).
26. C. Colston, *supra* n. 16, at 3.
27. As according to Art. 914 GCC the plaintiff must prove fault of the infringer, the damage suffered by the plaintiff, and a causal link between the wrongful act and the damage, in order to claim compensation.
28. For further references http://plato.stanford.edu/entries/intellectual-property/#HisIntPro.
29. At http://plato.stanford.edu/entries/intellectual-property/#HisIntPro.
30. Further reference to the history and development of IP laws in Greece will take place in the following chapters.
31. For further information *see* Ch. 1.

- L. ΒΡΝΣΤ/1893 referring to trademarks.
- L. ΓΥΠΓ/1909 with regard to dramatic works.
- L. 3092/24, ratify the International Convention of Paris.
- L. 2527/1920, for the protection of patents.
- L. 2387/20, regulating literacy and artistic works.

IV. IP Regimes at International Level

38. The industrial revolution and the internationalization of trade led to international cooperation between States over procedural and substantive law matters and to the development of international organizations who deal with intellectual property protection.[32] The first international IP Convention is the Paris Industrial Property Convention of 1883, which was revised in Stockholm (1967), while the Berne Convention of 1886[33] established protection for literary, dramatic, musical, and artistic works. The Berne Convention provided that copyright protection arises automatically on the creation of a work and is administered by the World Intellectual Property Organization (WIPO) in Geneva. The Madrid Agreement of 1891 established a system of deposit for trademarks registered nationally with WIPO. The first international convention regarding the related rights was the Rome Convention of 1961, for the Protection of Performers, Phonograms, and Broadcasting Organizations. In 1973 the European Patent Convention (EPC) was enacted, while in 1994, during the Round of Uruguay, the Agreement on Trade-Related Aspects of Intellectual Property Rights (TRIPS) was established, administered by the World Trade Organization (WTO). The WIPO Conventions of 1996, also referred to as 'Internet Conventions', regulate the rights of authors in their literary and artistic works in relation to the new technological developments and the evolution of the Internet.

V. IP Law in Greece

A. *Basic Legal Framework*

39. The basic statutory sources of IP law in Greece are the following:[34]

- Copyright and related rights: L. 2121/1993 and L. 4481/2017.
- Patents and utility models: L. 1733/1987.
- Trademarks: Articles 121–183 L. 4072/2012.
- Unfair Competition: L. 146/1914.
- Topographies of semiconductor products: PD 45/1991.
- Greece has also ratified many international conventions regarding IP rights.

---

32. C. Colston, *supra* n. 16, at 8.
33. This was revised in 1908, in 1948, and in 1971.
34. A detailed analysis of the relevant legal framework will take place in the following chapters of this book.

B. Conditions for the Existence of IP Rights

40. There are two possible systems for an IP right to be acquired and protected: the formal and the substantial system. The formal system requires certain formalities, which are not a prerequisite according to the substantial system.[35] There is also the filing system, according to which typical formalities are not imperative for the acquisition of the right but serve as a type of publicity,[36] Copyright is based on the substantial system, whereas industrial property rights, with the exception of distinctive marks, are based on the typical system.[37]

C. Duration of Protection

41. The period of protection provided by IP law varies according to the type of IP right. The duration of protection for trademarks is ten years from application, that can be renewed unlimited times. Copyright protection lasts for as long as the author lives plus seventy years after his death. As for patents, they are valid for twenty years.

VI. IP Law in Relation with Other Fields of Law

A. IP Law and Constitutional Law

42. IP rights are protected by the Greek Constitution, which provides that property is protected by the State (Article 17).[38] Furthermore, IP rights fall into the scope of Articles 2,[39] 5(1)(2),[40] 14(1),[41] and 16(1)[42] of the Constitution.[43]

B. IP Law and Civil Law

43. IP law is part of Private Law (Civil and Commercial Law).[44] However, we need to draw the reader's attention to the fact that the term 'property' in IP law does not have the same meaning as the term 'property' in the Civil Code (CC), which

---

35. A. Liakopoulos, *Industrial Property*, 111 (Athens 2000 (in Greek)).
36. *Ibid.* An example of an IP right that is acquired through the filing system is company names.
37. *Ibid.*
38. This opinion, which was the prevailing in the doctrine, has also gained ground in the jurisprudence over the past years. IP rights are also protectable under Art. 1 of the Additional Protocol of the European Convention for the Protection of Human Rights and Fundamental Freedoms, and under Art. 17 para. 2 of the Charter of Fundamental Rights of the European Union (2007/C 303/01).
39. Respect and protection of the human value.
40. Free development of personality.
41. Freedom of expression.
42. Freedom of art, science, research, and teaching.
43. D. Kallinikou, *Copyright and Related Rights*, 9–10 (Athens 2008 (in Greek)).
44. N. Rokas, *supra* n. 25, at 9.

provides that only tangible goods enjoy an exclusive right with absolute effect (Article 947 CC).[45] Nevertheless, the protection of IP rights can find ground on Article 60 CC, which provides that a person who suffered an infringement to his intellectual creations may ask for injunctive relief and bring an action for damages, according to the general provisions on torts (Articles 914 et seq. CC).[46]

C. IP Law and Competition/Antitrust Law

44. Competition/Antitrust law regulates the structure of the market and the conditions under which competition takes place. The goal of competition law is to prevent monopolies or oligopolies, or at least to ensure that they will behave in a way that it will not distract effective competition. Competition law protects the economic freedom and the freedom to compete. Competition rules may be used for the preservation of liberty and the dispersal of economic power.[47] Also, in the EU, competition rules serve as a means of establishing and preserving the internal market, by prohibiting actions that could lead to its fragmentation and by encouraging trade between the Member States.[48] The legal framework for the protection of competition is L. 3959/2011 while the Hellenic Competition Commission[49] is the competent authority regarding the enforcement of competition rules. Also, since Greece is a member of the EU, Articles 101–102 of the TFEU have a direct effect within the Greek State.

45. In a free market, there should be no monopolistic rights and, hence, profits; a business can use the technology and ideas of another business. This is exactly where the principles of IP law and antitrust law diverge.[50] However, one of the limits regarding the freedom of the holders of IP rights, concerning the economic exploitation of their rights, is the preservation of effective competition in the relevant markets. According to the above, the holder of a patent or a copyright who has a dominant position in the relevant market, cannot abuse his/her position by refusing access to his patent or copyright to third parties, under a reasonable and non-discriminatory remuneration. In general IP law and competition law, both encourage innovation and competition.

---

45. As it has been interpreted Art. 60 GCC does not recognize an absolute right in every intellectual creation; the conditions under which an intellectual creation will be the object of an absolute right must be determined by a special law, *see* A. Liakopoulos, *supra* n. 35, at 4 with further references.
46. *Ibid.*, 4–5.
47. A. Jones & B. Suffrin, *EU Competition Law*, 16–17 (4th ed., OUP 2010), G. Amato, *Antitrust and the Bounds of Power*, 2–3 (Hart Publishing 1997).
48. R. Whish, *Competition Law*, 22–23 (6th ed., OUP 2008), D. Tzouganatos, *The Scope of Protection of Competition Law*, in *Competition Law*, 17–18 (D. Tzouganatos ed., Athens 2013 (in Greek)).
49. At http://www.epant.gr/main.php?Lang=en.
50. For a general reference *see* H. Ullrich *The Interaction Between Competition Law and Intellectual Property Law: An Overview*, in *European Competition Law Annual 2005: The Interaction between Competition Law and Intellectual Property Law*, xxviii et seq. (C.-D. Ehlermann/I. Atanasiu eds, Hart Publishing 2007). *See also* E. Mastromanolis, *Agreements Regarding Intellectual Property Rights. Technology Transfer*, in *Competition Law*, 377 et seq. (D. Tzouganatos ed., Athens 2013).

46. IP law along with competition law and consumer protection law form the so-called economic law (*droit du marché*).

Chapter 1. Copyright and Related Rights

D. Kallinikou

§1. Sources of Law and Legislation

47. The sources of Greek copyright law are national legislation and international conventions ratified by Greece. The primary legislative provisions on copyright were Articles 432, 433, and 471 of the old penal code (1834) providing only penal sanctions. Article 432 punished illegal 'reprinting' of printed works where this took place without the permission of the author and without 'elaboration or redrafting'. Article 433 permitted the extension of this protection to foreigners on condition of reciprocity and Article 471 included, under the offence of the 'theft', the works of 'the human intellect'. The first legislative acts on copyright were the L. ΓΥΠΓ/1909 for the protection of dramatic works and in particular the L. 2387/1920 for the protection of creators in general. These acts, together with various amendments, served as the basic law on copyright until the year 1993, when the L. 2121/1993 on 'Copyright, Related Rights and Cultural Matters' was voted. Law 2121/1993 entered into force on 3 March 1993, date of the publication in the Official Gazette (OG A 25/4.3.1993). Prior provisions were repealed by Article 72(1) of L. 2121/1993. Greece belongs to traditional literary and artistic property countries and the human dimension is primordial in L. 2121/1993.

48. L. 2121/1993[51] is the main statutory source of copyright in Greece, considered as a landmark in the legal history, covering the whole field of copyright and related rights. Further acts brought amendments including implementation of the European Community Directives on copyright and related rights. L. 2121/1993 was recently amended by L. 4481/2017[52] implementing the Directive 2014/26/EU on collective management of copyright and related rights. L. 4481/2017 entered into force on 20 July 2017, date of the publication in the Official Gazette (OG A 100/20.7.2017). This law establishes an autonomous collective management framework, brings amendments to L. 2121/1993 and includes provisions concerning infringement of copyright and related rights on the Internet, reproduction for private use, and public lending by libraries.

49. The main legal provisions amending L. 2121/1993[53]and L. 4481/2017 are the following:

51. For the English translation of L. 2121/1993 *see* www.opi.gr and www.wipo.int/wipolex.
52. For the English translation of L. 4481/2017 *see* www.grammo.gr.
53. For the analysis of L. 2121/1993 in English language *see* G. Koumantos & I. Stamatoudi, *Greek Copyright Law, Sakkoulas Publications* (2014), passim. L. Kotsiris, *Greek Copyright Law* (IUS 2012), passim. A. Liakopoulos, *Intellectual Property Law in Greece*, 57 et seq. (Kluwer Law International-Sakkoulas 1999), G. Koumantos, *The New Greek Law on Authors' Rights and Neighbouring Rights*, 205 (RIDA 159/1984); *'News from Greece'*, RIDA 162/1999 p. 53. *G. Koumantos-P. Koriatopoulou-Aggeli, 'News from Greece'*, RIDA 200/2004 p. 141. *E. Deligianni, 'News from Greece'*, RIDA 200/2009 p.173. For the analysis of L. 4481/2017 in English and French language

(a) Article 4 of L. 2173/1993 concerning the resale right (OG A 208/16.12.1993).
(b) Article 59 of L. 2218/1994 concerning the collective management (OG A 90/13.6.1994).
(c) Article 3 of L. 2435/1996 concerning the reproduction for private use and in particular the right of information entitled to collecting societies (OG A 189/20.8.1996).
(d) Article 8 of L. 2557/1997 implementing the Directive on satellite broadcasting and cable retransmission, as well as the Directive on the term of protection (OG A 271/24.12.1997).
(e) Article 7 of L. 2819/2000 implementing the Directive on the legal protection of databases (OG A 84/15.3.2000).
(f) Article 14 of L. 3049/2002 concerning the reproduction for private use and the equitable remuneration (OG A 212/10.9.2002).
(g) Article 81 of L. 3057/2002 implementing Directive 2001/29 on the harmonization of certain aspects of copyright and related rights in the information society (OG A 239/10.10.2002).
(h) L. 3524/2007 implemented Directive 2001/84 on the resale right and Directive 2004/48 on the enforcement of intellectual property rights (OG A 15/26.1.2007).
(i) Article 46 of L. 3905/2010 concerning collective management and other copyright issues (OG A 219/23.12.2010).
(j) L. 4212/2013 implementing Directive 2011/77[54] and Directive 2012/28 on orphan works (OG A 257/3.12.2013).
(k) Article 235(2) of L. 4281/2014 concerning the reproduction for private use and, in particular, the exemption of specific foreign companies from the payment of equitable remuneration (OG A 160/8.8.2014).
(l) L. 4481/2017 (Article 1–54) implementing Directive 2014/26 on collective management and providing amendments to L. 2121/1993 on issues not related to collective management, i.e., provisions for enforcement on the Internet, reproduction for private use, public lending right (OG A 100/20.7.2017).
(m) Article 13 of l. 4505/2017 amending subparagraph 2 of paragraph 1 of Article 54[55] of L. 4481/2017 (OG A 189/8.12.2017).
(n) Article 79 of L. 4509/2017 adding a subparagraph at the end of paragraph 3 of Article 17[56] of L. 4481/2017. According to the above subparagraph rights revenue and any income arising from the investment of rights revenue cannot be seized (OG A 201/22.12.2017).

---

see D. Kallinikou-P.Koriatopoulou, 'News from Greece', RIDA 254/2017 p. 107-132. For the implementation of Directive 2001/29 in English language *See B. Linder and T. Shapiro, 'Copyright in the Information Society-A guide to National Implementation of the European Directive'* Edward Elgar, 2011, *'Greece'* by *E. Vagena*, pp. 233–250.

54. Directive 2011/77/EU amended Directive 2006/116/EC on the term of protection of copyright and related rights.
55. Article 54 of L. 4481/2017 concerns repealed and amended provisions of L. 2121/1993.
56. Article 17 of L. 4481/2017 concerns rights revenue of collective management organization.

(o) Article 127 of L. 4514/2018 amending Article 54 paragraph 10 subparagraph 1 of L. 2121/1993, [57] concerning the appointment of a temporary commissioner in case there is a chance that the collective management organizations are unable to fulfil their financial obligations. The total renewal and duration of service of the temporary commissioner is fixed up to six months (OG A 14/30.1.2018).
(p) Article 45 of L. 4531/2018 amending L. 2121/1993, L. 4481/2017, and PD 311/1994, concerning the entrustment of collective management, exceptionally and temporarily, to a Special Department of Urgent Management set up in the Hellenic Copyright Organization (OPI) (OG A 62/5.4.2018).

50. Greece ratified several international conventions applicable to copyright and related rights. It should be noted that according to Article 28(1) of the Greek Constitution the international conventions, after their ratification by statute and their coming into effect according to their respective conditions, are an integral part of domestic Greek law and prevail over any contrary provision of the law. The international conventions ratified by Greece are the following:

(a) Universal Copyright Convention, done in Geneva in 1952, and its Protocols 1, 2, and 3. It was ratified by Decree-Law 4254/1962 (OG A 166/17.10.1962).
(b) Berne Convention for the Protection of Literary and Artistic Works, Paris Act of 24 July 1971. It was ratified by L. 100/1975 (OG A 162/1.8.1975). It should be noted that Greece has ratified all the revised texts of the Berne Convention since 1921. Greece is a member of the Berne Union and has also ratified the Convention establishing the WIPO adopted on 14 July 1967 by L. 100/1975.
(c) Convention relating to the Distribution of Program-Carrying Signals Transmitted by Satellite, done in Brussels on 21 May 1974. It was ratified by L. 1944/1991 (OG A 56/22.4.1991).
(d) International Convention for the Protection of Performers, Producers of Phonograms and Broadcasting Organizations, done in Rome on 26 October 1962. It was ratified by L. 2054/1992 (OG A 104/30.6.1992).
(e) Convention for the Protection of Producers of Phonograms against Unauthorized Duplication of their Phonograms of 29 October 1971. It was ratified by L. 2148/1993 (OG A 96/16.6.1993).
(f) Agreement on Trade-Related Aspects of Intellectual Property Rights (TRIPS Agreement), ratified by L. 2290/1995 (OG A 28/9.2.1995).
(g) WIPO Copyright Treaty (WCT) adopted in Geneva on 20 December 1996. It was ratified by L. 3184/2003 (OG A 228/26.9.2003).
(h) WIPO Performances and Phonograms Treaty (WPPT) adopted in Geneva on 20 December 1996. It was ratified by L. 3183/2003 (OG 227/26.9.2003).

51. The main regulations applicable in the area of copyright and related rights are the following:

---

57. It is to be noted that para. 10 was added to Art. 54 of L. 2121/1993 by Art. 15 of L. 4463/2017 (OG A 42/30.3.2017) and amended, with effect from 30 Mar. 2017, by Art. 54 para. 15a of L. 4481/2017 (OG A 100/20.7.2017).

(a) PD 311/1994 concerning the Copyright Organization (OG A 165/6.10.1994) as amended by L. 2557/1997 (Article 8(3)), L. 2819/200 (Article 7(13)), L. 3905/2010 (Article 46 (9–13)) and L. 4531/2018 (Article 45).
(b) MD ΥΠΠΟ/ΔΙΟΙΚ/98546/12.10.2007 concerning the reproduction of copyrighted works for the benefit of the blind and deaf-mute and extension of the arrangement to other categories of people with disabilities (OG B 2065/24.10.2007).
(c) MD 10100/D3B/4020/27.7.2007 concerning the determination of the procedure for the imposition and collection of the administrative fine provided for in Articles 65A and 66 of L. 2121/1993 as modified by Article 2 of L. 3524/2007 (OG B 1670/22.8.2007).
(d) MD P48-7542/ΑΣ 3540/22.3.2008 establishing the Coordination Committee for monitoring and coordinating Intellectual Property Rights (OJ B 575/3.4.2008).
(e) PD 42/2015 concerning administrative fines for violation of the provisions of L. 2121/1993 by collective management organization (OG A 71/3.7.2015).This Presidential Decree was repealed by Article 54 paragraph 14 of L. 4481/2017 but still applies to pending cases before the Administrative Authorities.
(f) MD ΥΠΠΟΑ/ΓΔΔΥΗΔ/ΔΔΑΑΔ/ΤΥΕΦΤΠ/150793/14199/13406/1043/27.4.2017 concerning the appointment of a temporary commissioner for a collective management organization (OG B 202/28.4.2017).
(g) MD ΥΠΠΟΑ/ΓΔΔΥΗΔ/ΔΔΑΑΔ/ΤΥΕΦΤΠ/445018/36062/34174/2303/27.10.2017 concerning the extension of the term of service of the temporary commissioner (OG B 541/30.10.2017).
(h) MD ΥΠΠΟΑ/ΓΔΔΥΗΔ/ΔΔΑΑΔ/ΤΥΕΦΤΠ/42270/3639/3477/197/30.1.2018 establishing the Committee for the disclosure of an Internet infringement of copyright and related rights (OG B 64/7.2.2018).
(i) MD ΥΠΠΟΑ/ΓΔΔΥΗΔ/ΔΔΑΑΔ/ΤΥΕΦΤΠ/42269/3638/3476/196/30.1.2018 concerning the establishment, the operation and responsibilities of the Committee for the disclosure of an Internet infringement of copyright and related rights, as well as the determination of the amount of money to be paid by the complaint upon his application to the Committee (OG B 351/7.2.2018).
(j) MD ΥΠΠΟΑ/ΓΔΔΥΗΔ/ΔΔΑΔ/ΤΔΥΕΦ/61840/5094/4171/240/13.2.2018 establishing the procedure for imposing and levying the fine imposed by the Committee for the disclosure of an Internet infringement of copyright and related rights (OG B 683/27.2.2018).

§2. Subject Matter of Protection

I. Criteria and Different Categories of Protected Works

52. Copyright protects the work as an immaterial (intangible) good, having a unique character, and not the physical object in which the work is embodied. Article 2 of L. 2121/1993 contains the basic rules on the subject matter of copyright protection. More specifically according to Article 2(1) the term 'work' designates:

any original intellectual literary, artistic or scientific creation, expressed in any form, notably written or oral texts, musical compositions with or without words, theatrical works accompanied or unaccompanied by music, choreographies and pantomimes, audiovisual works, works of fine art, including drawings, works of painting and sculpture, engravings and lithographs, works of architecture and photographs, works of applied art, illustrations, maps and three-dimensional works relative to geography, topography, architecture or science.

53. It becomes apparent from the broad wording of the provision and the indicative enumeration of the 'works' that, in the context of Greek copyright legislation, any original intellectual creation that is expressed in any form is protected. The prevailing criteria are the protection of the form and the originality.

54. The principle that copyright protects the form of expression of ideas and not the idea itself is classical. The idea is common property and free and belongs to the public domain, only the form given by the author is protected by copyright. This principle is expressly included in Article 2(3) of L. 2121/1993 concerning computer programs, as follows: 'Ideas and principles which underlie any element of a computer program, including those which underlie its interfaces, are not protected under this Law.' This principle is also found in major copyright treaties. The TRIPS Agreement and the WCT state that copyright protection extends to 'expressions' and not to 'ideas, procedures, methods of operation or mathematical concepts'. As a result of the idea/expression dichotomy, copyright does not preclude others from using ideas or information. Ideas are freely accessible to the public in order not to impede future creative activity. However, the idea/expression dichotomy is sometimes difficult to apply in practice.

55. The criterion of originality is a substantive requirement for protection but the law does not define 'originality'. A specific definition of originality is introduced only for computer programs and databases according to the *acquis communautaire*. A computer program is protected if it is original in the sense that it is the author's personal intellectual creation (Article 2(3) of L. 2121/1993). Databases which, by reason of the selection or arrangement of their contents, constitute the author's intellectual creation are protected as such by copyright (Article 2(2a) of L. 2121/1993).

56. Different criteria have been used by Greek theory[58] and jurisprudence[59] to determine whether a work is to be considered as original or not. The personal

58. G. Koumantos, *Copyright Law*, 105–113 (Athens-Komotini 2002 (in Greek)). L. Kotsiris, *Copyright Law and acquis communautaire*, 63–67 (Athens-Thessaloniki 2017 (in Greek)). M. Marinos, *Copyright Law*, 76–82 (Athens-Komotini 2004 (in Greek)). D. Kallinikou, *supra* n. 43, at 34–38. P. Koriatopoulou-Aggeli-H. Tsigou, *Copyright* (Athens 2008 (in Greek)), P. Koriatopoulou-Aggeli, *Originality*, 419–424, L. Kotsiris-E. Stamatoudi, *Law on Copyright* (Athens-Thessaloniki 2009 (in Greek)), E. Stamatoudi, *Art. 2 of Law 2121/1993*, 31–56.
59. SMCFI of Athens 7483/2007, *ChrID* 2008, 67. CA of Athens 3252/2002, *ChrID* 2003, 465, AP 152/2005, *NoV* 2005, 1782.

element of the creation as a product of human mind constitutes the criterion of originality. A work is original when it is the result of the personal contribution when it expresses the author's personality when it represents some individuality. Another criterion applied is the 'statistical uniqueness'. According to this criterion a work is original if under the same circumstances and the same aims no other person would create the same work.[60] Jurisprudence has accepted that the work must present some individual peculiarity, measured by statistical uniqueness or a minimum creative style being unlike other already known and self-evident works.[61] The element of originality is different from the element of novelty. In order for a work to be original, it does not have to be new. Originality is subjective and is a key condition for copyright protection, while the element of novelty is based on objective criteria and is not a requirement for protection.

57. As it has already been mentioned, the enumeration of protected works according to Article 2(1) of L. 2121/1993 is indicative. The provision refers to the three basic categories of works (literary, artistic, or scientific), also giving types or examples of protected works:

- Written texts, such as books and other writings.
- Oral texts, such as sermons and speeches.
- Musical compositions, with or without words.
- Theatrical works accompanied or unaccompanied by music, such as plays and operas.
- Choreographies and pantomimes.
- Audiovisual works, such as cinematographic works, artistic movies, cartoons, video clips, or documentaries.
- Works of fine art, including drawings, works of painting and sculpture, engravings, and lithographs.
- Works of architecture, such as buildings, churches, bridges, designs of parks or gardens.
- Photographs.
- Works of applied arts, such as lamps, jewellery,[62] carpets, furniture.
- Illustrations, maps,[63] and three-dimensional works relative to geography, topography, architecture, or science.

58. This enumeration covers the basic categories of works, but the non-exhaustive list implies that any intellectual creation, as long as it is original, can be characterized as protected work, irrespective of whether it is included in the non-exhaustive list of Article 2(1) of L. 2121/1993. Jurisprudence has accepted that the concept of work comprises the imaginary form of a mythical hero,[64] chessboard

60. SMCFI of Athens 328/2010, *DIMEE* 2010, 89 comments by P. Koriatopoulou-Aggeli, AP 513/2008, *NoV* 2008, 2484, AP 1118/2006, *NoV* 2006, 1140.
61. AP 118/2006, *NoV* 2006, 1140, CA of Athens 3252/2002, *ChrID* 2003, 465.
62. SMCFI of Athens 745/2008 ChrID 2009, 162164 comments by D. Kallinikou.
63. CA of Thessaloniki 1710/2011, *DIMEE* 2012, 74 comments by M. Kannelopoulou-Boti.
64. SMCFI of Athens 3455/1997, *EEmpD* 1999, 597.

pawns,[65] an odd suitcase,[66] a woodcut artistic work in the form of a lion,[67] a dictionary,[68] jewels,[69] and other similar items.

59. The non-exhaustive list of Article 2(2) of L. 2121/1993 does not comprise the title, but it can be protected by copyright if it is original. Original is a title that personalizes the work and fits the content and, more generally, when it has a distinctive quality and individuality. A title is not original when it provides a general characterization and is used in an entire category of works, i.e., Criminal Law, Introduction to Philosophy, Introduction to operating systems.

60. Photography includes colour slides and any image produced by a similar medium or method, such as computer-processed photographs. The subject matter of the photograph is the photograph itself and not the item or person shown. Originality in photographs is judged with leniency and, for this reason, the law does not make any reference to the Community definition, according to which photograph is the 'author's own intellectual creation'.[70] Applying the criteria on the originality of photographs are the colour contrasts and combinations, the selection of location and time, the lightning, the relation between the object and the environment space, the photo angle, and the photo editing.[71]

61. The concept of audiovisual work includes all cinematographic films, irrespective of whether they are artistic films, documentaries, advertising films, or video clips, as well as works produced by media similar to those of cinema, such as TV-film and video-films.[72]

62. The concept of architectural work[73] comprises structures, both as to their external form (buildings, churches, bridges) and as to the layout (decoration, garden architecture), as well as the relevant prior drawings, including preliminary drawings, sketches, and models. Protection does not concern those elements of architectural works stemming from technical and mechanical measurements. Copyright does not protect architects as engineers but as creators.

63. Apart from the above-mentioned criteria no further qualifications are required for copyright protection. According to Article 2(4) of L. 2121/1993, copyright protection applies 'regardless of the value of the work and its destination and regardless of the fact that the work is possibly protected under other provisions'.

65. SMCFI of Athens 4348/1998, *NoV* 1998, 1095.
66. SMCFI of Athens 2519/1997, *EEmpD* 1997, 358.
67. CA of Athens 448/1981, *EEmpD* 1982, 321.
68. CA of Athens 7013/1999, *DEE* 2000, 45. MMCFI of Athens 5821/2010, ChrID 2011, 377-380 comments by D. Kallinikou.
69. SMCFI of Athens 7475/2008, *ChrID* 2009, 162 comments by D. Kallinikou.
70. MMCFI of Athens 5821/2010, *ChrID* 2011, 377 comments by D. Kallinikou.
71. CA of Thessaloniki 488/2015 DIMEE 2016, 90–93.
72. For the protection of videogames as audiovisual works *see* MMCFI of Athens 2221/2015, ChrID 2015, 699-702 with comments by. S. Stauridou.
73. For the concept of works of architecture *see* K. Katsouli, *The Protection of Woks of Architecture in Particular by Copyright*, 33 et seq. (Athens 2011 (in Greek)).

Copyright protects the work regardless of its artistic or aesthetic merit and of its illegal or immoral character. The courts, when they have to consider intellectual property issues, should not be converted into academies. The judges do not express their views on the value of the artistic creation. The artistic value of the work is of no interest to copyright law. The illegal or immoral character of a work is of no interest to copyright law either. The adaptation of a work realized without the authorization of the creator is illegal and infringes copyright. However, adaptation in itself is protected by copyright law, because protection is independent of the illegal character of the work. The protection of a work does not depend on its immoral content either. Copyright is not interested in the moral disapproval of the creation. Matters of morality differ from time to time and from place to place. Insults to honour and related offences are of interest to criminal law but are outside the scope of copyright.

64. It should also be noted that Greek legislation follows the principle of the 'unity of art' because the work is protected regardless of its 'destination'. The practical use of a work is an element that the judge has to not take into consideration if he has to decide whether to protect it or not. Designs and models may be protected by copyright as 'works of applied art'. As it has already been mentioned 'works of applied art' are expressly contained in the indicative list of Article 2(1) of L. 2121/1993. PD 259/1997 introducing specific rules for the protection of industrial designs and models permits, by Article 30, the cumulative protection under existing copyright law.

65. Furthermore, no quantitative requirements are needed for a work to be protected by copyright. 'Short works', i.e., titles and slogans, may be protected by copyright legislation if they meet the substantive criteria of the 'work'.

66. No formalities, i.e., publication, fixation, or registration, are needed for the acquisition or the exercise of copyright. The principle of protection without formalities is valid for all kinds of works. Article 1(1) of L. 2121/1993 provides that 'authors shall have, with the creation of the work, the right of copyright in that work … ', while Article 6(2) stipulates that economic and moral rights 'shall be vested in the author of a work without resort to any formality'. The deposit of copies to the National Library, the Parliament Library, and Public Libraries is a purely administrative procedure that aims to preserve cultural heritage and enrich national archives but does not constitute a requirement in order to obtain or safeguard copyright.

67. Copyright legislation excludes certain works from protection. According to Article 2(5) of L. 2121/1993 copyright protection does not apply to official works expressive of the authority of the State, notably legislative, administrative, or judicial texts, nor it applies to expressions of folklore, news information, or simple facts[74] or data.

74. Historical events and facts are not protected: AP 711/2017, DIMEE 2017, 582–587 comments by M. Sinanidou.

68. It is also common, under Greek law, to protect derivative works and collections. According to Article 2(2) of L. 2121/1993 the term 'work' designates in addition 'translations, adaptations, arrangements and other alterations of works or expressions of folklore, as well as collections of works or collections of expressions of folklore or of simple facts and data, such as encyclopaedias and anthologies, provided the selection or the arrangement of their contents is original'. The above-listed works in no way prejudice rights in the pre-existing works, which are used as the object of the alterations or the collections. Databases are also specifically protected, provided the selection or the arrangement of their contents constitutes the author's intellectual creation. Databases are protected, according to the '*acquis communautaire*', not only by copyright as original works but also by the sui generis right. Directive 96/9 on the legal protection of databases is implemented by Article 7 of L. 2819/2000.

69. Expressions of folklore are excluded from the protection afforded by copyright because they go back much further in time than the term of legal protection granted by the international conventions and the national law. They can, however, obtain the protection of copyright as derivative works, such as translations, adaptations, arrangements, and other alterations, i.e., translation of folk story, adaptation of folk music composition. Collections of expressions of folklore, e.g., digital compilation of folk songs, are also protected, provided the selection or arrangement of their content is original. Expressions of folklore may be also protected by the Directive 96/9 on the legal protection of databases.

70. Copyright law does not regulate the similar matter of *restoration of old texts* (i.e., ancient texts). The need to restore old texts or old drawings mainly stems from the fact that the text or drawing has been destroyed or worn. It has been maintained that there is no copyright in the restored text because there is no intellectual creation and the initial form of another creator is simply given to the public.[75] It is, however, held that there is copyright in a critic's comments and in those sections that are lost and, therefore, are completed by the person attempting restoration.[76] The possibility to protect the restored text is supported by a scientific opinion accepting that the restoration of texts (in this case, a manuscript of Solomos poems) constitutes intellectual work because 'the restorer creates' as well.[77] The Single-Member Court of First Instance (SMCFI) of Athens has held in Judgment 11672/1995[78] that the restoration of manuscripts in Arabic of four books of Arithmetica of the famous ancient mathematician Diophantus is an original intellectual work. Originality consists in restoring the entire discovered text, supplementing gaps, and commenting. This position taken by jurisprudence is accurate because the restoration of an ancient text carries the element of the personal contribution of the scientist who intervenes in the old text to bring out its true form and constitution.

75. T. Ioannou-K. Lykiardopoulos, *Copyright Law*, 108 (Athens 1962 (in Greek)).
76. G. Koumantos, *supra* n. 58 at 159.
77. I. Passias, *NDik* 1958, 504.
78. SMCFI of Athens 11672/1995, unreported.

II. Special Categories of Works

A. Computer Software

71. Greece transferred, in national legislation, the relevant Directive 2009/24/EC[79] on the legal protection of computer programs by Article 2(3) and Articles 40–45 of L. 2121/1993. Computer programs and their preparatory design material are considered works within the meaning of the provisions on copyright protection. A computer program is protected if it is original in the sense that it is the author's personal intellectual creation. Copyright protects the expression in any form of computer program. Ideas and principles which underlie any element of the computer program, including those which underlie its interfaces, are not protected under copyright law. The term of protection covers the whole of the author's life and seventy years after his death according to the general rule of duration.

72. An interesting point is made by Judgment 30766/1996 of the SMCFI of Athens,[80] according to which an original creation includes the musical selection, expression, and rendition of traditional rhythms in a specific personal manner, so that the user of tunes in which the computer program is embodied can be accompanied by an imaginary multi-instrument orchestra, each playing a specific instrument at a specific time and in the specific manner of his choice. According to Judgment 2182/2006 of the MMCFI of Athens,[81] a program is protected on the condition that it comprises originality and the personal intellectual contribution of its author and an element of creative style over the minimum acceptable limit, in order to differentiate from already known works by the shaping of thoughts and the peculiarity of the manner of collection, classification and arrangement of the material. This individual peculiarity of the work is measured by the statistical uniqueness of the creation. In the same spirit, the SMCFI of Katerini, in Judgment 881/2006,[82] held that the description of the program is necessary, *inter alia*, for the determination of originality, in the sense of personal intellectual contribution of its author, the special individuality or the creative style that differentiates it from other similar programs, or, in any event, the possibility that a third party could not create the same program at the same time.

73. Concerning limitations, special provisions are included in Article 42 of L. 2121/1993:

(1) In the absence of an agreement to the contrary, the reproduction, translation, adaptation, arrangement, or any other alteration of a computer program do not require authorization by the author or necessitate payment of a fee, where the

79. Directive 2009/24/EC repealed the Directive 91/250/EEC on the legal protection of computer programs.
80. SMCFI of Athens 30766/1996, *DEE* 1997, 94.
81. MMCFI of Athens 2182/2006, *DEE* 2006, 1020.
82. SMCFI of Katerini 881/2006, *EpiskED* 2006, 593.

said acts are necessary for the use of the program by the lawful acquirer in accordance with its intended purpose, including correction of errors.[83]

(2) Reproduction which is necessary for the purposes of loading, displaying, running, or storage of the computer program shall not fall under the restriction of the previous paragraph and shall be subject to authorization by the author.[84]

(3) The making of a backup copy by a person having a right to use the computer program may not be prevented by contract, insofar as it is necessary for the use of the program, and shall not necessitate an authorization by the author or the payment of a fee.[85]

(4) The person having a right to use a copy of a computer program shall be entitled, without the authorization of the author and without payment of a fee, to observe, study, or test the functioning of the program in order to determine the ideas and principles which underlie any element of the program, if he does so while performing any of the acts which he is entitled to do. Any agreement to the contrary shall be prohibited.[86]

(5) Reproduction of a computer program for private use other than in the circumstances specified in the above-mentioned points (3) and (4) is prohibited.

74. Decompilation is regulated in Article 43 of L. 2121/1993: The person having the right to use a copy of a computer program is entitled to carry out the acts referred to in Article 42(1) and (2) without the authorization of the author and without the payment of a fee when such acts are indispensable to obtain the information necessary to achieve the interoperability of an independently created computer program with other programs, provided that the information necessary to achieve interoperability has not previously been easily and readily available to the person having the right to use the computer program, and provided that these acts are confined to the parts of the original program which are necessary to achieve the said interoperability.

75. The above-mentioned provisions do not permit the information obtained through its application: (a) to be used for goals other than to achieve the interoperability of the independently created computer program (b) to be given to others, except when necessary for the interoperability of the independently created computer program (c) to be used for the development, production, or marketing of a computer program substantially similar in its expression to the initial program or for any other act which infringes copyright.

76. The economic right for computer programs created by an employee in the execution of the employment contract, or following instructions given by the employer, is transferred *ipso jure* to the employer, unless otherwise provided by contract.

83. Article 42(1) of L. 2121/1993.
84. Article 42(2) of L. 2121/1993.
85. Article 42(3) of L. 2121/1993.
86. Article 42(4) of L. 2121/1993.

77. Agreements contrary to the above-mentioned provisions of Article 42(3) and (4) of L. 2121/1993 as well as to Article 43 are null and void.

78. Copyright in computer programs does not preclude the protection by other legal provisions relating, notably, to patents, trademarks, unfair competition, trade secrets, protection of semiconductor products, and the law of contract.

B. Databases

79. Articles 2(2a) and 45A of L. 2121/1993 harmonize the national legislation to Directive 96/9 on the legal protection of databases.[87] 'Database' is a collection of independent works, data, or other materials arranged in a systematic or methodical way and individually accessible by electronic or other means. According to Article 2(2a) of L. 2121/1993 databases are protected by copyright, provided the selection or arrangement of their contents, constitute the author's intellectual creation. The copyright protection does not extend to the contents of databases and does not prejudice any rights subsisting in those contents themselves.

80. Article 45A of L. 2121/1993 recognizes the sui generis right of the maker[88] of the database according to the relevant provisions of the Directive 96/9/EC. The maker of the database is the individual or legal entity who takes the initiative and bears the risk of investment. The database contractor is not considered as maker. The maker of a database has the right to prevent extraction and/or re-utilization of the whole or of a substantial part, evaluated qualitatively and/or quantitatively, of the contents of that database which shows that there has been qualitatively and/or quantitatively a substantial investment in the obtention, verification, or presentation of the contents

81. The law provides the definition of extraction and re-utilization. According to Article 45A(2) of L. 2121/1993 'extraction' means the permanent or temporary transfer of all or a substantial part of the contents of a database to another medium by any means or in any form, and 're-utilization' means making available, in any form, all or a substantial part of the contents of a database to the public by the distribution of copies, by renting, online, or other forms of transmission. The first sale of a copy of a database within the Community by the right holder or with his consent shall exhaust the right to control resale of that copy within the Community. Public lending is not an act of extraction or re-utilization.

82. The sui generis right of the maker of a database is effective regardless of whether the said database or the content thereof are protected by the provisions on

87. For the implementation of Directive 96/9 in Greece *see* M. Kanellopoulou-Botti, *The Legal Protection of Databases*, 85–91 (Athens 2004 (in Greek)).
88. For the analysis of Art. 45A of L. 2121/1993 and the sui generis right *see* T. Synodinou, *The Legal Protection of Databases*, 245 et seq. (Athens-Thessaloniki 2004 (in Greek)), V. Dromazos, *The Legal Protection of Digital Technology Applications*, 193–217 (Athens 2009 (in Greek)).

copyright or other provisions. Protection on the basis of the sui generis right does not prejudice potential rights on their content. The sui generis right of the maker of a database may be transferred and its exploitation may be assigned by licence or contract. The repeated and systematic extraction and/or re-utilization of immaterial parts of the content of the database are not allowed if they involve actions opposed to the normal exploitation of the database or unjustifiably prejudice the lawful rights of the maker of the database.

83. Specific provisions refer to the rights and obligations of lawful users, to the exceptions, to the sui generis right, and to the term of protection. The term of protection is fifteen years from 1 January of the year following the date of completion. In the case of a database which is made available to the public in whatever manner before the expiry of the period provided for above, the term of protection by that right expires fifteen years from 1 January of the year following the date when the database was first made available to the public. Any substantial change, evaluated qualitatively and/or quantitatively, to the contents of a database, including any substantial change resulting from the accumulation of successive additions, deletions, or alterations, which would result in the database being considered to be a substantial new investment, evaluated qualitatively and/or quantitatively, qualifies the database resulting from that investment for its own term of protection.

84. It is well known that the ECJ, in Case C-444/02 of 9 November 2004 *Fixtures marketing Ltd v. Organismos Prognostikon Agonon Podosfairou (OPAP),* answered several questions referred for a preliminary ruling by the Court of First Instance of Athens concerning the sui generis protection of databases. The ECJ ruled that the term 'database', as defined in Article 1(2) of Directive 96/9, refers to any collection of works, data, or other materials separable from one another without the value of their contents being affected, including a method or system of some sort for the retrieval of each of its constituent materials. A fixture list for a football league such as that at issue in the above case constitutes a database within the meaning of Article 1(2) of Directive 96/9. The expression 'investment in ... the obtaining ... of the contents of a database' in Article 7(1) of Directive 96/9 must be understood to refer to the resources used to seek out existing independent materials and collect them in the database. It does not cover the resources used for the creation of materials which make up the contents of a database. Therefore, in the context of drawing up a fixture list for the purpose of organizing football league fixtures, it does not cover the resources used to establish the dates, times, and the team pairings for the various matches in the league.

85. Case law recognizes the sui generis database protection to maps contained in directories with information for drivers and professionals.[89] The sui generis protection is also recognized concerning hunting maps.[90]

89. SMCFI of Athens 6544/2006, *DIMEE* 2007, 90 comments by M. Kanellopoulou-Botti.
90. AP 1051/2015, *EEmpD* 2016, p. 454.

§3. OWNERSHIP

I. The Author

86. Article 6(1) of L. 2121/1993 provides that the initial owner of the economic right and the moral right of a work is the author, i.e., the person who actually created the work. Greece follows the principle of many civil-law countries that only the natural person who creates the work is the author.[91] A legal person cannot be considered as author with the exception of specific cases of anonymous or pseudonymous works. According to Article 11 of L. 2121/1993 any person who lawfully makes available to the public anonymous or pseudonymous works is deemed as the initial holder of the economic and moral right towards third parties. When the true author of the work reveals his identity, he acquires the above-mentioned rights in the condition they are so as a result of the actions of the fictitious right holder. The moral right belongs to the fictitious right holder as that is compatible with his status.

II. Works Made for Hire

87. A special provision deals with the case of employed authors in line with the above-mentioned principle that the initial owner of the rights is the author as a natural person. According to Article 8 of L. 2121/1993 the initial holder of the economic and moral rights of the work is the author. Only those economic rights that are necessary for the fulfilment of the purpose of the contract are transferred to the employer, if there is no stipulation to the contrary. Concerning works created by employees under any work relation of the public sector or a legal entity of public law in the execution of their duties, the economic right of the author is transferred to the employer, unless provided otherwise by contract. The same rule is laid down for computer programs created by an employee in the exercise of his duties or following instructions given by his employer (Article 40 of L. 2121/1993). In that case, unless otherwise provided by contract, all the author's economic rights are transferred to the employer.

III. Joint Works and Works Created by Several Persons

88. Article 7 of L. 2121/1993 contains provisions concerning different type of works created by a plurality of authors.

89. The term 'joint work' or 'work of joint authorship' designates any work which is the result of the direct collaboration of two or more authors. The initial right holders in respect of economic and moral rights in a joint work are the authors of that work. The rights are equally shared by the co-authors, unless otherwise

91. MMCFI of Athens 5417/2000, *EpiskED* 2000, 221 comments by K. Mitka.

agreed.[92] Joint works are those created with the 'direct collaboration of two or more authors' who are the initial joint beneficiaries of the property and moral right on the work. Collaboration, within the meaning of this provision, is the joint effort of two or more natural persons for the creation of a single work, i.e., musical dramatic works such as opera, scientific works written by two or three authors, computer programs compiled by more than one person in the context of a working group. Collaborating persons do not include persons who provide the author with some ideas or have an ancillary contribution or helped in the creation of the work only by their financial contribution. A necessary condition for a work of joint authorship is the unity of effort of all collaborating authors, whose personal contribution is directed to the creation of an entity. The individual contributions of the various authors in the final entity sometimes can be distinguished in the work as a whole, e.g., music from lyrics in musical-lyrical works, and other times cannot, in which case the work cannot be separately exploited, e.g., a scientific article published in a journal under the names of two authors who jointly collaborated for the entire work without distinguishing who wrote what.

90. A 'collective work' designates any work created by the independent contribution of several authors acting under the intellectual direction and coordination of one natural person. The natural person is the initial right holder of the economic and the moral right in the collective work. Each author of a contribution is the initial right holder of the economic right and the moral right in his own contribution, provided that the related contribution is capable of separate exploitation.[93] In the context of this provision, the category of collective works can comprise audiovisual works since, pursuant to Article 9 of L. 2121/1993, the director is presumed to be the author of such works. Collective works differ from joint works in that, in the case of collective works there is a person responsible for the intellectual direction, initiative, and coordination of the authors while in the case of joint works, all authors work together to create a single work.

91. A 'composite work' is a work which is composed of parts created separately. The authors of all the parts are the initial co-right holders of the rights in the composite work and its author is the exclusive initial holder of the rights of the part of the composite work that he has created, provided that the related part is capable of separate exploitation.[94] A composite work is made up by joining more than one work, e.g., a musical composition accompanying a poem recited by an artist. The SMCFI of Athens, in Judgment 11923/1998,[95] held that a teaching book consisting of texts and dialogues in English, photographs, and sketches constitutes a composite work. According to this judgment, the relations of the joint beneficiaries of a composite work are governed by the provisions on civil companies or, if no contractual bond exists between them, by the provisions of Civil Law on joint ownership.

92. *See* Art. 7(1) of L. 2121/1993.
93. *See* Art. 7(2) of L. 2121/1993.
94. *See* Art. 7(3) of L. 2121/1993.
95. SMCFI of Athens 11823/1998, *NoV* 1998, 1474.

92. According to Article 9 of L. 2121/1993 the principal director of an audiovisual work is considered as its author. This presumption is legal and rebuttable in the sense that it is possible to be proven that other authors of an audiovisual work, i.e., scriptwriter or the director of photography, contributed to the director's artistic work. Although the director is presumed the author of the audiovisual work, Article 34(2) of L. 2121/1993 provides that other persons are considered as authors of audiovisual contributions. These persons are the author of the screenplay, the author of the dialogue, the composer of music, the director of photography, the stage designer, the costume designer, the sound engineer, and the monteur. According to the Greek legislation the producer of audiovisual work is not recognized or presumed as author. The economic right is transferred to the producer by the director and the other authors of audiovisual contributions.

IV. Presumption of Authorship or Ownership

93. Greek law contains a presumption of authorship or ownership similar to one provided for in Article 15(1) of the Berne Convention. According to Article 10 of L. 2121/1993 the person whose name appears on a copy of a work in a manner usually employed to indicate authorship is presumed to be the author of that work. The same is applied when the name that appears is a pseudonym, provided that the pseudonym leaves no doubt as to the person's identity. This provision is applied *mutatis mutandis* to the holders of related rights with regard to their protected subject matter, as well as to the database makers for their sui generis right.

94. In the case of collective works, computer programs, or audiovisual works, a presumption of ownership is introduced in favour of the natural or legal person whose name or title appears on a copy of the work in a manner usually employed to indicate the right holder.

§4. Scope of Exclusive Rights

I. Moral Rights

95. Greek legislation always recognized the moral right which safeguards the personal connection between the author and his work. The protection of moral rights is an issue of fundamental importance in the context of the 'information society' in which there is a danger of modification, distortion, and mutilation of protected works and performances.

96. Greek Law 2121/1993, in Article 4, provides a wide protection of moral right. In particular, the protection of the moral right, apart from the right of divulgation (publication), the right of paternity of the work, and the right of integrity is reinforced by the recognition of two new rights: the right of access to work and the right of rescission. The list of moral rights provided in Article 4 is indicative. It is stipulated that 'The moral rights shall confer *notably* the following rights ...'.

According to Article 4(3) of L. 2121/1993 the moral right is independent of the economic right and shall remain with the author even after the transfer of the economic rights.

97. Article 12(2) of L. 2121/1993 provides that the moral right is not transferable between living persons. After the death of the author the moral right passes to his/her heirs. However, it should be noted that an 'indirect' mode of transfer is provided in Article 16 of L. 2121/1993 stipulating that the author may consent for an action or omission which, otherwise, would constitute an infringement of his moral right. In other words this provision recognizes the consent of the author, in that case, as a mode of exercise of the moral right and must be in writing according to Article 14 of L. 2121/1993.

98. The moral right, after its explicit provision in the above-mentioned Article 4 of L. 2121/1993, is independent of the right of personality protected by Article 57 of the GCC.[96] Nevertheless, Greek case law[97] accepts the exclusive or additional application of Article 57 concerning the right of personality if related conditions are satisfied.

A. *Right of Divulgation*

99. According to Article 4(1)(a) of L. 2121/1993 the author has the power to decide on the time, place, and manner in which the work shall be made accessible to the public. L. 2121/1993 does not define the concept of divulgation. Under the previously applicable law, the term had a broad meaning and included any communication of the work to the public in any manner, such as publication, public performance, radio and television broadcasting, or theatrical performance. This broad meaning is also accepted by the currently applicable law. As a result, it is held that divulgation comprises any manner in which the work is made accessible to the public. The power of divulgation is significant because it initiates the economic right. When the author decides to divulgate his work, economic exploitation and the exercise of the relevant powers of the economic right usually follow. The work becomes economic property and economic benefits are drawn therefrom. The exercise of the power of divulgation removes the intellectual creation from the personal sphere of

96. P. Nikolopoulos, *The Evolution of Greek Case Law on Moral Right, Symposium in Memoriam of George Koumantos – The Work of George Koumantos and the Current Issues in Copyright*, 90 (ALAI, Athens-Thessaloniki 2011). *See also* O. Garoufalia, *The Infringement of Moral Right and of the Right or Personality in Digital Environment*, 58 (Athens 2009 (in Greek)). E. Papapetropoulou-Taliadourou, *Moral Right of the Author and the Value of the Human Being*, 58 et seq. (Athens 2010 (in Greek)). For the conflict between the two rights *see* E. Alafragkis, *Conflict Between the Right of Personality and the Moral Right of the Creator of a Work Protected by Copyright*, 257 et seq. (Athens-Thessaloniki 2011 (in Greek)).

97. CA of Athens 7013/1999, *DEE* 2000, 45 comments by K. Kyprouli. CP of Athens 1478/1997, *ArxN* 1998, 236. *See also* P. Koriatopoulou-Aggeli-H. Tsigou, *Copyright supra, Right of Personality* by *P. Koriatopoulou-Aggeli,* at 146.

the author and delivers it to the public. Therefore, the economic function of copyright begins and the author is financed through the relevant exploitation of the work.

100. Jurisprudence[98] has held that the owner of the medium of a personal journal acquires neither the economic right to divulgate the work, since he does not invoke or prove any written agreement transferring such power, nor the moral right on the work, since it is not transferable *inter vivos* and, after the death of the author, it devolves to his heirs, subject to Article 16 of L. 2121/1993.

101. As regards the problem of termination of the right of divulgation, two views have been put forward in science: One view holds that this right is not exhausted with the initial divulgation, so that the author preserves the power to decide on each specific manner and form of divulgation, even after the first licence to present the work to the public.[99] This view is based on the arrangements of Article 4(1)(a) of L. 2121/1993, which recognizes, to the author, the power to decide on the time, place, and manner in which the work will be made accessible to the public, as well as on the right of rescission, recognized for literary or scientific works by Article 4(4)(e) of L. 2121/1993. This position takes up great practical importance in the digital environment because it enables the author to control any use of the work on the Internet, even after the initial divulgation. The other view maintains that the right of divulgation is exhausted with the initial divulgation, but exhaustion relates only to each specific manner of divulgation.[100]

102. Jurisprudence has upheld the latter view in the case of television broadcasting of a musical work: 'the power to divulgate ... is not perpetual, but is exhausted with the initial divulgation of the work. However, divulgation relates only to each specific manner of divulgation separately ... The defendant was not authorized by the company ... to which the plaintiff has assigned his rights from the exploitation of the song, but this failure does not prejudice the power to divulgate such work ... because, as already mentioned, the work has been repeatedly broadcast on television and the power to divulgate such work in this manner had already been exhausted with the initial divulgation (television broadcasting)'. [101]

B. Right of Paternity

103. Article 4(1)(b) of L. 2121/1993 gives the author the power to demand that his/her status as the author of the work is acknowledged and, in particular, to the extent that it is possible that his/her name be indicated on the copies of his/her work and noted whenever his/her work is used publicly, or, on the contrary, if he/she so wishes, that his/her work be presented anonymously or under a pseudonym. The

98. SMCFI of Athens 32992/1997, *EEmpD* 1999, 409–410.
99. D. Kallinikou, *Basic Issues of Law 2121/1993 on Copyright and Related Rights*, 51 (Athens 1994 (in Greek)).
100. G. Koumantos, *supra* n. 58 at 255. M. Marinos, *supra* n. 58 at 170.
101. SMCFI of Athens 3343/1998, unreported.

author can require that his/her name is mentioned both on the copies of his/her work and in any public usage. The publisher is obliged to write the name of the author on all copies and mention his/her name in all advertising material. The same is true when the book is presented in newspapers, magazines, or television media. For theatrical works, the name of the author must be mentioned in all advertising.

104. Article 4(1)(b) of L. 2121/1993 stipulates that the name is mentioned 'to the extent possible'. The view has been put forward in science that agreements on the non-mentioning of all the names of authors could be considered valid when such mention would complicate the presentation of the work in practice. However, there is a trend to the contrary in jurisprudence and courts have held that it is prejudicial to the moral right, specifically the power of acknowledgment of paternity, not to mention the name of the author in encyclopaedias,[102] as well as on the cover or label of records or cassettes comprising compilations of song extracts.[103] Therefore, it must be held that the author can always require that his/her name is mentioned on all copies or in any usage of the work and that the non-mention of the name can be accepted only in extreme instances, when there are practical difficulties in mentioning all the names of authors or when the method of broadcasting complicates the relevant mention, provided that there is a written agreement of the parties. Jurisprudence has held that the non-mention of the name of the music composer in a television broadcast of the work prejudices the power of acknowledgement of paternity and that the name of the author could be mentioned at least orally, even if we assume that that the written mention would be difficult because of the prefabrication of titles for all episodes.[104]

105. A special arrangement is made for photographers. Article 38(4) of L. 2121/1993 makes it mandatory to mention the name of the photographer in all publications of the photograph. Concerning translators, according to Article 33(7) of L. 2121/1993 their name must be indicated on the main title page of the work. If the publisher agrees, the translator's name may also be indicated on the outer cover of the work.

C. Right of Integrity

106. According to Article 4(1)(c) of L. 2121/1993 the author has the power to prohibit any distortion, mutilation, or other modification of his work and any offence to him due to the circumstances of the presentation of the work in public.[105] Offences referring to the 'circumstances of presentation' of the work to the public do not relate to offending the 'essence' of the work, but to placing the work in a

102. SMCFI of Athens 1444/1935, *Themis* 1936, 33–38 comments by G. Mihailidis-Nouaros.
103. SMCFI of Athens 1293/1987, *NoV* 1987, 1423–1426 comments by D. Kallinikou. CA of Athens 631/1990, *EllDni* 1991, 206.
104. SMCFI of Athens 3343/1998, *supra.*
105. *See* A. Papadopoulou, *The Right of Integrity* 63 et seq. (Athens-Thessaloniki 1997 (in Greek)), I. Kikkis, *The Moral Right of the Author in Digital Environment*, 107 (Thesis, University of Nantes-France 2004 (in French)).

place that is unsuitable for its character or to unjustifiably relocating it from its initial position to another place. Moreover, offences due to the 'circumstances of presentation' can relate to qualitative criteria, such as the bad performance of musical work, or the use of the work for advertising purposes without the permission of the author or the distribution, without the consent of the music composer, of recordings in the form of gift accompanying printed matter (also known as premiums), especially when they have no relation to the character of the work and the personality of the author. In the event that the author assigns the exploitation of the work to a third party, the power of protection remains directly linked to his/her personality since the moral right is non-transferrable under Article 12(2) of L. 2121/1993. However, the author may allow, in writing, some contractual limitations relating to the exercise of the moral right, specifically the power of protection. He may, i.e., authorize the correction of spelling mistakes in the publication contract, authorize the translator to make certain changes to the work in order to translate it in another language in the translation contract, etc.

107. The relationship between the right of integrity and the right of ownership seems to be very important in architectural works. The Greek jurisprudence has been concerned with the matter of interventions of the owner in an architectural work, specifically the addition of a fourth floor in a luxury hotel, despite the disagreement of the architect. The judgment held[106] that the specific building met the requirements of protection of the architectural work but the exercise of a moral right by the architect did not have any legal foundation, nor was it in line with the principles of good faith, because the amendment to the work was not material, since it did not change the general outline of the building, while, for the owner, the addition of a new floor would lead to a significant increase in the hotel's revenue and would prevent the financial collapse of the business. The conflict between the right of ownership and the moral right is resolved by weighing the conflicting interests and the dominance of the one considered to be the strongest. The criteria taken into consideration to reach either solution include, in addition to the technical features of the architectural work, whether the change is dictated by a public authority, i.e., the urban planning office. In this case, the owner is obliged to accept the administrative measures and, in reality, there is no conflict of interest between the owner and the architect. The functionality of a building and the purpose of use are elements that must be considered by the judge who will decide on the basis of striking a balance between the interests of both parties. Changes made to serve functional and technical or construction needs are allowed on the basis of good faith.

108. The limits allowing additions or changes are fuzzy. An obstacle to the exercise of the right of integrity can also be placed by Article 281 of the GCC on the abuse of rights. Even in cases when the right of ownership prevails, the owner must act in such a way as to cause the least possible alteration to the architectural work. A more practical solution is to seek the opinion of the architect on the changes, provided of course that the architect wants to agree to the relevant amendments. Article

106. SMCFI of Athens 4714/1971, *EEmpD* 1971, 462–466 comments by K. Asprogerakas-Grivas, *see also* SMCFI of Athens 276/2001, *NoV* 2001, 1332.

16 of L. 2121/1993 may be applied further since it provides for certain deviations from the principle of non-transferability of such moral right *inter vivos*. More specifically, according to such provision, 'the consent of the author to actions or omissions that would otherwise constitute a prejudice to the moral right is a manner of exercise of such right and is binding for the author'. In the context of this provision, the contract for the preparation or construction of the architectural work may contain contractual limitations of the architect's right of integrity, i.e., the architect may allow changes to the architectural work in specific instances, depending on the purpose of use or the functionality of the building, provided that the consent of the author does not run contrary to ethics and does not excessively bind his freedom (Articles 178 and 179 of the GCC).

D. *Right of Access*

109. This right permits the author to remain in contact with his work, even when the economic right has been transferred or when ownership of the physical carrier into which the work has been incorporated belongs to someone else, in which case, access must be effected with the least possible nuisance to the right holder. In Greece, the right of access finds, for the first time, legislative establishment in the regulation of Article 4(1)(d) of L. 2121/1993, while under the system of the law previously in force, this was grounded in the right of personality, in the absence of a special regulation. The practical application of this is to be found in the case of works of single incorporation, e.g., visual works. The reason why the author seeks to have access to his/her work may stem from the need which he/she feels to see his/her work again for sheer pleasure or to use it as a source for items which will be useful to him for his subsequent creative work. The Court of Appeal (CA) of Athens[107] recognized the right of access in the case of architectural designs and photographs contained in the archive of a famous architect in favour of his daughter acting as an heir after the death of his father.

E. *Right of Rescission*

110. The right of rescission, also known as the right to change one's mind, is regulated for the first time in Greek legislation. More specifically, in Article 4(1) of L. 2121/1993 a right is recognized to the author, exclusively and only in the case of literary or scientific works, to rescind contracts transferring the economic right or exploitation contracts and licences. However, in order to reconcile the interests of authors and publishers, the law sets certain strict conditions: the right of rescission may be exercised only if this is necessary for the protection of the personality of the author because of a change in his convictions or the circumstances and on condition of payment of compensation to the counterparty for positive damage. Article 4(2) of L. 2121/1993 further stipulates that rescission takes effect after the payment of

107. CA of Athens 1819/2016 *NoV* 2017, 79–95 comments by D. Kallinikou.

this compensation and that in the event of an author later wishing to transfer the economic right or generally to exploit the same or a like work, he must offer the former counterparty the opportunity to exploit the work on terms identical or similar to those which were in force at the time of rescission. The purpose of these provisions is that the author should be able to withdraw his work when this no longer reflects his/her convictions or corresponds to the political, social, or other circumstances, but with the restrictions described above.

II. Economic Rights

111. The list of rights conferred on the author by the economic right according to Article 3 of L. 2121/1993 has an indicative character. In particular, the author has, among other rights, 'notably' the exclusive and absolute right to permit or prohibit (a) the fixation and direct or indirect, temporary or permanent reproduction of his work by any means, and in any form, in whole or in part (b) the translation (c) the arrangement, adaptation, and alteration of his work (d) the distribution of the original or copies of his work (e) the rental or public lending (f) the public performance (g) the broadcasting or rebroadcasting of his work to the public by radio or television, by wireless means or by cable or by any kind of wire or by any other means or by satellite (h) the communication to the public of his work by any means, including the making available to the public of his work in such a way that members of the public may access this work from a place and at a time individually chosen by them and (i) the import of copies of the work produced without the creator's consent or the import of copies from a country outside the European Community when the right over such imports had been retained by the author through contract.

III. Right of Reproduction

112. Article 3(1)(a) of L. 2121/1993 confer upon the authors the right to authorize or prohibit 'the fixation and direct or indirect, temporary or permanent reproduction of their works by any means and in any form, in whole or in part'. It is to be noted that the law recognizes the fixation and reproduction right. Concerning reproduction right this provision implements Article 2 of Directive 2001/29. The right of the author to prevent others from making copies of his works is the most basic right under copyright. For example, the making of copies of a protected work is the act performed by a publisher who wishes to distribute copies of a text-based work to the public, whether in the form of printed copies or digital media such as CD-ROMs. Therefore, the right to control the act of reproduction is the legal basis for many forms of exploitation of protected works.

113. *Fixation* is certainly not the same as creation, which can be purely esoteric. Fixation means the first incorporation of the work in a media, which is the basis for the reproduction of the work in one or more copies. Another view maintains that in order to be fixated, the work must be susceptible to performance, e.g., theatrical work, musical composition, choreography, or pantomime.[108] The concept of fixation is more often used in the field of related rights. The law refers to this concept in Article 3 concerning the author's economic right, in order to make this provision in line with the corresponding arrangements on related rights, where the right of fixation is expressly provided for. In any event, even if the relevant reference was not made in Article 3, the act of fixation could be considered as included in the process of reproduction.

114. Reproduction is the production of one or more copies of the work, usually on the basis of incorporation into a media by fixation. Such copies may be, e.g., books, photocopies, microfilm, pictures, records, cassettes, CDs, etc. Reproduction can be made using any means, such as mechanical, phonographic, magnetic, audio, cinematic, electronic, digital, photochemical, or any publishing art means, e.g., typesetting, photocopy, linotype, etc., as well as in any form, physical or non-physical, in open or non-open line. The act of reproduction includes both temporary and permanent copies. Reproduction is sometimes made by hand, such a copy of a painting or other art forms. Of particular importance these days is the *digital reproduction*, which enables the production of more accurate and truer copies to an unlimited extent, while it also provides increased room for processing and alteration of the copies.

115. Jurisprudence[109] has held that the fragmentary reproduction and release of musical works on recordings in the form of digital discs requires the permission of the beneficiary and that the same is true for the reproduction of a live recording.

116. Architectural works are usually reproduced in two ways: architectural drawings may either become the subject of reproduction of other drawings, photographs, or images or be used for the construction of a similar building.

IV. Right of Translation and Adaptation

117. The acts of translating or adapting a work protected by copyright also require the authorization of the owner of rights. According to Article 3(1)(b) of L. 2121/1993 the author has the right to authorize or prohibit the translation of his work. Article 3(1)(c) confers upon the author the right to authorize or prohibit the arrangement, adaptation, or other alteration of his work. 'Translation' means the expression of a work in a language other than that of the original version. 'Adaptation' is generally understood as the modification of a work to create another work, such as adapting a novel to make a motion picture or the modification of a work to make it suitable for different conditions of exploitation, e.g., by adapting an instructional textbook originally prepared for higher education into an instructional textbook intended for students at a lower level. Translations and adaptations are works protected by copyright. Therefore, in order to reproduce and publish a translation or

---

108. G. Koumantos, *supra* n. 58 at 217.
109. SMCFI of Athens 2159/1999, *DEE* 1999, 719.

adaptation, authorization must be obtained from both the owner of the copyright in the original work and of the owner of the copyright in the translation or adaptation. In recent years, the scope of the right of adaptation has been the subject of discussion because of the increased possibilities for adapting and transforming works which are embodied in digital format. With digital technology, manipulation of text, sound, and images by the user is quick and easy. Discussions have focused on the appropriate balance between the rights of the author to control the integrity of the work by authorizing modifications, on the one hand, and the rights of users to make changes which seem to be part of a normal use of works in digital format, on the other.

V. Right of Distribution

118. Article 3(1)(d) of L. 2121/1993 confers upon the author the right to authorize or prohibit the distribution of the original or copies of his work to the public, in any form, by sale or otherwise. The distribution right is exhausted within the Community only where the first sale or other transfer of ownership in the Community of the original or copies is made by the right holder or with his/her consent. This provision is in accordance with the principle of Community exhaustion of the distribution right and implements, in Greek legislation, the relevant provision of Article 4(2) of Directive 2001/29.

VI. Rental and Public Lending Right

119. Article 3(1)(d) of L. 2121/1993 implements the relevant Articles 2 and 3(1) of the Directive 2006/115 on rental right, lending right, and certain related rights. The rental and public lending have the meaning provided by the above-mentioned Directive. 'Rental' means 'making available for use, for a limited period of time and for direct or indirect economic or commercial advantage'. 'Lending' means 'making available for use, for a limited period of time and not for direct or indirect economic or commercial advantage, when it is made through establishments which are accessible to the public'. The author has the right to authorize or prohibit the rental or public lending concerning the original or copies of his/her works. These rights are not applicable to architectural works and works of applied art. The principle of Community exhaustion does not apply. In accordance with Article 1(2) of the Directive 2006/115 these rights are not exhausted by any sale or other act of distribution of the original or copies.

120. The SMCFI of Athens, in Judgment 12729/1997,[110] prohibited the rental of videocassettes by persons not authorized by the initial author throughout the term of the exclusive exploitation contract between the initial author and the exclusive

110. SMCFI of Athens 12729/1997, *DEE* 1997, 829.

assignee Greek company. The CA of Athens, in Judgment 8532/2006,[111] acknowledged that music incorporated into a film is an autonomous work and that the author of the musical work does not lose the economic right to copyright. Therefore, the music composer continues to hold and exercise the right of rental vis-à-vis the producer, on television.

121. As regards the right of public lending, it should be noted that L. 2121/1993 did not make use of Article 6 of Directive 2006/115/EC, which allows Member States to derogate from the exclusive public lending right, provided that authors at least obtain remuneration for such lending. Member States may exempt certain categories of establishments from the payment of the remuneration, such as public or university libraries. In Greece, the right of public lending is preserved its exclusive character and has not been restricted by law or administrative deed. In reality, it has been left for many years to the scope of action of beneficiaries or collective management organizations. However, Article 54(3) of L. 4481/2017 introduced a limitation providing that public lending right of works is permissible, without the authorization of the author and without remuneration, for libraries of primary and secondary education institutions (school libraries) and for academic libraries that are members of the Hellenic Academic Libraries Association.[112] There is no Greek jurisprudence on this right. It should also be noted that the State provides books free-of-charge to pupils and students of all educational levels, namely public schools and universities, and, consequently, there is no need to borrow certain categories of works and educational material.

VII. Right of Public Performance

122. On the basis of the right of public performance, the author has the right to authorize or prohibit the live performances of a work, such as n orchestra performance of a symphony in a concert hall. Public performance also includes performance by means of recordings, such as musical works embodied in phonograms. These works are considered publicly performed when the phonograms are played over recording equipment in discotheques, aeroplanes, restaurants, and shopping malls. According to Article 3(2) of L. 2121/1993 there is public use, performance, or communication of the work when the work, thereby, becomes accessible to a circle of persons wider than the narrow circle of the family and the immediate social circle of the author, regardless of whether the persons of this wider circle are the same or at different locations. A performance is public when effected in tuck shops, music halls, restaurants, or coffee shops, in the form of broadcasting radio and television shows, unless an employee of the shop simply listens to the radio. Jurisprudence[113] has held that the broadcasting of musical compositions and songs in communal areas and hotel rooms[114] is public performance. A performance is public

111. CA of Athens 8532/2006, *DEE* 2007, 924.
112. *See infra* §6(E).
113. *See*, indicatively, SMCFI of Athens 2571/2004, 3092/2003, 2857/2004, unreported.
114. CA of Athens 16/2010, *DIMEE* 2010, 247.

even when the hotel manager does not intervene in the distribution of music programs but simply installs television or radio sets in the rooms, on the basis that, in this case, audiovisual, musical, or other works and the radio and television program, in general, are made accessible to a new audience. For hotels, rooms are the main element for the provision of services of such enterprises, and television sets and receivers are placed with an aim to gain profit and improve services to their customers. They are potential anonymous customers who, as a whole, fall into the concept of 'public', although each separate customer privately takes up a room for temporary residence or stay. By placing a television receiver or other similar device and the appropriate antenna, which will soon become technologically obsolete, the hotel business enables its customers to watch, listen to, or make use of the works broadcast via television programs. With the authorization he/she grants, the author or his/her beneficiary enable third parties to make use of the work, regardless of whether they will actually use it. This is also the position taken by the ECJ[115] on hotel rooms with television sets.

VIII. Right of Broadcasting

123. Article 3(1)(g) of L. 2121/1993 confers upon the author the right to authorize or prohibit the broadcasting or rebroadcasting of their works to the public by radio and television, by wireless means or by cable or any kind of wire, or by any other means, parallel to the surface of earth or by satellite. The concept of broadcasting comprises both by radio and television the broadcasting of works. In theory, a work is broadcasted by radio and television when it becomes accessible to the public via electromagnetic waves, transmitted by certain devices (transmitters) and received by other devices (receivers). A work is broadcasted by radio when the transmitted signal contains only sounds and by television when the signal contains sounds and images. Existing works or works performed live can be broadcasted by radio and television. The law also stipulates a special power for the rebroadcasting of works by radio and television. A critical element for the concept of broadcasting is the ability of a certain audience to receive the signal. Any expansion or differentiation of the audience constitutes a new method of exploitation of the work. When a show is broadcasted by satellite or cable it is considered to be a new broadcast of the work, requiring the permission of the author, even if this does not expand the audience but simply improves the quality of reception. The concept of broadcasting by radio and television is constantly changing, along with the developments in digital technology.

115. ECJ 7 Dec. 2006 (C-306/05) *SGAE v. Rafael Hoteles SA*. *See also* Order of the ECJ 18 Mar. 2010 (C-136/09) *Organismos Sillogikis Diacheirisis Dimiourgon Theatrikon kai Optikoakoustikon Ergon v. Divani Acropolis Anonimi Xenodocheiaki kai Touristiki Etairia*.

IX. Right of Communication to the Public

124. Greek legislation implemented the provision of Article 3 of the Directive 2001/29 concerning the right of communication to the public in Article 3(1)(h) of L. 2121/1993. According to this provision the author has the right to authorize or prohibit the communication, to the public, of his/her works, by wire or wireless means or by any other means, including making the works available to the public in such a way that members of the public may access them from a place and at a time individually chosen by them. The communication to the public is considered 'public' according to the above-mentioned provision of Article 3(2) of L. 2121/1993. The principle of Community exhaustion does not apply. It is expressly provided that the right of communication/making available to the public is not exhausted by any act of communication to the public. Communication to the public is considered as a broad concept, comprising every act except, of course, the distribution of copies, by which a work is made accessible to the public, namely to a number of persons with no special family, kinship or personal relationships. The national law, however, makes a special reference to public performance and television and radio broadcasting, which constitute more partial powers of the economic right. The concept of communication to the public explicitly comprises transmission on demand. In more detail, an exclusive right is recognized to the author to make his works available to the public by way of interactive on-demand transmissions, so that members of the public may access them from a place and at a time individually chosen by them.

125. Jurisprudence[116] has held that the right of reproduction and communication to the public is violated in the event of public broadcasting on the Internet and online communication of musical works, without the authorization of the beneficiary, by a radio station that has signed a radio broadcasting contract with the collective management organization for broadcasting solely by radio, at the frequencies of the specific station.

X. Right of Importation

126. Greek legislation includes the right to control importation of copies. Article 3(1)(i) of L. 2121/1993 confers upon the author the exclusive right to authorize or prohibit (a) the import of copies of his/her works produced abroad without his/her consent and (b) the import of copies from a country outside the European Community when the right over such import in Greece has been retained by the author through contract. Both cases are in accordance with the Community law, because the first case concerns infringed copies and the second case concerns imports made exclusively from non-Member States.

116. SMCFI of Athens 3413/2002, *ChrID* 2003, 652.

XI. Resale Right

127. Resale right (*droit de suite*) is recognized by Article 5 of L. 2121/1993, as amended by Article 1 of L. 3524/2007 implementing the Directive 2001/84. The resale right is provided for the benefit of the author for an original work of art. This right is an inalienable right *inter vivos* which cannot be waived, even in advance. The author has the right to receive a royalty based on the sale price obtained for any resale of the work subsequent to the first transfer of the work by the author. Resale right is applied to all acts of resale involving, as sellers, buyers, or intermediaries, art market professionals, such as sales room and art galleries and, in general, any dealer in works of art. The royalty is payable by the seller. In case an intermediary art market professional is involved, he shares liability with the seller for payment of the royalty. 'Original work of art' means works of graphic or plastic art. such as pictures, collages, paintings, drawings, engravings, prints, lithographs, sculptures, tapestries, ceramics, glassware, and photographs, provided they are made by the artist himself/herself or are copies considered to be original works of art. Copies of works of art, which have been made in limited numbers by the artist himself or under his authority, are considered to be 'original works of art' for the purposes of the resale right. Such copies would normally have been numbered, signed, or otherwise duly authorized by the artist.

128. According to Article 5(3) the royalty is set at the following rates:

(a) 5% for the portion of the sale price up to EUR 50,000.00;
(b) 3% for the portion of the sale price from EUR 50,000.01 to EUR 200,000.00;
(c) 1% for the portion of the sale price from EUR 200,000.01 to EUR 350,000.01;
(d) 0.5% for the portion of the sale price from EUR 350,000.01 to EUR 500,000.00;
(e) 0.25% for the portion of the sale price exceeding EUR 500,000.00.

The total amount of the royalty may not exceed EUR 12,500.00.

The above-mentioned sale prices are net of tax.

The royalty is payable to the author of the work and, after his death, to those entitled under him/her.

129. The management and protection of the resale right may be entrusted to collective management organizations operating by resolution of the Ministry of Culture, for the category of works of art including the photographs. For a period of three years after the resale, beneficiaries and collective management organizations may require from art market professionals to furnish any information that may be necessary in order to secure payment of royalties in respect of the resale. The Greek Chamber of Visual Arts is also entitled to collect information.

130. The term of protection of the resale right corresponds to that laid down for all works protected by copyright.

131. Authors who are nationals of third countries and their successors in title enjoy the resale right in accordance with national law only if legislation in the country of which the author or his/her successor in title is a national of permits resale right protection in that country for Greek authors or authors from other EU Member States and their successors in title. Authors who are not nationals of a Member State but who have their habitual residence in Greece shall also enjoy the resale right.

132. The resale right may come under the broader category of economic rights.[117] This right does not have an absolute or exclusive character. It is a contractual claim turning against certain persons, pursuant to the legislation. The resale right may also be compared to the right of the author to determine the destination of the work (*droit de destination*). From this viewpoint, the resale right follows, in a sense, the 'destination' of the medium in which the work has been incorporated, empowering the author to receive a percentage on every resale. It has been, however, maintained that the resale right is associated with the personality of the author, specifically with the moral right of paternity of the work. This view[118] is based on the following line of thinking: Even when the author waives all his right, even when his work becomes the subject of commercial transaction, it is not possible to alienate all rights of the author, because the paternity of the work always belongs to the initial beneficiary. The buyer of works of art is interested in the initial creation and pays money for the paternity of the work and its authenticity. The resale price of a work of art is shaped by many factors, including the paternity of the work and the fact that this work is the creation of this artist.

§5. Transfer

I. General Principles

133. It is a known fact that most of the time the author is not in a financial position to exploit the work himself/herself. He addresses to publishers, producers of sound and visual recordings, and other cultural enterprises which undertake the exploitation in question. L. 2121/1993 stipulates some general provisions on the transfer, the exploitation, and the exercise of the economic right. It provides, with the more complete protection of the author, for the possibility of the transfer of the economic right[119] and the non-transferability of the moral right. More precisely, Article 12 stipulates that the economic right may be transferred between living persons or *mortis causa.*[120] The moral right is not transferable between living persons. After the death of the author, the moral right passes to his heirs, who should exercise this right in compliance with the author's wishes, provided that such wishes

117. For the legal nature of the resale right *see* O. Garoufalia, *Works of Fine Art and their Legal Protection*, 310–311 (Athens 2001 (in Greek)).
118. M. Stathopoulos, UNESCO, Intergovernmental Copyright Committee, 23–27 (1997), Oral presentation.
119. *See* I. Nikolopoulos, *The Transmission of Copyright*, 31–36 (Athens 2005 (in Greek)).
120. For the transfer of economic right mortis causa *see* P.Nikolopoulos, *Right of Inheritance and Copyright* (Athens 2017 (in Greek)).

have been explicitly expressed. The Supreme Administrative Court [121] decided that after the death of the author, the Ministry of Culture cannot proceed to any act of exploitation without the authorization of the author's heirs.

134. The concept of exploitation contracts and licences is clarified, and certain rules are introduced which restrict the contractual freedom of the author, to protect him/her from the economically powerful counterparty. In this spirit, L. 2121/1993 establishes the written form as an element for the validity of all the relevant juridical acts (Article 14) and lays down certain interpretative rules on the duration, the purpose, and the extent and means of exploitation (Article 15). It also introduces an obligation on the person who acquires the right to the licence of exploitation to present the work to the public within a reasonable time and establishes a percentage fee as a principle which has force for all contracts (Article 32), with certain exceptions when in the nature of things another form of fee is required. Moreover, the rights of a person who undertakes to carry out the exploitation of a work may not be transferred between living persons without the consent of the author.

135. Article 13 of L. 2121/1993 distinguishes between exploitation contracts and licences. By the exploitation contracts the author entrusts economic rights to the other contracting party and the other party to the contract undertakes the obligation to exercise the rights thus entrusted. By the exploitation licence the author authorizes another party to exercise economic rights. The exploitation contract imposes to the contracting party the obligation for the exploitation of the work, while the licence only authorizes the contracting party to exercise the economic rights without imposing any obligation of exploitation of the work.

136. According to Article 13(3) exploitation contracts and licences may be exclusive or non-exclusive. Exclusive exploitation contracts and licences empower the other contracting party to exercise the rights conferred by the contract or licence, excluding any third person. Non-exclusive exploitation contracts and licences give the right, to the other contracting party, to exercise the rights conferred by the contract or licence parallel to the author and other contracting parties. In the absence of an agreement to the contrary, the other contracting party is entitled in his/her own name to seek legal protection against illegal infringements of the rights he/she exercises by third parties. According to Article 13(4), where doubt exists about the exclusivity of an exploitation contract or licence the contract or licence is deemed to be non-exclusive.

137. Particular attention should be drawn to Article 13(5) which stipulates that the contract or licence may in no circumstance confer any total right over the future works of the author and shall never be deemed to refer to forms of exploitation which were unknown on the date of the contract. Consequently, the conclusion of contracts which refer to future methods of exploitation is prohibited and, in the event of doubts, the agreement may never be regarded as including uses which did not exist at the time of the conclusion of the relevant juridical act. Thus, a contract

121. Supreme Administrative Court 3921/2015, DIMEE 2016, 411–413, comments by G. Kapellakou.

for a printed publication which was drawn up some years ago cannot be deemed to include new methods of exploitation of the work, such as reproduction on CD-ROM or CD-I.[122] According to Article 13(6) the rights of a person who undertakes to carry out the exploitation of a work or who acquires the possibility of exploitation may not be transferred among living persons without the consent of the author.

138. Article 14 deals with the form of legal acts and provides that the transfer of economic rights, the assignment or licensing of the right of exploitation, and the exercise of the moral right shall be null and void unless they are concluded in writing.[123] Nullity may be invoked only by the author.

139. Article 15 deals with interpretative rules concerning the transfer as well as the exploitation contracts and licences. The transfer of the economic right and exploitation contracts or licences contracts may restrict the rights they confer, their scope and duration, the geographical application, and the extent or the means of exploitation. If the duration of the transfer or of the exploitation contract or licence is unspecified, its duration is deemed to be limited to five years, provided conventional mores do not indicate otherwise. If the geographical application of the transfer or of the exploitation contract or licence is unspecified, the said legal acts are deemed to apply to the country in which they were concluded.

140. According to Article 15(4) if the extent and the means of exploitation which the transfer concerns or for which the exploitation or the exploitation licence is agreed are unspecified, the said acts refer to the extent and the means that are necessary for the fulfilment of the purpose of the contract or licence. This is the doctrine of the purpose[124] having its origin to German theory and case law.[125] The economic right is transferred for a specific purpose and only to the extent necessary for the implementation of the purpose pursued. In other words, it is considered that transfer is made only of the rights necessary for the counterpart in order to fulfil the purpose of the contract.

141. In all cases involving the transfer of the economic right or the granting of an exclusive exploitation licence, the person who acquires the right or the licence shall ensure that within a reasonable period of time the work is accessible to the public via an appropriate form of exploitation.[126]

142. Article 16 contains the provision concerning the consent of the author as exercise of the moral right: The granting of consent by an author for an action or an

122. *See* case law for broadcasting of old cinematographic works created before the enactment of Greek Law 2121/1993 and in particular CA of Athens 4499/2000, *KrEp* 1/2001, 253–268.
123. AP 711/2017, DIMEE 2017, 574–578 comments by *K.Vossos.*
124. *See*, indicatively, G. Koumantos, *supra* n. 58 at 327, P. Koriatopoulou-Aggeli, *The Contractual Limitations on Copyright Exploitation*, 8 (Athens 1994 (in Greek)).
125. CA of Athens 7545/1982, *EEmpD* 1983, 165. CA of Athens 143/2004, *DEE* 2004, 415 comments by *K. Kyprouli.*
126. Article 15(5) of L. 2121/1993.

omission which would otherwise constitute an infringement of his moral right is deemed to be a form of exercise of his moral right and is binding upon him.

143. The explanatory rule of Article 17 is also very important. Unless there exists prior agreement to the contrary, in writing, with the initial right holder of the economic right, the transfer of the ownership of the physical carrier into which the work has been incorporated, whether in the original form or in any form of copy, shall not constitute a transfer of the copyright or confer on the new owner any rights to exploit the work.

II. Rules Relating to Exploitation Contracts and Licences

A. Percentage Fee

144. Article 32 of L. 2121/1993 introduces the system of *percentage fee*. More precisely, the fee payable to the author by the other contracting party to legal agreements relating to the transfer of all or part of the economic right, the granting of the exploitation, or for the exploitation licence is obligatorily determined as a percentage, agreed freely between the parties. The computation of the percentage is based on gross revenues without exception or the gross expenditure or on the combined gross revenues and expenditure realized from the activity of the other contracting party in the course of the exploitation of the work. By way of exception, in the following circumstances, the fee may be agreed as a lump sum: (a) when it is practically impossible to establish the basis for the calculation of a percentage fee or when there are no means of monitoring the implementation of a percentage arrangement; (b) when the expenditure required for the calculation and the monitoring is likely to be out of reasonable proportion to the fee to be collected; (c) when the nature or the conditions of the exploitation make the implementation of a percentage impossible, notably when the author's contribution is not an essential element in the intellectual creation as a whole, or when the use of the work is secondary in relation to the object of the exploitation.

145. The obligatory percentage arrangement of the fee prescribed above is implemented in all circumstances, provided that the law does not stipulate otherwise, and provided that it does not concern works created by employees in the execution of the employment contract, computer programs or advertisement, in any form.

B. Publishing Contracts and Translators' Rights

146. In connection with Article 33 of L. 2121/1993, which contains certain special provisions on the percentage fee in the *publishing contract*, the following should be noted: it is expressly stipulated that the fee which the publisher owes to the author is to be agreed as a certain percentage.[127] The basis for the calculation of the percentage is the retail sale price of all the copies on sale. The level of the percentage is freely determined between the parties, with the exception of literary works, such as short stories, short novels, novels, poems, essays, critical essays, theatrical works, travel books, or biographies, which are being published in book form in its original language, excluding pocketbook editions; the fee payable to the author by the publisher after the sale of 1,000 copies cannot be less than 10% of the retail selling price of all the copies sold. By way of exception to the above provision, according to Article 33(2) the fee payable to the author may be agreed as a lump sum when the work is any of the following: (a) collective works; (b) encyclopaedias, dictionaries, or anthologies of the works of others; (c) school books; (d) albums, calendars, agendas, instructional books, printed games and educational material, e.g., maps and atlases; (e) prefaces, commentaries, introductions, presentations; (f) illustrations and photographic material in printed publications; (g) non-literary picture books for children; (h) luxury publications with a limited number of copies; (i) magazines or newspapers.

147. As to the distribution of the percentage fee where there is more than one author, Article 33(3) of L. 2121/1993 provides that this percentage fee is distributed among them in proportion to the contribution of each, if, of course, the relation between them has not been regulated differently. This provision is important because it is a deviation from the general regulation of Article 7(1) of L. 2121/1993 on works of joint authorship, which stipulates that the rights belong in equal measure to the co-authors if there is no agreement to the contrary. In the event of the rental or lending of copies by third parties, the fee for the granting of the necessary licence is distributed equally between the author and the publisher. This regulation, according to Article 33(4) of L. 2121/1993, does not afford very special protection to the author, since in effect it cedes, by law, half of the fee to the publisher.

148. According to Article 33(5) in a case where the author's fee is fixed as a percentage of retail sales, and unless some other method of monitoring is agreed, each of the copies to be sold shall be signed by the author. An alternative method of monitoring the number of copies sold shall be fixed in a PD, to be promulgated within six months of the entry into force of this law, on the recommendation of the Minister of Culture after consultation with the interested professional branches.

149. An important innovation is the introduction of the percentage fee in the *translation contract*. According to Article 33(6) of L. 2121/1993, the fee which the publisher must pay to the translator of a work for the translation, reproduction, and distribution of the work or copies thereof is to be agreed as a percentage of the retail selling price of all the copies sold. The level of the percentage is determined freely between the parties in all instances and no lower limit on the percentage of the retail

127. *See* A. Chiotelis, *Contract on Printed Edition*, 117–123 (Athens 1994 (in Greek)). A. Despotidou, *Legal Nature and Function of the Publishing Contract*, 402–412 (Athens-Thessaloniki 2003 (in Greek)). M. Markellou, *The Exploitation Contract of the Author*, 226–228 (Larcier 2012 (in French)).

selling price is stipulated. This regulation is contrary to the usual practice which imposes the payment of a lump sum fee to translators but is justified by the spirit of author protection with which the whole of L. 2121/1993 is imbued. In the translation contract, the provisions of Article 33(2), (4), and (5) of L. 2121/1993 also apply, *mutatis mutandis*. Consequently, the exceptions from a percentage fee which are stipulated for the publishing contract apply *mutatis mutandis* for the translation contract also. Thus, in the case of the translation of a dictionary, an encyclopaedia, school books, and those in the categories cited in Article 33(2), the fee paid to the translator may be agreed at a fixed sum.

C. Audiovisual Production Contracts

150. Article 34 of L. 2121/1993 establishes the rules relating to *audiovisual production contracts*. The contract dealing with audiovisual work between the producer and the author shall specify the economic rights which are to be transferred to the producer. If the aforementioned provision is not met, the contract shall be deemed to transfer, to the producer, all the economic rights which are necessary for the exploitation of the audiovisual work, pursuant to the purpose of the contract. The audiovisual work is deemed to be accomplished when the master from which copies for exploitation are to be made is approved by the author. No alteration, abridgement, or other modification can be made to the definite form of the audiovisual work, as the latter has been approved by the author, without his/her prior consent. The author of the audiovisual work has the right to a separate fee for each form of exploitation of the work. This fee is agreed as a percentage specified in the relevant contract. The calculation of the percentage is based on the gross revenues or gross expenditure realized in the course of the exploitation of the work. Short advertising films are exempted from this provision. When visual or audiovisual recordings carrying a fixation of an audiovisual work are the object of a rental arrangement, the author shall retain the right to an equitable remuneration in all cases. This provision is also applied in the case of a rental arrangement relating to sound recordings.

D. Rules Relating to Broadcasting by Radio and Television

151. Article 35 of L. 2121/1993 deals with rules relating to *broadcasting by radio and television*. In the absence of an agreement to the contrary, the rebroadcasting of a work by radio or television requires no consent from the author additional to that granted for the first broadcasting. However, when a broadcasting organization rebroadcasts a work it shall pay an additional fee to the author. For the first rebroadcast, the fee payable shall be at least 50% of the initial fee agreed for the first broadcast, and for each subsequent broadcast the additional fee shall be 20% of the initial fee. This provision is not applicable to the arrangements between collecting societies and users. In the absence of an agreement to the contrary, the contract between an author and a broadcasting organization does not empower the broadcasting organization to permit third parties to broadcast or rebroadcast, to the public, the work, which is the object of the contract, by wireless or by wire or by any other means, parallel to the surface of the earth or by satellite. Article 35 also implements the provisions of the Directive 93/83/EEC on satellite broadcasting and cable retransmission.

E. *Theatrical Performance Fee*

152. According to Article 36 of L. 2121/1993 concerning the *theatrical performance fee,* the rights of playwrights are determined as a percentage of gross receipts after deduction of the public entertainment tax. The fee is based on the gross receipts for the whole of the program of a performance of original works or translations or adaptations of ancient or more recent classical works, the minimum fee is 22% for performances in State theatres and 10% for performances in private theatres. For translations of modern works of the contemporary international repertory, the minimum fee is 5%. Where a program contains works by more than one playwright, the fee is shared among them in proportion to the duration of each playwright's work. The authorization to communicate a work to the public by satellite is acquired only by agreement.

F. *Musical Accompaniment of Films*

153. Article 37 of L. 2121/1993 deals with the fee for *musical accompaniment of films* The minimum fee payable to the composers of music and song accompaniment of films, shown to the public in cinema halls or other spaces, is 1% of the gross receipts after deduction of the public entertainment tax.

G. *Photographers' Rights*

154. Article 38 contains provisions for the *photographers' rights*:

- In the absence of an agreement to the contrary, a transfer of the economic right or exploitation contract or licence dealing with the publication of a photograph in a newspaper, periodical, or other mass media shall refer only to the publication of the photograph in the particular newspaper, periodical, or mass media specified in the transfer or exploitation contract or licence and to the archiving of the photograph. Every subsequent act of publication shall be subject to payment of a fee equal to half the current fee. The publication of a transferred photograph from the archive of a newspaper, periodical, or other mass media is permitted only when accompanied by a reference to the title of the newspaper or of the periodical or to the name of the mass media into whose archive the photograph was initially and lawfully placed.
- Where the publication of a photograph is facilitated by the surrender of the photographic negative, use shall be made of the negative, in the absence of an agreement to the contrary, only for the first publication of the photograph, after which the negative shall be returned to the photographer.

- The photographer retains the right to access and request the return of his/her photographs, which have been the object of an exploitation contract or licence arrangement with a particular newspaper, periodical, or other mass media and which have remained unpublished three months after the date of the exploitation contract or licence. Each act of publication of a photograph is accompanied by a mentioning of the photographer's name. This provision applies, likewise, when the archive of a newspaper or of a periodical or of another mass media is transferred.
- The owner of a newspaper or of a periodical shall not be entitled to publish a photograph created by a photographer employed by him/her, in a book or album publication without the employee's consent. This provision applies, likewise, to the lending of a photograph.

H. Nullity of Contrary Agreement

155. Article 39 contains a provision concerning the nullity of contrary agreement. Except where provided for elsewhere in law, any agreement which lays down conditions contrary to the provisions of the above-mentioned Articles 32–38 of L. 2121/1993, or which imposes a fee level lower than that prescribed in this section, is null and void in respect of those of its clauses which are deleterious to the authors.

§6. Limitations to the Scope of Economic Rights

I. General Principles

156. Greek legislation contains specific limitations on the economic right with regard to its content and extent (section IV of L. 2121/1993 Articles 18–28, 28A, 28B, 28C). These limitations are justified on grounds of social policy, research, or education and have as their purpose the protection of society as a whole. A reflection of these considerations can be seen in the provisions concerning the following cases: use of the work for the purpose of informing the public (Article 25), reproduction for teaching purposes (Article 21) and to meet other educational needs (Article 20), reproduction for judicial or administrative purposes (Article 24), the quotation of extracts with a view to the advancement of science and letters (Article 19), and public performance on special occasions (Article 27). Article 28A contains provisions concerning the reproduction for the benefit of blinds and deaf-mute and Article 28B concerns temporary acts of reproduction and Article 28C contains a clause of general application ('three-step test') Specific uses of computer programs are laid down in Articles 42–43 of L. 2121/1993 in conformity with the Directive on the legal protection of computer programs. Reproduction for private use is dealt with in Article 18 of L. 2121/1993, as amended. Article 27A implements the Directive on orphan works and contains provisions concerning the subject matter and scope of protection, the diligent search to identify the right holder, the end of orphan works status, as well as the permitted uses of orphan works.

II. Limitations Provided by Legislative Provisions

A. Reproduction for Private Use

157. Article 18 of L. 2121/1993, as amended by Article 14 of L. 3049/2002, Article 10(33) of L. 3207/2003, Article 46(8) of L. 3905/2010, and Article 54(2) of L. 4481/2017, regulates the reproduction for private use. This provision does apply to analogue and digital reproduction recognizing to the authors and to certain holders of related rights (performers, phonogram producers, and producers of audiovisual works) the right to an *equitable remuneration* if, for the free reproduction of the work, use is made of technical media, such as[128] audio or video recorders or audio/video recorders; magnetic tapes or other material suitable for the reproduction of sound or images or sound and images, including digital means, in particular CD-RW, CD-R, DVD and other storage media with a capacity of less than 1 terabyte (TB) or equal or more than 1 TB; computers, including tablets and smartphones with a random access memory (RAM) size of more than 4 gigabyte (GB); devices or components, whether or not computer-aided, used for digital copying, transcription or otherwise reproducing; photocopying machines and paper suitable for photocopies; scanners and printers. Items to be exported are excepted. It should be noted that reprography is also subject to the regulation of Article 18 of L. 2121/1993, as amended.

158. The equitable remuneration is determined as follows:

(a) With regard to computers, including those with a RAM of more than 4 GB, remuneration is set at 2% of their value. The remuneration shall be distributed to authors, performing artists, phonogram producers, as well as producers of audiovisual works and to publishers of printed forms. The distribution of the equitable remuneration rates on computers to the collective management organization of each category or sub-category of right holders, the means of collection of monies and payment shall be determined by resolution of the Copyright Organization, in accordance with paragraph 11 of Article 18(11) of L. 2121/1993.
(b) Remuneration for audio, video or audio/video recording devices, magnetic tapes or other media suitable for the reproduction of sound or images or sound and images, including digital duplication media other than storage media with a capacity less than 1 TB, as well as for devices or components, whether computer-aided or not and used for digital copying, transcription or otherwise reproducing, is set at 6% of the value. The remuneration shall be distributed as 55% to authors, 25% to performing artists, and 20% to producers of phonograms and producers of audiovisual works.
(c) To 4% of the value of photocopiers, scanners, printers using paper suitable for photocopying, and storage media with a capacity of less than 1 TB. The remuneration shall be distributed halfway between the authors and publishers. The

---

128. The enumeration of technical media is indicative.

concept of photocopying devices also includes any multifunction machine capable of copying. In any case, the value shall be calculated upon import or disposal from the factory.

159. The remuneration shall be paid by the importers or by the producers of those items,[129] it shall be entered on the invoice and shall be collected by collective management organizations operating with the approval of the Minister of Culture and Sport and covering, in whole or in part, the category of right holders concerned. Within the framework of Article 18 of L. 2121/1993, as amended, OPI may, on the basis of an expert study which takes into account technological developments, the Greek, EU and international markets, propose to the Minister of Culture and Sport provisions regarding technical means and their characteristics, the rate of remuneration on their value, the categories of right holders, and the remuneration rates per category.

160. The law requires, explicitly, that the permitted private copy concerns only lawfully published works. The term 'private use' does not include use by an enterprise, a service, or an organization. The freedom to make a reproduction for private use shall not apply when the act of reproduction is likely to conflict with normal exploitation of the work or prejudice the author's legitimate interests, and notably: (a) when the reproduction is an architectural work in the form of a building or similar construction; (b) when technical means are used to reproduce fine arts which circulates in a restricted number of copies, or when the reproduction is a graphical representation of a musical work. The three-step test is also applied according to the provision of Article 28C of L. 2121/1993.

161. The reproduction of an entire work, legal books in particular, with an aim to market them without the authorization of the authors does not constitute private reproduction but reproduction, in the context of a business which prevents the ordinary exploitation of the work and prejudices the legitimate rights of authors and publishers.[130]

162. Whoever imports or acquires intra-Community products or produces and offers technical equipment and media and/or paper suitable for photocopies which are subject to payment of equitable remuneration, shall, within thirty days from the end of each calendar quarter, declare in writing and under oath, pursuant to L. 1599/1986, to OPI: (a) the quantity and total value of technical means and/or photocopying paper imported or acquired within the Community or produced and made available in the immediately preceding calendar quarter by category and type of technical means and (b) that this is the actual quantity and total value without any concealment. Each collective management organization shall have the right to request, at any time from any debtor, by written notice, to declare in writing and

129. Foreign companies that are not established in Greece and they have received a special license according to Art. 29 (4a) of the Code of Customs are not obliged to pay the equitable enumeration for private use (Art. 235 (2) of L. 4281/2014 adding para. 12 to Art. 18 of L. 2121/1993).

130. CA of Larissa 130/2015, *ChrID* 2015, 762-765 comments by D. Kallinikou.

under oath, pursuant to L. 1599/1986, to OPI: (a) the quantity and total value of technical media and/or paper suitable for photocopying by category and type of technical media in detail, which are subject to payment of equitable remuneration and which, on a case-by-case basis, it imported or acquired within the Community or produced and made available and (b) that this is the actual quantity and total value without any concealment. Within one month of such notice, the debtor is obliged to submit to OPI the above-mentioned statement signed by him/her in the case of a sole proprietorship, or by his/her statutory representative in the case of a company. If the debtor fails to submit the above statement within the time limits specified or fulfils this obligation in an insufficient or incorrect manner, he shall pay twice the equitable remuneration provided for in Article 18(3) of L. 2121/1993. The collective management organizations are not entitled to request the same debtor to submit a new statement before the lapse of at least six months from the submission of the previous one. If the debtor fails to comply with the obligation to submit the declaration, the SMCFI, which considers the case following the interim measures procedure, shall order the person who has been summoned for the immediate submission of the declaration. In any case of non-compliance, a penalty of EUR 3,000–EUR 30,000 is imposed in favour of the requesting collective management organization.

163. In case the same category or subcategory of beneficiaries includes more than one collecting societies and they have not reached an agreement on the distribution of the percentage of reasonable remuneration between them by 1 April of each year, the distribution of the percentages of reasonable remuneration to the collective management organization of each category or subcategory of beneficiaries, the method of collection and payment, as well as any other relevant detail, are determined by resolution of the Copyright Organization. The resolution of the Copyright Organization is shaped according to the opinions of the concerned collecting societies, good faith, transaction ethics, and practices followed at international and community level. Collecting societies that do not agree with this resolution may apply to the SMCFI, under the procedure of injunction measures, to determine other distribution. However, debtors are obliged to pay the reasonable remuneration to collecting societies according to the resolution of the Copyright Organization. Such payment entails full settlement and discharge thereof.

164. Greek jurisprudence[131] has held that the provision of Article 18 of L. 2121/1993 is in line with Information Society Directive and does not infringe the principle of proportionality.[132] The Multi-Member Court of First Instance (MMCFI) of Athens held that smartphones fall within the equitable remuneration for private use.[133]

131. CA of Athens 2429/2007, unreported.
132. Greek case law is in line with the judgments of the CJEU: *See* AP 2097/2013 DIMME 2014, 395–402.
133. MMCFI of Athens 2373/2017, *ChrID* 2017, 752–757 comments by D.Kallinikou.

B. Quotation of Extracts

165. According to Article 19 of L. 2121/1993, quotation of short extracts of a lawfully published work by an author for the purpose of providing support for a case advanced by the person making the quotation or a critique of the position of the author is permissible without the consent of the author and without payment, provided that the quotation is compatible with fair practice and that the extent of the extract does not exceed that justified by the purpose. The quotation of the extract must be accompanied by an indication of the source of the extract and of the names of the author and the publisher, provided that the said names appear in the source. According to jurisprudence,[134] small extracts of foreign works may be quoted to corroborate the opinion of the quoting party or to criticize the opinion of the author. Quoting long extracts, however, makes the work competitive and, for this reason, it is illegal, even if the source is mentioned. In any event, quotation must be made to corroborate an opinion or criticize and should not be the sole source to write a new book or the simple conveyance of another work.[135] Quoting the entire work is illegal.

C. School Textbooks and Anthologies

166. Article 20(1) of L. 2121/1993 provides that the reproduction of lawfully published literary works of one or more writers in educational textbooks approved for use in primary and secondary education by the Ministry of National Education and Religions or another competent Ministry, according to the official, detailed syllabus, is permissible without the consent of the authors and without payment. The reproduction shall encompass only a small part of the total output of each of the writers. The provision is applicable concerning only the reproduction by means of printing. The reproduction shall not conflict with the normal exploitation of the work from which the texts are taken and must be accompanied by an indication of the source and of the names of the author and the publisher, provided that the said names appear in the source.

167. According to Article 20(2) of L. 2121/1993 after the death of the author it is permissible to reproduce his works in a lawfully published anthology of literary works of more than one writer, without the consent of the right holders and without payment. The reproduction shall encompass only a small part of the total output of each of the writers and shall not conflict with the normal exploitation of the work from which the texts are taken and must be accompanied by an indication of the source and of the names of the author and the publisher, provided that the said names appear in the source.

---

134. SMCFI of Athens 8753/1995, *EEmpD* 1995, 708.
135. SMCFI of Athens 1692/1994, *NoV* 1994, 1030.

D. Reproduction for Teaching Purposes

168. Article 21 of L. 2121/1993 permits, without the consent of the author and without payment, to reproduce articles lawfully published in a newspaper or periodical, short extracts of a work or parts of a short work, or a lawfully published work of fine arts exclusively for teaching or examination purposes at an educational establishment, in such measure as is compatible with the aforementioned purpose, provided that the reproduction is effected in accordance with fair practice and does not conflict with the normal exploitation. The reproduction must be accompanied by an indication of the source and of the names of the author and the publisher, provided that the said names appear on the source.

E. Libraries and Archives

169. It is permissible by Article 22 of L. 2121/1993, without the consent of the author and without payment, for a non-profit library or archive to reproduce one additional copy from a copy of the work already in their permanent collection, for the purpose of retaining that additional copy or of transferring it to another non-profit library or archive.[136] The reproduction shall be permissible only if an additional copy cannot be obtained in the market promptly, and on reasonable terms.

170. In Article 22 of L. 2121/1993, a second paragraph is added by Article 54(3) of L. 4481/2017, concerning public lending right. More precisely, public lending of works is permissible, without the authorization of the author and without remuneration, for libraries of primary and secondary education institutions (school libraries) and academic libraries that are members of the Hellenic Academic Libraries Association.[137] A Presidential Decree issued within one year after the entry into force of L. 4481/2017, upon proposal of the Ministers of Interior, Education, Research and Religious Affairs, and Culture and Sport, shall determine the remuneration received by right holders for the public lending right, the means and system of its collection and distribution, all libraries and entities which fall within the scope of the regulation, with the exception of the above-mentioned libraries (libraries of primary and secondary education institutions (school libraries) and academic libraries).

F. Orphan Works

171. Article 27A, added in L. 2121/1993 by Articles 7–8 of L. 4212/2013, determines the permitted uses of orphan works by publicly accessible libraries, educational establishments, or museums, as well as by archives, film or audio heritage institutions, and public service broadcasting organizations established in the Member States. These cultural entities are permitted to reproduce orphan works and

136. *See* D. Kallinikou, *Copyright and Libraries*, 143–151 (Athens 2007 (in Greek)).
137. It is to be noted that this provision is entered into force as of 4 Mar. 1993, namely since the entry into force of L. 2121/1993.

make them publicly available online in order to achieve aims related to their public interest missions; in particular, the preservation, restoration, and the provision of cultural and educational access to works and phonograms contained in their collections. Orphan works are works that are still protected by copyright but none of the right holders are identified or even if one or more of them is identified, none is located despite a diligent search for the right holders. The provision of Article 27A applies to works published in the form of books, journals, newspapers, magazines or other writings, cinematographic or audiovisual works, and phonograms, as well as to works embedded or incorporated in other works or phonograms contained in the collections of the above cultural organizations in order to achieve aims related to their public interest missions. For the purpose of establishing whether a work or phonogram is an orphan work, a diligent search for the right holders shall be carried out prior to the use of the work or phonogram. The sources that are appropriate for each category of works or phonograms in question are determined by resolution of the board of members of the Copyright Organization. The right holder has the possibility to put an end to the orphan work status and receive the payment of damages for the use that has been made of their works. It is provided that the payment of damages shall be the half of the legally required or normally payable remuneration for the use that has been made by the above cultural organizations.

G. Reproduction of Cinematographic Works

172. Article 23 of L. 2121/1993 provides that in cases where the holder of the economic right abusively withholds consent for the reproduction of a cinematographic work of special artistic value, for the purpose of preserving it in the National Cinematographic Archive the reproduction is permissible without his consent and without payment, subject to a decision by the Minister of Culture, taken in conformity with the prior opinion of the Cinematography Advisory Council.

H. Reproduction for Judicial or Administrative Purposes

173. According to Article 24 of L. 2121/1993 the reproduction of a work for use in judicial or administrative procedures is permitted without the consent of the author and without payment, to the extent justified for a particular purpose.

I. Reproduction for Information Purposes

174. Article 25 permits the following acts of reproduction without the consent of the author and without payment, to the extent justified for the particular purpose: (a) for the purpose of reporting current events by the mass media, the reproduction and communication to the public of works seen or heard in the course of the event; (b) for the purpose of giving information on current events, the reproduction and communication to the public by the mass media of political speeches, addresses, sermons, legal speeches, or other works of the same nature, as well as of summaries or extracts of lectures, provided the said works are delivered in public. Wherever possible, the reproduction and communication to the public are accompanied by an indication of the source and of the name of the author.

J. Use of Images of Works Sited in Public Places

175. According to Article 26 of L. 2121/1993, the occasional reproduction and communication by the mass media of images of architectural works, fine art works, photographs or works of applied art, which are sited permanently in a public place is permissible, without the consent of the author and without payment. Jurisprudence[138] has held that the occasional reproduction of the front of a building for advertisement purposes does not infringe the copyright of the architect and falls within the scope of application of the limitation provided by Article 26 of L. 2121/1993. The three-step test is not intended either to affect the substantive content of provisions falling within the scope of Article 26 or to extend the scope of the limitation provided for therein. The above use was secondary and not competitive with the normal exploitation of the architectural work.

K. Public Performance or Presentation on Special Occasions

176. According to Article 27 of L. 2121/1993 the public performance or presentation of a work is permissible, without the consent of the author and without payment, on the following occasions: (a) at official ceremonies, to the extent compatible with the nature of the ceremonies. An 'Official Ceremony' is any ceremony attended by institutional bodies performing State functions, i.e., national anniversary, reception of Heads of State or State officials, celebration of significant event, such as the new millennium, pursuant to Opinion No. 226/2000 of the Legal Council of the State, the opening and closing ceremonies of the Olympic Games;[139] (b) within the framework of staff and pupil/student activities at an educational establishment, provided that the audience is composed exclusively of the aforementioned persons, the parents of the pupils/students, persons responsible for the care of the pupils/students, or persons directly involved in the activities of the establishment. Public performance or presentation in educational establishments must be made by the staff or the pupils/students of the establishment and the audience must be composed exclusively of the parents of the pupils/students or persons responsible for their care or other persons directly involved in the activities of the establishment. In the absence of a more specific definition, educational establishments include public or private schools, universities, and schools, provided that they are supervised by the State. It was decided by the Three-Member Misdemeanor Court of Athens that public performance in a professional school of dance does not constitute an infringement of copyright because in that occasion music is publicly performed only for

138. MMCFI of Athens 3141/2015 ChrID 2016, 59–63 comments by S. Stauridou.

139. Concerts and carnival celebrations organized by municipalities are not considered as official ceremonies: AP 1/2009, *EllDni* 209, 1587.

educational purposes within the framework of student activities, according to the exception provided by Article 27 of L. 2121/1993.[140]

L. Exhibition and Reproduction of Works of Fine Art

177. According to Article 28 of L. 2121/1993, museums which own the physical carriers into which works of fine art have been incorporated are entitled, without the consent of the author and without payment, to exhibit those works to the public on the museum premises or during exhibitions organized in museums. The presentation of fine art to the public and its reproduction in catalogues to the extent necessary to promote its sale is permissible, without the consent of the author and without payment. In the above-mentioned cases reproduction is permissible, provided such reproduction does not conflict with the normal exploitation of the work and does not unreasonably prejudice the legitimate interest of the author.

M. Reproduction for the Benefit of Blinds and Deaf-Mute

178. Article 28A implements Article 5(3)b of the Information Society Directive and provides that the reproduction of the work is allowed for the benefit of blinds and deaf-mutes, for uses which are directly related to the disability and are of a non-commercial nature, to the extent required by the specific disability. By decision of the Minister of Culture[141] the conditions of application of this provision may be determined, as well as the application of this provision for other categories of people with a disability.[142]

N. Exception from the Reproduction Right

179. Article 28B implements Article 5(1) of Directive 2001/29 concerning temporary acts of reproduction. It provides that temporary acts of reproduction which are transient or incidental, which are an integral and essential part of a technological process, and whose sole purpose is to enable: (a) a transmission in a network between third parties by an intermediary or (b) a lawful use of a work or other protected subject matter, and which have no independent economic significance, are exempted from the reproduction right.

---

140. Three-Member Misdemeanor Court of Athens 2485/2017, PoinikaXronika 2017, 549.

141. Ministerial Decision ΥΠΠΟ/ΔΙΟΙΚ/98546/12.10.2007 concerning the reproduction of copyrighted works for the benefit of the blind and deaf-mute and extension of the arrangement to other categories of people with disabilities.

142. For the interpretation of Article 28A as well as of the Ministerial Decision *see* V. Antoniadis, *Limitations to the Scope of Copyright for the Benefit of People with Disabilities*, 131–147 (Athens 2018 (in Greek)).

O. Clause of General Application Concerning the Limitations

180. Article 28C entitled 'clause of general application concerning the limitations' contains the three-step test. Under this provision all limitations provided for in section IV of Greek Law on Copyright (Articles 18–28B of L. 2121/1993, as amended) is only applied in certain special cases which do not conflict with the normal exploitation of the work or other protected subject matter and do not unreasonably prejudice the legitimate interests of the right holder. The three-step test has also been taken into consideration in the drafting of certain provisions on limitations. It is addressed to the legislator and also to the judge and, therefore, can be directly applied in judicial practice.

§7. DURATION OF PROTECTION

181. Copyright does not have force indefinitely, but it has a limited *duration*. With the elapse of a certain length of time prescribed by law, a work becomes common property; it belongs to the public domain and may freely be the object of exploitation. This time limit is to be justified mainly on the grounds of the protection of society as a whole. The recognition of the institution of copyright, as we have noted above, ensures that the author will be able to exploit his work for economic purposes, thus supporting the cultural production of each country and of humanity in general. But at some point in time, the work must be disseminated freely so that it can become the possession of the whole of humanity. In accordance with Article 7 of the Berne Convention, copyright lasts as long as the author lives, and for fifty years after his death. In recent years, there has been a tendency towards the lengthening of the term of the protection. Certain legislations and Directive 2006/116 establish a term of protection of seventy years after the death of the author. L. 2121/1993 in Article 29(1), as amended by Article 8 of L. 2557/1997, follows this contemporary trend towards the lengthening of the term of protection and stipulates that copyright lasts for the whole of the life of the author and for seventy years after his death, calculated from 1 January of the year after the author's death. The duration of protection is valuable for economic and moral rights. However, concerning moral right, the law provides in Article 29(2) that after the expiry of the duration of copyright protection, the State, represented by the Minister of Culture, may exercise the rights relating to the acknowledgement of the author's paternity and the rights relating to the protection of the integrity of the work.

182. In regard of works of joint authorship, according to Article 30 of L. 2121/1993, as amended by Article 54(4) of L. 4481/2017, copyright lasts as long as the life of the last surviving author and seventy years following his death, calculated from the 1 January of the year after the death of the last surviving author. The term of protection of musical compositions with lyrics is the same as the one mentioned above, provided that both contributions, by the composer and the lyricist, have been created specifically for the specific musical composition with lyrics.

183. In the case of anonymous or pseudonymous works,[143] the term of protection lasts for seventy years calculated from 1 January of the year after that in which the work is lawfully made available to the public. However if, during this period, the author discloses his identity or when the pseudonym adopted by the author leaves no doubt as to his identity, then the general rule of term is applied.

184. In case of audiovisual works,[144] the term of protection expires after the death of the last of the following persons to survive: the principal director, the author of the screenplay, the author of the dialogue and the composer of the music specifically created for use in the audiovisual work.

185. According to Article 31(2) of L. 2121/1993 implementing the Community rule provided in Article 1(5) of Directive 2006/116, where a work is published in volumes, parts, instalments, issues, or episodes and the term of protection runs from the time when the work was lawfully made available to the public, the term of protection runs for each such item separately.

§8. Related Rights

186. Greek L. 2121/1993 provides for the protection of related rights: performers, producers of sound or visual or audiovisual recordings, broadcasting organizations.[145] A specific protection is recognized in favour of publishers of printed matters.[146] In conformity with the Directive 2006/116[147] a specific provision, added to L. 2121/1993 by Article 8(9) of L. 2557/1997, recognized a related right in case of previously unpublished works.

I. Performers

187. According to Article 46(1) of L. 2121/1993 the term 'performers' designates the persons who in any way act or perform works, such as actors, musicians, singers, chorus singers, dancers, puppeteers, shadow theatre artists, 'variety performers or circus artists'. The acts which may be authorized or prohibited by performers are the following: (a) fixations of their performance; (b) concerning the fixation of their performances, the direct or indirect, temporary or permanent, reproduction by any means and in any form, in whole or in part; (c) distribution to the public of the fixation of their performance, by sale or other means. The law follows the principle of the Community exhaustion of the distribution right; (d) rental and public lending of the fixation of their performances. The principle of Community exhaustion does not apply for rental and public lending right; (e) radio or television

143. *See* Art. 31(1) of L. 2121/1993.
144. *See* Art. 31(3) of L. 2121/1993.
145. *See* Arts 46–53 of L. 2121/1993.
146. *See* Art. 52 of L. 2121/1993.
147. *See* Art. 4 of Directive 2006/116.

broadcast of the illegal fixation, by any means such as wireless waves, satellite, cables, as well as the presentation to the public of the recording with the illegal fixation of their performances; (f) radio or television broadcast by any means, such as wireless waves, satellite, cables, of their live performances, except where the said broadcast is a rebroadcast of a lawful broadcasting (e) communication of their live performances to the public by any means other than radio or television transmission (h) making available to the public the fixations of their performances, by wire or wireless means, in such a way that members of the public may access them from a place and at a time individually chosen by them. This right is not exhausted by any act of making available to the public.

188. It is prohibited to transfer, during the lifetime of the performer, and to waive the rights referred to above. The administration and protection of the aforementioned rights may be entrusted to a collecting society

189. Subject to contractual clauses to the contrary explicitly specifying those acts which are authorized, the above-mentioned acts are presumed to be authorized in a circumstance where the performer enters with a party operating such acts into an employment contract having as object the operation of those particular acts. The performer retains, at all times, the right to remuneration for the operation of each of these acts, whatever the form of exploitation of his performance. In particular, the performer retains the right to an equitable remuneration for rental, without being able to wave this right, if he/she has given to the producer of sound or visual, or sound and visual recordings, the authorization for the rental of the recordings carrying the fixation of his performance.

190. In case a performance is effected by an ensemble, the performers making up the ensemble elect and appoint, in writing, one representative to exercise the above-mentioned rights. This presentation does not encompass orchestral conductors, choir conductors, soloists, main role personages, and principal directors. If the performers making up an ensemble fail to appoint a representative, the above-mentioned rights are exercised by the director of the ensemble.

191. Performers are also protected concerning their moral right and, in particular, the right of paternity and the right of integrity.[148] After the death of a performer moral right pass to his heirs. Article 16 of L. 2121/1993, concerning the consent of the author as exercise of the moral right, is applicable *mutatis mutandis* to the moral right of performers. The dubbing of the voice over from Greek to Albanian language without the authorization of the actor constitutes an alteration of the performance and, therefore, an infringement of the moral right of the performer and, in particular, of the right of integrity.[149]

148. *See* Art. 50 of L. 2121/1993. *See also* K. Kyprouli, *The Related Rights of Performers*, 200–223 (Athens-Thessaloniki 2000 (in Greek)).

149. CA of Athens 761/2016: DEE 2017, 48–51 with comments by K. Kyprouli; ChrID 2017 293-296 with comments by Th. Chiou.

192. When sound recordings are used for radio or television broadcast or for communication to the public, the performers have a right of equitable remuneration. According to Article 49(1) of L. 2121/1993, as amended by Article 54(6a) of L. 4481/2017, when sound recordings are used for a radio or television broadcast by any means, such as wireless waves, satellite, or cable, or for communication to the public the user shall pay a *single and equitable remuneration* to the performers whose performances are carried on the recordings and to the producers of the recordings. This remuneration is payable only to collective management organizations. The collective management organizations are responsible for negotiating and agreeing on the remuneration levels, raising the claims for the payment and collecting the remuneration from the users. Without prejudice to the obligatory assignment of the administration of rights and the collection of the remuneration by collective management organizations, the right of performers to the equitable remuneration prescribed under paragraph is not assignable.[150] The collected remuneration is distributed in the order of 50% to the performers and 50% to the producers of the recordings. The distribution of the collected remuneration among the various performers and among the various producers is effected pursuant to agreements among them that are contained in the rules of each collecting society.[151]

193. According to Article 49(5) of L. 2121/1993, as amended by Article 54(6b) of l. 4481/2017, in case of visual or audiovisual recordings used for radio or television broadcast by any means, such as wireless waves, satellite or cable or communication to the public, the user shall pay equitable remuneration to the performers whose performances are carried on the recordings.

194. The criteria on the basis of which the judge can determine the level of equitable remuneration mainly include (a) the extent of the contribution of the use of the devices on which the performance or presentation has been recorded in the revenue of radio and television organizations, as regards the specific radio and television broadcast (advertising revenue, number of listeners or receivers, area of reception, length and number of uses); (b) the effects of the radio and television broadcasting of recordings on the employment of performers or performing artists, e.g., fall in the sales of sound recordings due to frequent radio and television broadcasting of musical works and performances. For music, e.g., account may be taken of the costs of the radio station if, instead of the music repertory broadcast daily, it employed singers, orchestra, musicians, etc. during its live program. The level of reasonable remuneration is determined on the basis of rating zones.

195. Jurisprudence[152] has acknowledged the right of equitable and single remuneration to performers or performing artists and producers of sound recordings, for the presentation to the public, of radio and television programs made in hotel rooms[153] and communal areas. In more detail, these judgments have held that the

150. *See* Art. 49(2) of L. 2121/1993.
151. *See* Art. 49(3) of L. 2121/1993.
152. SMCFI of Thessaloniki 30021/2003 and 20578/2007 unreported.
153. CA of Athens 915/2010, *DIMEE* 2010, 240.

purpose and destination of the radio and television broadcasting are for private persons to receive the transmission in their homes or other private premises for personal use. For this use, royalties have been paid to beneficiaries by radio and television stations. When, however, one of the recipients of the broadcast (the hotel manager), using a central distributing receiver (antenna) in the context of his business activity, makes the radio and television broadcast accessible to other persons, specifically persons with whom he is not associated with family ties, who are not members of his immediate social environment, at premises provided by him or for which he is responsible, then there is a new audience and, therefore, a different destination of the radio and television broadcast, which justifies the payment of another remuneration. Such a presentation is a public presentation, different from radio and television broadcasting. Therefore, the broadcast of radio and television shows within a business and before an audience, namely the persons who transact with the businessman (provided that there are no family or immediate social ties between them and the businessman), from a television or radio receiver placed in hotel rooms, in order to watch or listen to radio and television shows via a central antenna serving the entire building, is a new usage and a separate form of public presentation.

196. The MMCFI of Athens in its Judgment 3089/2014 ruled that the uploading of ninety-five films by the film producer on his web channel that is hosted by YouTube without the actors' and their collecting society written consent and licence, infringes the actors' related rights and is in breach of related rights of performers and in particular an infringement of the right reproduction and making available to the public. The court found that there was also an infringement of the moral right of performers and, especially, of the right to prohibit any form of alteration of their performances. The judgment was confirmed by the CA of Athens.[154]

II. Producers of Phonograms and Audiovisual Works

197. Producers of sound or visual or audiovisual recordings are granted the rights provided in Article 47 of L 2121/1993. According to Article 47(3) of L. 2121/1993 'producer of sound recordings' (phonogram producer) designates any natural or legal person who initiates and bears the responsibility for the realization of the first fixation of a series of sounds.[155] The term 'producer of visual or sound and visual recordings' (producer of audiovisual works)[156] designates any natural or legal person who initiates and bears the responsibility for the realization of the first fixation of a series of images with or without sound.

154. CA of Athens 1701/2016: NoV 2017, 324-339 comments by D. Kallinikou; DIMEE 2016, 584–591 comments by M. Sinanidou.
155. Concerning the definition of the phonogram producer *see* SMCFI 2512/2010, *DIMEE* 2010, 512. *See also* K. Kolotourou, *The Related Rights of the Phonogram Producers*, 36–43 (PhD Thesis – National and Kapodistrian University of Athens 2017 (in Greek)).
156. E. Deligianni, *The Protection of Producers of Audiovisual Works According to Greek Law*, 31–34 (Thessaloniki 1996 (in Greek)).

198. The phonogram producers (producers of sound recordings) have the right to authorize or prohibit: (a) the direct or indirect, temporary or permanent, reproduction by any means and in any form, in whole or in part, of their phonograms; (b) the distribution to the public of the above recordings by sale or other means. The principle of Community exhaustion is applied. The distribution right is not exhausted within the Community in respect of the said recordings except where the first sale in the Community is made by the right holder or with his consent; (c) the rental and public lending of the said recordings. These rights are not exhausted by any sale or other act of distribution of the said recordings; (d) the making available to the public, by wire or wireless means, in such a way that members of the public may access them from a place and at a time individually chosen by them concerning their phonograms. This right is not exhausted by any act of making available to the public in the sense of this provision; (e) the import of the said recordings produced abroad without their consent, or the import from a country outside the European Community when the right over such import in Greece had been retained by the producer through contract. The producers of phonograms also have the right to *single and equitable remuneration* according to the above-mentioned Article 49(1) of L. 2121/1993, as amended by Article 54(6a) of L. 4481/2017.[157]

199. The producers of audiovisual works (producers of visual or sound and visual recordings) have the right to authorize or prohibit: (a) the direct or indirect, temporary or permanent, reproduction by any means and form, in whole or in part, of the original and copies of their films; (b) the distribution to the public of the above recordings, by sale or other means. The principle of Community exhaustion is applied. The distribution right is not exhausted within the Community in respect of the said recordings except where the first sale in the Community is made by the right holder or with his consent; (c) the rental and public lending of the said recordings. Such rights are not exhausted by any sale or other act of distribution of the said recordings; (d) the making available to the public, by wire or wireless means, in such a way that members of the public may access them from a place and at a time individually chosen by them concerning the original and the copies of their films. This right is not exhausted by any act of making available to the public in the sense of this provision; (e) the import of the said recordings produced abroad without their consent, or the import from a country outside the European Community when the right over such import in Greece had been retained by the producer through contract; (f) the broadcast of the said recordings by any means including by satellite or cable, as well as the communication to the public.

III. Radio and Television Organizations

200. Radio and television organizations have the right to permit or prohibit: (a) the transmission of their broadcasts by any means such as wireless waves, satellites

157. Concerning the application of Art. 49(1) of L. 2121/1993 to radio broadcast *see* SMCFI of Thessaloniki 11980/2012, *DIMEE* 2012, 213 comments by E. Vagena.

or cable; (b) the communication of their broadcasts to the public in places accessible to the public against payment of an entrance fee; (c) the fixation of their broadcasts on sound or sound and visual recordings, regardless of whether the broadcasts are transmitted by wire or by air, including by cable or satellite broadcasting; (d) the direct or indirect, temporary or permanent, reproduction by any means and in any form, in whole or in part of the fixation of their broadcasts, whether those broadcasts are transmitted by wire or over the air, including cable or satellite (e) the distribution to the public of the recordings containing the fixation of their broadcasts, including the copies thereof, by sale or other means. The principle of Community exhaustion is applied. The distribution right is not exhausted within the Community in respect of devices containing the recording of their broadcasts except where the first sale in the Community is made by the right holder or with his consent; (f) the rental or public lending concerning the recordings containing the fixation of their broadcasts. Such rights are not exhausted by any sale or other act of distribution of the said recording; (g) the making available to the public, by wire or wireless means, in such a way that members of the public may access them from a place and at a time individually chosen by them concerning the fixation of their broadcasts. This right is not exhausted by any act of making available to the public, in the sense of this provision.

IV. Publishers of Printed Matter

201. According to Article 51 of L. 2121/1993 publishers of printed matters have the right to authorize or prohibit the reproduction by photocopying, electronic or any other means, of the typesetting and pagination format of the works they have published if the said reproduction is made for exploitation purposes. Judgment 26196/1999 of the SMCFI of Athens[158] refers to the related right of publishers. The judgment accepted the petition for injunction measures lodged by a publishing house against a publishing company that made photographic reproductions of the entire work (Grand Dictionary of the Greek Language) and marketed it in the same artistic form, using the same typeset as that used in the initial publishing house.

V. Protection of Previously Unpublished Works

202. Previously unpublished works are protected according to Article 51A of L. 2121/1993. Any person who, after the expiry of copyright protection, for the first time lawfully publishes or lawfully communicates to the public a previously unpublished work benefits from a protection equivalent to the economic rights of the author. The term of protection is twenty-five years from the time when the work was first lawfully published or lawfully communicated to the public and is calculated from 1 January of the year after the first publication or communication to the public. This provision implements Article 4 of the Directive 2006/116 on the term of protection.

158. SMCFI of Athens 26196/1999, *NoV* 2001, 73.

VI. Regulations Concerning the Form of Licence, Limitations and Duration

203. According to Article 52 of L. 2121/1993, as amended by Article 3 and 4 of L. 4212/2013, related rights are subject to the following rules: (a) Agreements concerning such rights are valid only when concluded in writing. (b) The limitations applicable to the economic right attaching to copyright are likewise applicable by analogy to related rights. (c) The term of protection of the economic rights of performers prescribed lasts for fifty years from the end of the year in which the performance occurs but in no case expires before the death of the performer. However, if the fixation of the performance, otherwise than in a phonogram, is lawfully published or lawfully communicated to the public within this period, the performers' rights expire fifty years from the date of the first publication or the first communication to the public, whichever is the earlier. If the fixation of the performance in a phonogram is lawfully published or lawfully communicated to the public within this period, the performers' rights expire seventy years from the date of the first publication or communication to the public, whichever is the earlier. The above provisions implement Article 1(2)(a) of Directive 2011/77. (d) The rights of phonogram producers (producers of sound recordings) expire fifty years after the fixation is made. However, if the phonogram has been lawfully published within this period, the said rights shall expire seventy years from the date of the first lawful publication. If no lawful publication has taken place within the period mentioned in the first sentence, and if the phonogram has been lawfully communicated to the public within this period, the said rights shall expire seventy years from the date of the first lawful communication to the public. The above provisions implement Article 1(2)(b) of Directive 2011/77. However, where through the expiry of the term of protection granted pursuant to this paragraph in its version before the amendment by Directive 2001/29 on the harmonization of certain aspects of copyright and related rights in the information society, the rights of producers of phonograms are no longer protected as on 22 December 2001, this paragraph shall not have the effect of protecting those rights anew. This provision implements Article 11(2) of the Information Society Directive. (e) The rights of producers of audiovisual works (producers of sound and visual recordings) shall expire fifty years after the fixation is made. However, if lawful publication or lawful communication of the device is made to the public within such period, such rights shall expire fifty years from the date of first publication or first communication to the public, whichever comes first. (f) Protection of the rights of radio or television organizations and of publishers lasts for fifty years from the end of the year in which the first radio or television broadcast occurs or in which the last edition of the work is published. (g) The rights of editors provided in Article 51 expire fifty years after the last edition of the work.

204. Article 52, as amended by Article 4(2) of L. 4121/2013 implementing Article 1(2)(c) of Directive 2011/77, contains provisions concerning the 'use it or lose it clause' to help the performers. If, fifty years after the phonogram was lawfully published or, failing such publication, fifty years after it was lawfully communicated to the public, the phonogram producer does not offer copies of the phonogram for sale in sufficient quantity or does not make it available to the public, by wire or wireless means, in such a way that members of the public may access it from a place and at a time individually chosen by them, the performer may terminate the contract linking him with the producer of phonogram under the conditions prescribed in the above provision.

VII. Protection of Copyright

205. Article 53 of L. 2121/1993 confirms the independence of copyright and related rights. It is provided that the protection recognized to the right holders of related rights shall leave integral the copyright protection and shall in no case affect it. In no circumstance shall any of the provisions of the aforementioned articles concerning the related rights be interpreted in such a manner as to lessen or prejudice that protection. Where the performers, the producers of sound or visual, or sound and visual recordings, the radio or television organizations, and the publishers acquire the right of copyright over a work in addition to the related right, the copyright and the related right shall apply parallel to each other and shall confer the powers deriving from each right.

§9. Administration by Collecting Societies

206. Articles 1–54 of L. 4481/2017 regulate collective management of copyright and related rights, as well as the multi-territorial licensing for online rights in musical works, implementing, in Greece, Directive 2014/26/EU on collective management. The legal framework on collective management provided by L. 2121/1993 was repealed by Article 54(1) of L. 4481/2017, as amended by Article 13 of L. 4505/2017. The aim of the above provisions of L. 4481/2017 is to ensure a high standard of governance, financial management, transparency, and reporting.[159] Article 2 of L. 4481/2017 outlines the scope of application and covers the collective management organizations, the collective protection organizations, the entities owned and controlled by a collective management organization, the agents of collective management organizations, the independent management entities, and the independent management entities with a dominant position in the Greek market.[160]

207. Article 3 of L. 4481/2017 gives the definition of the terms used for the application of the law on collective management according to Article 3 of the Directive on collective management. The definitions provided are the following: collective management organization, collective protection organization, independent management entity, right holder, member, statute, object of protection, operating licence, General Assembly of Members, rights revenue, management fees, representation agreement, user, repertoire, multi-territorial licence, online rights in musical works, OPI. For the purposes of Articles 1–54 of L. 4481/2017 'collective management organization' means 'any organization authorized by law or by way of assignment, licence or any other contractual arrangement to manage copyright or

159. *See also* recital 9 of Directive 2014/26.
160. Article 50 of L. 4481/2017.

rights related to copyright on behalf of more than one right holder for the collective benefit of those right holders, as its sole and main purpose, and which fulfils one or both of the following criteria: a) it is owned or controlled by its members b) it is organized on a non-profit basis'.[161]

208. According to Article 8(1) and (2) of L. 4481/2017, collective management organizations may operate in any legal form under the terms of the above definition. Where they operate in the form of an incorporated company all of the shares shall be nominal. Collective management organizations may also operate in the form of an urban cooperative.

209. Any collective management organization, collective protection organization, and independent management entity in a dominant position is required to obtain an operating licence issued by the Minister of Culture and Sport in accordance with the procedure of Article 4 of L. 4481/2017.

210. Collective management organizations have the competencies provided indicatively by Article 6 of L. 4481/2017 as follows: (a) to manage the economic right; (b) to enter into agreement with the users; (c) to secure for authors and other right holders the percentage fee referred to in Article 32(1) of L. 2121/1993; (d) to collect the remuneration and distribute it to right holders, to prepare and publish the annual transparency report; (e) to grant multi-territorial licences for online rights in musical works, provided that they meet the legal requirements and take all relevant appropriate measures according to the law; (f) to initiate administrative, judicial, or extrajudicial proceedings for the legitimate protection of the rights of right holders notably taking court actions, lodging of complaints, and appearing as civil plaintiffs; (g) to obtain from users all information needed for computation, collection, and allocation of remuneration; (h) to provide social, cultural, or educational services for the benefit of right holders; (k) to exercise the right of the right holder to grant or refuse authorization to a cable operator for retransmission through cable or other transmission materials; (l) to conclude representation agreements and give the other collective management organization any information relating to the management of the rights provided by L. 4481/2017 or the L. 2121/1993 (m) to conduct in collaboration with the public authority the inspections in shops for the sale, rental and lending of copies, or public performance of works, in order to protect against infringements of the rights protected (n) to organize conferences on copyright and related rights and to participate in such conferences.

211. Article 7(1) of L. 4481/2017, based on the repealed Article 55(2) of L. 2121/1993, establishes a presumption in favour of collective management organizations, collective protection organizations, as well as independent management entities in dominant position (in the Greek market) which had been established until the date of entry into force of L. 4481/2017.[162] The above legal persons are presumed to have the competence to manage or protect the rights of all works or

161. Article 3(a) of L. 4481/2017.
162. Article 50 of L. 4481/2017.

objects of protection or all right holders in respect of whom or which they declare, in writing, that they have been entrusted with the respective powers or that the right to equitable remuneration has been transferred to them or that they act under power of attorney or other contractual agreement. The presumption is valid both for the civil and criminal protection of right holders. The Introductory Report to L. 2121/1993 shows that the purpose of the provision establishing the presumption was to 'safeguard the legitimate power of the organization to manage and provide judicial protection to works and authors, without the need to produce thousands of documents which would have been necessary under the general procedural provisions and without risking the dismissal of the action due to vagueness which, in such matters, would be impossible to set aside'. Insofar as a collective management organization operating with a licence granted by the Minister of Culture and Sport exercises rights which are subject to mandatory collective management, the presumption covers all right holders, both foreign and Greek, as well as all their works or other subject matter. If in the above case, there are more collective management organizations for a specific category of right holders, the presumption applies to the extent that the rights are jointly exercised by all relevant collective management organizations in accordance with the specific provisions of law. Regardless of whether their competence rests on a transfer of rights or on power of attorney, or on any other contractual agreement, collective management organizations and collective protection organizations are entitled to initiate judicial or extrajudicial proceedings in their own name and to exercise, in full legitimacy, all the rights transferred to them, or for which they hold power of attorney or any other contractual agreement. When seeking the legal protection of the courts for works and right holders, collective management organizations or protection organizations are not required to provide an exhaustive list of all of the works which have been the object of the unlicensed exploitation or without payment of the equitable remuneration, it is sufficient to provide only a sample list of works.[163]

212. The General Assembly of Members is convened once a year and is organized according to the rules laid down in Article 9 of L. 4481/2017. These rules delineate the powers of the General Assembly, the right of the members to participate in and to vote at the General Assembly, the right to appoint another person or entity as a proxy holder to participate in and to vote on his behalf. The powers of the General Assembly may be exercised by the Assembly of Delegates under the conditions of Article 9(7) of L. 4481/2017 or by the Supervisory Board if the collective management organization does not have a General Assembly of Members. Specific rules are established regarding the General Assembly of Members of the independent management entities with a dominant position in accordance with Article 9(9) of L. 4481/2017.

213. The Supervisory Board is the body exercising the supervisory function pursuant to Article 10 of L. 4481/2017. The main power is to monitor the activities and the performance of the duties of the persons who manage the business of the organization. The Supervisory Board may consist of three to nine members. Specific

163. Article 7(2) of L. 4481/2017.

rules are laid down concerning the Supervisory Board of the independent management entities with a dominant position in accordance with Article 10(8) and (9) of L. 4481/2017. Pursuant to recital 24 of Directive 2014/26 collective management organizations should have a supervisory function appropriate to their organizational structure.

214. Collective management organizations are required to act in the best interest of the right holders whose rights they represent and not impose on them any obligations which are not objectively necessary for the protection of their rights and interests or for the effective management of their rights. The rights and obligations of right holders are described in Articles 12–16 of L. 4481/2017 and must be provided for in the statute of the collective management organization. In accordance with Article 12 of L. 4481/2017 right holders have the right to authorize a collective management organization to manage their economic rights or the powers deriving therefrom, or categories of powers or types of works or object of protection of their choice, for the territories of their choice, irrespective of the Member State of nationality, residence, or establishment of either the collective management organization or of the right holder. Such authorization may be granted by transfer of the right or the relevant powers for the purpose of management, either by power of attorney or any other contractual agreement. The authorization in question is given in writing and for a specified period of time, which may not exceed three years. In case of ambiguity it is presumed that the authorization concerns all works, including future works, for a time period not exceeding three years. Right holders have the right to terminate, in whole or in part, the authorization to manage rights or categories of powers, or types of works or object of protection of their choice, for the territory of their choice, as well as the right to withdraw from the collective management organization any of the rights, categories of rights, types of works, and other subject matter of their choice upon sending three-months' notice in writing. Collective management organizations must inform their members about their rights. This information has to be posted on the website of the collective management organization and be communicated to the right holder by e-mail. Article 13 of L. 4481/2017 implements Article 6 of the Directive 2014/26 and provides for objective, transparent, and non-discriminatory membership criteria. A collective management organization shall accept right holders and entities representing right holders, including other collective management organizations and associations of right holders. The membership requirements shall be included in the statute and posted on the organization's website. In case where a collective management organization refuses to accept a request for membership, it shall provide the right holder with a clear explanation of the reasons for its decision. The representation of the different categories of members in the decision-making process must be fair and balanced. Collective management organizations have to facilitate its members to electronic communication including for the purposes of exercising members' rights. They must also keep record of its members and regularly update those records at least once a month. Article 14 of L. 4481/2017 recognizes to right holders the right to grant licences for non-commercial use of any rights, categories of rights or types of works, or any subject matter of their choice. Article 15 of L. 4481/2017 describes the rights of right holders who are not members of a collective management organization but have a direct legal relationship by law or by assignment, licence or any other contractual arrangement with them. According to Article 16 of L. 4481/2017, right holders who have entrusted the management of all their works to a collective management organization have the obligation to inform, in writing, about the works they have published, in any way, as well as of any new work published after the assignment of management to the organization.

215. Articles 17–19 of L. 4481/2017 contain specific provisions concerning rights revenue, deductions, and distribution of amounts due to right holders. Collective management organizations have to be diligent in the collection and management of rights revenue. They must keep separate in their accounts: (a) revenues collected and any income due to right holders and (b) any own assets and income arising from such assets, management fees, or from other activities. Collective management organizations are not permitted to use rights revenue or income arising from the investment of rights revenue for purposes other than the distribution to right holders.[164] Deductions must be reasonable in relation to the services provided by the collective management organizations right holders and established on the basis of objective criteria. Management fees shall not exceed, in total and on average, 20%[165] of the gross rights revenue of the collective management organization. The distribution of amounts to right holders must be made in proportion, to the extent possible, to the actual use of their works. Articles 20 and 21 of L. 4481/2017 lay down the rules applied for rights management, deductions, and payments under representative agreements.

216. Articles 22–25 of L. 4481/2017 contain provisions concerning the relations between collective management organizations and users. According to Article 22 of L. 4481/2017, collective management organizations and users must conduct negotiations for the licensing of rights in good faith and provide each other with all the necessary information. Licensing terms must be based on objective and non-discriminatory criteria. Collective management organizations, in order to allow users to use the works of their repertoire, shall request from them a percentage fee in accordance with Article 32 of L. 2121/1993. In case of non-payment of a licence fee or disagreement as to the amount of the remuneration required by the collective management organization, the user, before any use, must advance to the collective management organization the requested amount of remuneration or the amount determined and awarded by provisional order of the SMCFI, at the request of the user or the collective management organization, in accordance with the procedure of interim measures, as usually paid in similar cases or where there are no similar cases, as the court deems equitable. Following a lawsuit filed by the collective management organization or by the user, the SMCFI shall definitively determine the

164. According to Art. 79 of L. 4509/2017 adding a subparagraph at the end of para. 3 of Art. 17 of L. 4481/2017 rights revenue or any income arising from the investment of rights revenue cannot be seized.

165. Concerning collective management organizations, the annual gross revenue of which does not exceed the amount of EUR 500,000, management fees must not exceed in total and on average 25% of the gross revenue of such collective management organization.

amount of the remuneration. Specific provision[166] regulates the dispute between the user and the collective management organization in respect of the amount of equitable remuneration referred to in Article 49 of L. 2121/1993. In that case the SMCFI shall determine the amount by provisional order, at the request of the user or the collective management organization, and shall provisionally award up to half the amount of the equitable remuneration determined by the court. The definitive amount of equitable remuneration and the payment terms are determined by the SMCFI. The banking system is used for financial transactions of users with collective management organizations.

217. Article 23 of L. 4481/2017 provides the basic rules for the tariffs. Right holders must receive appropriate remuneration for the use of their works. Tariffs must be reasonable in relation to, *inter alia*, the economic value of the use of the rights in trade, taking into account the nature and scope of the use of the works and other subject matters, as well as in relation to the economic value of the service provided by the collective organization to the user. Tariffs are prepared by decision of the Board of Directors of the collective management organization and made available to the public through the website of the collective management organization according to Article 23(2) of L. 4481/2017. For the formulation and implementation of their tariffs collective management organizations apply objective criteria and refrain from any arbitrary and discriminatory acts. Judgment 578/2002 of the SMCFI[167] made an interim determination of the remuneration corresponding to the business of the user by taking into account various criteria, such as the fact that, for this business, music was not necessary but just useful, that it was a tavern half of which consisted of outdoor space and was situated outside the city centre, that the business was average in the winter and fairly good in the summer, and that the music was played during specific hours of the day. The court concluded that the commensurate remuneration payable in similar instances amounts to EUR 210 annually (without taxes), as opposed to EUR 35,276 demanded by the collective management organization. Article 23 of L. 4481/2017 also provides the possibility of collective management organizations to enter into agreements with the users for the determination of tariffs or to submit the disputes to arbitration.

218. Article 24 of L. 4481/2017 concerns the obligation for users to provide information in a specified format to collective management organizations on the use of the works and rights represented by the collective management organization. In the event the user fails to meet the obligation above, the collective management organization may impose on him/her a 10% surcharge on the remuneration due. If the user breaches the obligation more than twice, the collective management organization may opt to either impose a 15% surcharge on the remuneration due or terminate the agreement.

219. Articles 25–27 of L. 4481/2017 contain transparency rules. These rules require collective management organizations to provide information: (a) to right

166. Article 22 (7) of L. 4481/2017.
167. SMCFI of Trikala 578/2002, *DIKI* 2002, p. 1140.

holders on the management of their rights; (b) to other collective management organizations on the management of rights under representation agreement; and (c) to right holders, other collective management organizations, and users on request. Article 28 of L. 4481/2017[168] describes, in detail, the information that must be public concerning the statute and the structure of collective management organization, including the membership terms and terms of termination of authorization to manage rights, standard licence contracts, agreements with user associations, method of distribution of the amounts to right holders, management fees and basis for their calculation, policy on deductions from revenues and income, list of representative agreements, use of non-distributable amounts, including allocation of funds for social, cultural and educational services, the decision to impose a sanction on the collective management organization,[169] the rights and the repertoire, as well as the annual transparency report. The information must be published on the website of the collective management organization in a readable format.

220. Articles 29–30 of L. 4481/2017 concern reporting rules. Collective management organizations must draw up and make public an annual transparency report for each financial year, no later than eight months following the end of the year. The annual transparency report is published on the website of the collective management organization and contains all the information described in Article 30 of. L. 4481/2017, implementing the Annex to the Directive 2014/26. Managers of the collective management organization have to do so in a sound, prudent, and appropriate manner. In accordance with Article 31 of L. 4481/2017, collective management organizations must put in place and apply procedures to avoid conflicts of interest. The above procedure includes at least an annual individual statement by the persons who manage the business of the collective management organization to the General Assembly or to the Supervisory Board of the independent management entity in a dominant position.

221. Articles 33–41 of L. 4481/2017 lay down the requirements for multi-territorial licensing concerning online rights in musical works. These provisions implement the Articles 23–32 of Directive 2014/26. More precisely, Articles 33–37 set out the conditions for multi-territorial licensing for online rights in musical works, the transparency rules, the accuracy of multi-territorial repertoire information, the monitoring use of online rights in musical works, and the accurate and timely payment to right holders. Article 38 of L. 4481/2017 concerns the rules and agreements between collective management organizations for multi-territorial licensing and, in particular, the non-exclusive nature of the mandate, the management on a non-discriminatory basis, as well as the transparency requirements. Article 39 of L. 4481/2017 imposes the obligation to accept the representation of another collective management organization for multi-territorial licensing if the requested collective management organization is already granting or offering to

168. Article 28 is also applied to independent management entities in dominant position (in the Greek market) which had been established until the date of entry of L. 4481/2017 (*See* Art. 50 of L. 4481/2017).

169. In case there is such a decision.

grant multi-territorial licences. Article 41 sets out special provisions facilitating the licensing of online rights in musical works required by a broadcaster to communicate or make available to the public its radio and television programs simultaneously with or after initial broadcast, as well as any online material, including previews, produced by or for the broadcaster which is ancillary to the initial broadcast of its radio or television program.

222. Collective management organizations have to make available, effective and timely, complaint procedures to their members and to the collective management organizations on whose behalf they manage rights under a representation agreement; in particular, concerning authorization to manage rights and termination or withdrawal of rights, membership terms, collection of amounts due to right holders, deductions, and distributions.[170] Specific provisions of L. 4481/2017 permit the disclosure of potential violations,[171] give the possibility for alternative dispute resolution procedure [172] and establish sanctions for violation of the legislation by collective management organizations or independent management entities.[173] The sanctions imposed, cumulatively or alternatively, for any violation of the legislation (L. 4481/2017 and L. 2121/1993) are: (a) an administrative fine of EUR 2,000–EUR 20,000, and (b) temporary or definitive revocation of the operating licence.[174] The ministerial decision (MD) imposing the fine is an enforceable title.[175] In case of revocation of the operating licence, the Minister of Culture and Sport assigns, exceptionally and temporarily, the management of the rights to the OPI for a time that does not exceed two years.[176] The OPI is the national competent authority to exchange information concerning matters relevant to collective management organizations and respond to any request for information by authorities of other EU Member States.[177] Personal data are protected according to Article 49 of L. 4481/2017. Greek legislation also contains specific provisions concerning the collective management by independent management entities in dominant position[178] and the so-called 'Commissionaire for Reorganization' appointed by judicial decision in the event a collective management organization or an independent management entity

170. Article 42 of L. 4481/2017.
171. Article 43 of L. 4481/2017.
172. Article 44 of. L./2017.
173. Article 46 of Ll. 4481/2017.
174. The procedure for imposing the sanctions is provided by Art. 46 of L. 4481/2017.
175. Article 47 of L. 4481/2017.
176. These duties are entrusted to a Special Department of Urgent Management set up in the Hellenic Copyright Organization (Art. 51A added to L. 4481/2017 by Art. 45 (7) of L. 4531/2018).
177. Article 48 of L 4481/2017.
178. Article 50 of L. 4481/2017 states as follows: 'Independent management entities that either existed or are established after the entry into force of this law and which engage in collective management of copyright or related rights and which are in a dominant position in the Greek market in the category they represent, are obliged to include in their statutes provisions regarding the General Assembly of Members and a supervisory board in accordance with Article 9 (9) and Article 10 (8). The provisions of this law relating to collective management organizations, including the relevant provisions of Articles 7 and 28 and the provisions on mandatory collective management, as well as the provisions of the law 2121/1993, including article 69 (2) of Law 2121/1993, as this paragraph was replaced by article 7 (13) of Law 2819/2000 shall also apply to the management entities which had been established until the date this law came into force'.

in dominant position fails to meet its financial obligations towards its creditors, including right holders who have entrusted them with the management of their rights, on a general and permanent basis.[179] The Minister of Culture and Sport may also appoint a temporary commissioner, provided that there is a strong chance that the collective management organization is unable to fulfil its obligations and, in particular, to collect and distributes to right holders the sums it receives on their behalf.[180]

§10. Infringement and Remedies

223. Greek L. 2121/1993, as amended by L. 3524/2007, by Article 46 of L. 3905/2010, and by Articles 52 and 54(7–9) of L. 4481/2017, contains provisions concerning enforcement of rights, such as measures to prevent infringement, injunctions, civil and penal sanctions. The following statutes are also applicable to the general question of enforcement: Greek Civil Code (GCC), Criminal Code, Code of Civil Procedure, Competition Law, and Customs legislation. Directive 2004/48/EC on the enforcement of intellectual property rights was implemented in Greece by L. 3524/2007. A special judicial system was created, concerning civil procedures, in order to enforce copyright and related rights.[181] Copyright cases are introduced to special chambers for the first instance cases in Athens, Piraeus, and Thessaloniki. Concerning jurisdiction of the three-member courts, appeals against the decisions of these first instance courts are tried before the special chamber of the CA in Athens.

224. The concept of 'infringement' is not defined by law. It has been held, however, that infringement of copyright or related rights arises from provisions relating to the scope, the subject matter, and the content of such rights. In more detail, infringement of copyright and related rights is 'any act whose subject matter and content are identical to the subject matter and content of copyright or related right, to the extent that they are protected by law, on condition that the act is not carried out by the beneficiary or with his consent or does not fall under the legitimate limitations of the economic right.'[182] This definition shows that acts of infringement correspond to the subject matter of the right and the powers of the economic or moral right of the author or to the content of related rights recognized by law. On the contrary, the violation of contractual obligations assumed by the other party vis-à-vis

179. Article 51 (1) of L. 4481/2017. A Commissionaire for Reorganization may also be appointed in the event of actual or threatened failure to meet the financial obligations on the part of a collective management organization or an independent management entity in dominant position or in the event of a serious financial or management problem liable to jeopardize the rights of right holders (Art. 51(2) of L. 4481/2017).

180. *See* Art. 54 (10) of l. 2121/1993, as amended.

181. D. Kallinikou, *Greece's Specialized Intellectual Property Courts Regime – Study on Specialized Intellectual Property Courts*, 55–59 (Joint Project between IIPI-USPTO 2012 (in English)).

182. G. Koumantos, *supra* n. 58 at 427. CA of Athens 6234/2007, *EllDni* 2008, 584. CA of Thessaloniki 1286/2007, *EpiskED* 2007, 525.

the author in the context of exploitation contracts does not constitute an infringement of copyright or related rights. The consequences of the violation of obligations stemming from the contract are provided for by Contractual Law. It has been held, however, by jurisprudence that the exploitation of the work for a non-contractually foreseen use or the transgression thereof constitutes an infringement of the right, e.g., reproducing and making available to the public more works of arts (paintings) than those stipulated in the contract. It can be maintained that infringement also comprises the violation of contractual claims stemming from the law, such as the equitable remuneration prescribed in Articles 18 and 49 of L. 2121/1993.

I. Measures Preventing Infringement

225. The measures preventing infringement provided by Articles 59–63 of L. 2121/1993 are the following:

- Imposition and adherence to specifications for the equipment and other materials used in the making of reproductions of works with a view to prevent or limit the use of such equipment and materials for purposes which conflict with the normal exploitation of copyright and related rights (Article 59 of L. 2121/1993).
- Use of control systems making compulsory the use of equipment or systems which permit the designation of reproduced or used works and the extent and frequency of the reproduction or use, subject to such methods not causing unjustifiable harm to the lawful interests of users (Article 60 of L. 2121/1993).
- Circulation of visual or sound, or visual and sound recordings carrying on their outer casing or in another prominent position a special mark or control label of any type supplied by the competent collecting society, indicating that their distribution on the market or their circulation does not constitute an infringement of the rights of the author (Article 61 of L. 2121/1993).
- Prohibition of decoding encrypted programs without the permission of the broadcasting organizations which transmit encrypted programs by wire or over the air, or by any other means, including by cable or satellite[183] (Article 62 of L. 2121/1993).
- Stopping an infringement or its continuation: According to Article 63(1) of L. 2121/1993 where a potential infringement of copyright is identified, such as where there is a clear intention to offer an unlawful public performance of a theatrical or cinematographic or a musical work, the competent local police authority shall prohibit the infringing act when requested to do so by the author or right holder. When requested, the prosecuting authorities shall grant the police authority any necessary mandate. The same applies when the public presentation of a work has been in progress for more than two days without payment of due remuneration.

183. Council of Appeal Court Judges of Athens 1408/2017, PoinikaXronika 2018, 62.

- Municipal licence: According to Article 63(2) of L. 2121/1993, the granting of a municipal licence permitting the use of musical instruments or certifying the suitability permission for the use of premises for the performance of musical or other works, whose administration is entrusted to a collecting society competent to authorize the public performance of works, is conditional on the deposition by the applicant of a written authorization for the performance, issued by that collecting society. The simplification of procedure for the use of music and musical instruments provided by Article 29 of L. 4442/2016 does not affect the obligations or licences related to copyright legislation.[184]

226. It is to be noted that the above provisions of Article 63(1) and (2) of L. 2121/1993 are applied, *mutatis mutandis*, to infringements of the related rights referred to in Articles 46, 47, and 48 of L. 2121/1993.

II. Civil Sanctions

227. In case of infringement or threat of infringement of copyright or related rights, the author or the right holder may claim the recognition of this right, the discontinuation of the infringement, and its omission in the future. The discontinuation of the infringement may include, at the request of the applicant: (a) recall from the channels of commerce the goods that they have found to be infringing protected rights of and, in appropriate cases, with regard to materials and implements principally used in the creation or manufacture of those goods; (b) definitive removal from the channels of commerce; or (c) destruction. The rights of the first sentence of this paragraph shall be exercised by right holders against intermediaries whose services are used by a third party to infringe rights under this law.

228. A person who, by intent or negligence, infringes copyright or a related right of another person indemnifies that person for compensation and moral damage caused. It is provided that the payment of damages shall not be less than twice the legally required or normally payable remuneration for the form of exploitation which the infringing party has effected without a licence. This provision setting the minimum compensation at a level no less than twice the remuneration has been broadly applied by courts.[185] The purpose of this provision is to contribute to overcoming difficulties relating to proving the damage.

229. Instead of seeking damages, and regardless of whether the infringement was committed by intent or negligence, the author or the right holder of the related right may demand either the payment of the sum accrued by the infringing party from the unlicensed exploitation of a work, or of the object of a related right, or the profit gained by the infringing party from such an exploitation.

184. Article 29(4) of L. 4442/2016 (OG A 230/7.12.2016 and Art. 7(4) of MD 16228/17.5.2017 (OG B 1723/18.5.2017).
185. AP 872/2009, *ChrID* 2010, 298 comments by D. Kallinikou.

230. For each act of omission contributing to an infringement, the court may impose a fine from EUR 880 to EUR 2,900 payable to the author or to the right holder of the related rights.

231. The civil sanctions are applied accordingly in the case that the debtor did not pay the remuneration provided by Article 18(3) of L. 2121/1993, as amended, to a collecting society.

232. The civil sanctions are also applied in case of infringement of intellectual property of the author of a database and of the sui generis right of the maker of a database.

III. Injunction, Provisional Measures and Evidence

233. According to Article 64, as amended by Article 2(4) of L. 3524/2007 implementing the Enforcement Directive, in case of alleged infringement of copyright or related rights or the sui generis right of database maker, the SMCFI orders the precautionary seizure of items in the possession of the alleged infringer. Instead of precautionary seizure, the court may order the detailed description of such items, including the taking of photographs. Article 687(1) of the Code of Civil Procedure is applied in such cases and a provisional order is issued according to Article 691(2) of the Code of Civil Procedure.

234. The court orders injunction measures or precautionary evidence without needing to specify the works infringed or in threat of infringement.

235. The court may also issue against the alleged infringer an injunction intended to prevent any imminent infringement of the rights or to forbid, on a provisional basis and subject, where appropriate, to a penalty payment under Article 947 of the Code of Civil Procedure for each infringement or continuation of the infringements of that right. The court may order the precautionary seizure or delivery up of the goods suspected of infringing rights so as to prevent their entry into or movement within the channels of commerce.

236. In the case of an infringement committed on a commercial scale, the court may order the precautionary seizure of the property of the alleged infringer, including the blocking of his/her bank accounts. The court may order the communication of bank, financial or commercial documents, or appropriate access to the relevant information.

237. The above injunction measures may, in appropriate cases, be taken without the defendant having been heard, under Article 687(1) of the Code of Civil Procedure, in particular, where any delay would cause irreparable harm to the right holder. In that event, if the decision or the order of the court is not notified to the defendant before or during its enforcement, it shall be notified on the first business day following the enforcement; otherwise, any relevant procedural acts shall be null and void.

238. Where the provisional measures are revoked due to any act or omission by the applicant, or where it is subsequently found that there has been no infringement or threat of infringement of the rights under this law, the court may order the applicant, upon request of the defendant, to provide the defendant appropriate compensation for any injury caused by those measures.

239. Article 64A added to L. 2121/1993 by Article 81(8) of L. 3057/2002, implementing Article 8(3) of the Information Society Directive, provides that right holders may apply for an injunction against intermediaries whose services are used by a third party to infringe a copyright or related right. It is the same for the sui generis right of a database maker. The SMCFI of Athens in Decision 4658/2012,[186] ordered temporarily, technical measures in order to make impossible to the subscribers of the responders,[187] the digital downloading of works which are included in the websites with the Internet addresses (domain names) (www ... www ...) and IP addresses (IP ... IP ...). The court warned each of the responders with a EUR 5,000 fine for each violation of the decision. However, the SMCFI of Athens, in Decision 13478/2014, rejected the request of five collective management organizations for an injunction that would oblige ISP's to block websites infringing copyright and related rights of their members. The rejection of website blocking was justified on the grounds of fundamental freedoms and conflict with the principle of proportionality.[188] In that case the court also refused to deliver the requested Internet traffic data relating to the infringing websites because this request was not in conformity with the legislation related to data protection and confidentiality of communications. It is to be noted that this legislation was recently amended by Article 52(2) of L. 4481/2017[189] and the confidentiality may be waived for the purpose of ascertaining copyright or related rights infringement.

240. Article 63A, added in L. 2121/1993 by Article 2(3) of L. 3524/2007, implements Articles 6 and 8 of the Enforcement Directive. It provides that on application by a party which has presented reasonably available evidence sufficient to support its claims of infringement or threat of infringement of the rights, if specified evidence lies in the control of the opposing party, the court may order, on application by this party, that such evidence be presented by the opposing party. In the case of

---

186. SMCFI of Athens 4658/2012, *ChrID* 2012, 373 comments by D. Kallinikou.
187. The respondents were companies providing Internet access services.
188. SMCFI of Athens 13478/2014 'Website blocking in Greece: How does it work there?' (in English) by Jannos Paramythiotis, ipkitten.blogspot.com *DIMEE* 2015 p. 253 by E. Vagena. *See also* Th. Chiou, Copyright and website blocking: the principle of proportionality in the digital world, *ChrID* 2016 pp. 230–239.
189. According to Art. 52(2) of L. 4481/201, para. d is added after para. 1(c) of Art. 4 of L. 2225/1994, as amended by Art. 11 (1) of L. 4416/2016, as follows: 'd. Confidentiality may be waived for the purpose of ascertaining felony copyright or related rights infringement, as provided for in L. 2121/1993'.

an infringement committed on a commercial scale, the court may also order, on application by a party, the communication of banking, financial, or commercial documents under the control of the opposing party. The existence of a substantial number of copies shall be considered to constitute reasonable evidence of an infringement committed on a commercial scale. In any event, the court shall ensure the protection of confidential information. If a party is summoned to produce the evidence referred to in the above paragraph and unjustifiably fails to produce such evidence, the claims of the party that sought the production or notification of evidence shall be considered as confessed.

241. In the context of proceedings concerning an infringement of rights, and in response to a justified and proportionate request of the claimant, the chairman of a multi-member court or the judge of a single-member court may order, even before the hearing date, that information on the origin and distribution networks of the goods or services which infringe an intellectual property right be provided by the infringer and/or any other person who: (a) was found in possession of the infringing goods on a commercial scale; (b) was found to be using the infringing services on a commercial scale; (c) was found to be providing on a commercial scale services used in infringing activities; or (d) was indicated by the person referred to in the above points (a), (b), or (c) as being involved in the production, manufacture, or distribution of the goods or the provision of the services. Any party that unjustifiably violates an order of the court under the above paragraph shall be sentenced to pay, in addition to legal costs, a monetary fine of EUR 50,000–EUR 100,000, which shall devolve to the tax office.

IV. Administrative Sanctions

242. Article 65A, added in L. 2121/1993 by Article 2(9) of L. 3524/2007, refers to administrative sanctions.

243. Any person who, without being entitled to and in violation of the provisions of the law on copyright and related rights, reproduces, sells, or, otherwise, distributes to the public or possesses with the purpose of distributing a computer program is, irrespective of other sanctions, subject to an administrative fine of EUR 1,000 for each illegal copy of the computer program.

244. A street vendor or a standing person (outside a shop) caught distributing to the public, by sale or by other means, or in possession, with the intention of distributing, of sound recordings on which a work protected by copyright law has been recorded, is imposed an administrative penalty equal to the product of the items of illegal recordings by EUR 20 for each sound recording according to the seizure report drafted during the arrest of the infringer. The minimum of the administrative penalty is defined to EUR 1,000. The same applies to the reproduction and distribution of physical carriers of sound in shops.[190] Whoever, without any legitimate right and in violation of the provisions of the law, reproduces phonograms stored on any technical storage media, including hard disks, whether embedded or not on a computer, shall pay an administrative fine of EUR 1,000.[191]

245. The competent authorities for the control of enforcement of these stipulations and of the enforcement of the provided sanctions are the Unit of Special Controls (IPEE), the Police, and the Customs authorities, which inform the right holders via the OPI after the finding of the violation.

246. A common decision issued by the Ministry of Finance and the Ministry of Culture defines the procedure of the penalty enforcement and collecting, the competent collecting services and any other detail necessary for the application of the present article.[192]

V. Criminal Sanctions

247. Law 2121/1993 introduces a criminal law system by virtue of which criminal proceedings can be applied against all acts which constitute copyright/related rights' infringement.[193] The penalties provided by the legislation are very severe.

248. Any person who, in contravention of the provisions of the L. 2121/1993, as amended, or of the provisions of lawfully ratified multilateral international conventions on the protection of copyright, unlawfully makes a fixation of a work or of copies, reproduces them directly or indirectly, temporarily or permanently, in any form, in whole or in part, translates, adapts, alters, or transforms them, or distributes them to the public by sale or other means, or possesses with the intent of distributing them, rents, performs in public, broadcasts by radio or television or any other means, communicates to the public works or copies by any means, imports copies of a work illegally produced abroad without the consent of the author, and, in general, exploits works, reproductions, or copies being the object of copyright or acts against the moral right of the author to decide freely on the publication and the presentation of his work to the public without additions or deletions, shall be liable to imprisonment of not less than one year and to a fine from EUR 2,900 to EUR 15,000.

249. The sanctions listed above are applicable to any person who, in contravention of the provisions of law or of the provisions of lawfully ratified multilateral

190. This provision is added to Art. 65A by Art. 46(6) of L. 3905/2010.
191. This provision is added to Art. 65 A by Art. 54 (8b) of. L. 4481/2017.
192. Ministerial Decision 10100/D3B/4020/27.7.2007 concerning the determination of the procedure for the imposition and collection of the administrative fine provided for in Arts 65A and 66 of L. 2121/1993 as modified by Art. 2 of L. 3524/2007.
193. *See* Art. 66(1) and (2) of L. 2121/1993 as amended by Art. 81(9) and (10) of L. 3057/2002.

international conventions on the protection of related rights, commits the infringing actions[194] provided by Article 66(2) of L. 2121/1993.

250. Aggravating circumstances are the great financial gain or the damage caused, the commitment of the acts by profession or at a commercial scale, and the dangerousness of the infringer.

251. The same sanctions are imposed against any person who did not pay the remuneration provided for by Article 18(3) of L. 2121/1993 as well as against the debtor who, after the issuance of the decision of the SMCFI, does not submit the declaration under the provisions of Article 18(6) of L. 2121/1993.

252. Criminal sanctions are imposed for unlawful extraction and/or re-utilization of the whole or part of the contents of the database. Any person who proceeds to extraction and/or re-utilization of the whole or of a substantial part of the contents of the database without the authorization of the author is punished by imprisonment for at least one year and a fine of EUR 3, 000–EUR 15,000.[195]

253. Specific provisions of Article 66 regulate the consequences of the unreserved payment of the administrative fines provided by Article 65A. When the object of the infringement refers to computer programs, the culpable character of the action is raised if the infringer proceeds in the unreserved payment of the administrative fine and the infringement concerns quantity up to fifty computer programs. When the object of infringement concerns sound recordings in which works protected by copyright have been recorded, the unreserved payment of the administrative fine shall result in non-prosecution and any prosecution shall be dismissed, if the infringement concerns quantity up to 500 illegal sound recording carriers.[196] When the object of infringement concerns sound recordings stored on any technical storage media or computer, the unconditional payment of the administrative fine by the offender under the conditions of paragraph 2 of Article 65A shall result in non-prosecution and the dismissal of any prosecution, provided that the offence relates to up to 1,000 musical compositions.[197] The payment of the administrative fine and the non-prosecution or the dismissal of criminal prosecution do not relieve the infringers from the duty of paying off the copyright and related rights or from the duty of compensating and paying the rest expenses of these rights, according to the provisions of the relevant laws.[198] In case of recidivism during the same financial year the administrative fine provided by Article 65A of L. 2121/1993 doubles.

194. Infringing actions in that case concern the rights of performers, producers of phonograms, producers of audiovisual works, and broadcasting organizations.
195. Article 66 (9) of L. 2121/1993 as amended by Art. 54 (9c) of L. 4481/2017.
196. Article 66 (11) of L. 2121/1993 as amended by Art. 54 (9d) of L. 4481/2017.
197. Article 66 (11A) of L. 2121/1993 added by Art.54 (9e) of L. 4481/2017.
198. Article 66 (12) of L. 2121/1993 as amended by Art. 54 (9d) of L. 4481/2017.

VI. Technological Measures and Rights Management Information

254. Article 66A of L. 2121/1993 on technological measures implements Article 6 of the Information Society Directive. It provides legal protection against circumvention of effective technological measures and against the provision of devices and products or services to this effect.

255. Article 66B of L. 2121/1993 concerning rights management information implements Article 7 of the Information Society Directive. It provides protection against illegal activities carried out in order to remove or alter the electronic rights management information and against distribution, importation for distribution, broadcasting, communication, or making available to the public of works or other protected subject matter from which such information has been removed or altered without authority.

256. According to Article 66A(1) of L. 2121/1993 the expression 'technological measures' means any technology, device, or component that, in the normal course of its operation, is designed to prevent or restrict acts, in respect of works or other subject matter, which are not authorized by the right holder of any copyright or any related right as well as the sui generis right of the database maker. Technological measures are deemed to be 'effective' where the use of a protected work or other subject matter is controlled by the right holders through application of an access control or protection process, such as encryption, scrambling or other transformation of the work or other subject matter, or a copy control mechanism, which achieves the protection objective. This provision implements Article 6(3) of the Information Society Directive.

257. The law prohibits the circumvention, without the permission of the right holder, of any effective technological measure when such an act is made in the knowledge, or with reasonable grounds to know, that he/she is pursuing that objective.

258. It is also prohibited without the permission of the right holder, the manufacture, import, distribution, sale, rental, advertisement for sale or rental, or possession for commercial purposes of devices, products, or components or the provision of services which: (a) are promoted, advertised, or marketed for the purpose of circumvention of; or (b) have only a limited commercially significant purpose or use other than to circumvent; or (c) are primarily designed, produced, adapted, or performed for the purpose of enabling or facilitating the circumvention of any effective technological measures.

259. Criminal sanctions are imposed for those who act in violation of the above provisions by imprisonment of at least one year and a fine of EUR 2,900–EUR 15,000. Civil sanctions and injunction measures are also applied.

260. Right holders have the obligation to give to the beneficiaries the measures to ensure the benefit of the limitation (exception) to the extent necessary and where that beneficiaries have legal access to the protected work or subject matter concerned.[199] The limitations (exceptions) provided for in section IV of L. 2121/1993, as exists, are related to reproduction for private use, on paper or any similar medium (Article 18), reproduction for teaching purposes (Article 21), reproduction by libraries and archives (Article 22 paragraph 1), reproduction for judicial or administrative purposes (Article 24), as well as the use for the benefit of people with disability (Article 28A). If the right holders do not take voluntary measures including agreements between right holders and third parties benefiting from the exception, the right holders and third parties benefiting from the exception may request the assistance of one or more mediators selected from the list of mediators drawn up by the Copyright Organization. The mediators make recommendations to the parties. If no party objects within one month from the forwarding of the recommendation, all parties are considered to have accepted the recommendation. Otherwise, the dispute is settled by the CA of Athens, trying at first and last instance. These provisions do not apply to works or other subject matter available to the public on agreed contractual terms in such a way that members of the public may access them from a place and at a time individually chosen by them.

261. According to Article 66B (1) of L. 2121/1993 the expression 'rights management information' means any information provided by right holders which identifies the work or other subject-matter protected by a related right or the sui generis right of database maker, and which identifies the author or any other right holder, or information about the terms and conditions of use of the work or other subject matter, and any numbers or codes that represent such information. This provision implements Article 7(2) of the Information Society Directive.

262. It is prohibited for any person knowingly performing without the permission of the right holder any of the following acts: (a) the removal or alteration of any electronic rights management information; (b) the distribution, importation for distribution, broadcasting, communication, or making available to the public of works or other subject matter protected by a related right or the sui generis right of database maker, from which electronic rights management information has been removed or altered without authority, if such person knows, or has reasonable grounds to know that by so doing he is inducing, enabling, facilitating or concealing an infringement of any copyright or related right or the sui generis right of database maker.

263. The violation of the above provisions is punishable by imprisonment of at least one year and a fine of EUR 2,900–EUR 15,000, and entails the civil sanctions and injunction measures provided by law.

---

199. Article 66A(5) of L. 2121/1993 implementing Art. 6(4) of Directive 2001/29. For the analysis of this provision *see* E. Vagena, *Technological Protection and Digital Management of Copyright*, 235 (Athens 2011 (in Greek)). T. Synodinou, *Copyright and New Technologies*, 169 (Athens-Thessaloniki 2008 (in Greek)). *See also* V. Bandi-Markouti, *The Relation Between Personal Data and Copyright in Digital Environment*, 241 (Athens 2012 (in Greek)).

VII. Publication of Decisions

264. According to Article 66C of L. 2121/1993, decisions of civil or criminal courts concerning copyright and related rights may, at the request of the applicant and at the expenses of the infringer, order the appropriate measures to be taken for the propagation of information relating to the decision, including the posting of the decision, as well as its publication, in summary or in its entirety, in the mass media or the Internet.

VIII. Code of Ethics

265. Article 66D of L. 2121/1993 provides that the business or professional associations concerned, as well as collective management organizations, prepare codes of ethics with the purpose of contributing, at national, community, or international level, to the enforcement of the rights and recommend the use of codes in optical discs in order to identify the origin of their manufacture. The codes of ethics and any evaluation of their implementation shall be forwarded to the EU Commission.

IX. Sanctions for Infringement of Copyright and Related Rights on the Internet

266. In case of copyright or related rights infringement on the Internet, the right holder may follow the procedure described in Article 66E of L. 2121/1993, as this article was added to L. 2121/1993 by Article 52 of L. 4481/2017. For the purposes of Article 66E right holder means the right holder whose right has been infringed on the Internet, as well as any collective management or protection organization entrusted with the management or protection of copyright and related rights. The procedure does not apply to infringements by end users through downloading or streaming or peer-to-peer file sharing, which allow for direct exchange between end users of works in digital form or in the case of cloud computing.

267. A Committee of three members for the disclosure of an Internet infringement of copyright and related rights is being established by decision of the Minister of Culture and Sport.[200] The Committee consists of three members, namely the Chairman of the Board of Directors of OPI, the Vice Chairman of the Board of Directors of OPI as his deputy, a representative of the National Telecommunications and Post Commission (EETT) and his deputy, both appointed by the Chairman of EETT, and a representative of the Personal Data Protection Authority and

200. Ministerial Decision ΥΠΠΟΑ/ΓΔΔΥΗΔ/ΔΔΑΑΔ/ΤΥΕΦΤΠ/42270/3639/3477/197/30.1.2018 establishes the Committee for the disclosure of an Internet infringement of copyright and related rights.

his deputy, both appointed by the Chairman of the Personal Data Protection Authority. The term of the office of the Committee is three years.[201]

268. The right holder submits, either in person or by electronic means, a request to the Committee to end the infringement. Within ten days the Committee decides either to close the case for specific reasons described in paragraph 5 of Article 66E or to continue with the proceedings. In case of continuation of the procedure, the Committee informs access providers on the Internet and where possible, the hosting service provider and the administrators and/or owners of the websites referred to in the application. The addressee of this notification may voluntarily comply with the applicant's request or be granted a licence. Alternatively, it may object to the Committee within five days from the date of receipt of the notification by sending, at the same time, all the evidence showing, in particular, that there is no infringement. The Committee examines the case and notifies the addressee of the notification and the applicant of its decision: (a) either it shall close the case by reasoned act where no infringement has been established; or (b) where such infringement is established, it shall issue a reasoned decision whereby it requests the addressees to comply with it within a time limit not exceeding three business days from the date of service of the decision. In case of infringement, the Committee requests the addressee to remove the infringing content from the site on which it had been illegally posted or to disclose the access to it. If the site on which the content is hosted on a server located within the Greek territory, the Commission requests the addressees of the notification to remove that content. In the case of large-scale infringements, the Committee may decide to discontinue access to infringing content instead of its removal. If the site is hosted on a server outside of the Greek territory, the Committee requests the Internet access provider to discontinue access to the content. In case of non-compliance with the operative part of the decision the Committee shall impose a fine amounting from EUR 500 to EUR 1,000 for each day of non-compliance.[202]

269. The commencement of the procedure before the Committee does not suspend or affect the exercise of claims for the same dispute before the courts. If an action has been brought by the same applicant with the same claim before the courts, the Committee shall close the case. Any decision issued by the Committee shall be without prejudice to the right of the parties concerned to seek the protection of their legitimate interests before the courts.

201. Ministerial Decision ΥΠΠΟΑ/ΓΔΔΥΗΔ/ΔΔΑΑΔ/ΤΥΕΦΤΠ/42269/3638/3476/196/30.1.2018 determines the establishment, the operation, and responsibilities of the Committee for the disclosure of an Internet infringement of copyright and related rights, as well as the amount of money to be paid by the complaint upon his application to the Committee.

202. Ministerial Decision ΥΠΠΟΑ/ΓΔΔΥΗΔ/ΔΔΑΔ/ΤΔΥΕΦ/61840/5094/4171/240/13.2.2018 establishes the procedure for imposing and levying the fine imposed by the Committee for the disclosure of an Internet infringement of copyright and related rights.

Chapter 2. Patents

L.I. Athanassiou

§1. Introductory Remarks: Basic Characteristics of Greek Patent Law

I. European Orientation: National Patent, EPC, European Unitary Patent

270. The legal framework for patents is provided by L. 1733/1987 *on transfer of technology, inventions, and technological innovation*. The above statute replaced the previous L. 2527/1920 'on patents', in order to harmonize the national substantive legislation with the EPC of 1973. The objective was to create a modern legal infrastructure facilitating the dissemination of technological information, the development of national industry and innovation, and, generally, the promotion of the national economy.[203] Law 1733/1987 was recently amended by L. 3966/2011,[204] which modified Article 17 and added new Articles 17A–17Z, as part of compliance measures implementing Directive 2004/48/EC *on the enforcement of intellectual property rights*.[205]

271. Greece has also ratified the EPC by L. 1607/1986. The said convention does not establish a separate European industrial property right (as it was the purpose of the Community Patent) but, instead, a bundle patent which splits into several national rights after grant, with effect in those Member States for which the applicant has requested protection.[206] The owner of a European patent enjoys, in Greece,[207] the same rights and the same protection[208] as the owner of the Greek patent granted by the national Patent Office.[209] However, it has to be underlined that the two patents are legally independent of each other, as far as their existence, their

203. A. Sinanioti, *The Harmonization of the Patent Law with the European Patent Convention and the L. 1733/1987*, 29 (EEmpD 1988 (in Greek)), *See also* K. Lymperopoulos, *The New Law for the Protection of Patents*, 30 EllDni 11 (1989) (in Greek)).

204. OG A 118/24.5.2011.

205. OG L 157/30.4.2004, 45.

206. AP 1344/2012 ChrID 2013, 139 also Arm. 2013, 1096, MMCFI of Athens 668/2016, EllDni 2016, 519, MMCFI 3362/2012 EEmpD 2012, 702, MMCFI of Athens 5249/2005, EEmpD 2006, 154, SMCFI of Athens 3882/2007 ChrID 2007, 994.

207. When the applicant is a Greek citizen, the application for the grant of a European patent shall be obligatorily submitted to the Greek Patent Office (OBI), unless claiming the priority of an earlier Greek application (Art. 23(1) L. 1733/87). Since the date of its publication, the European patent application in Greece has the same effects as the Greek patent application (Art. 23(2)). The owner of the European patent shall supply OBI with the relevant certified Greek translation of the text on the basis of which the European Patent Office has granted the European patent or has maintained it with modifications (Art. 23(5)). The European patent is not valid in Greece unless the above translation is submitted (Art. 23(6)).

208. A European patent may be declared null in Greece only on the grounds of Art. 138 para.1 of L. 1607/1986 (Art. 23 (8) L. 1733/87).

209. Article 23(4) L. 1733/1987.

functioning, and their validity are concerned. *That means that any decision, assessment, or legal order concerning the European patent does not affect the validity of the national one and does not provide a legal basis to contest the existence or validity of the latter.*[210]

The European Unitary Patent was put into effect by the adoption of Regulation 1257/2012 in order to facilitate cooperation between Member States by creating a patent protection regime with unitary effect on the basis of Article 118(1) TFEU.[211,212]

The European Unitary Patent is of a unitary nature, meaning that it provides uniform protection and produces the same results in all the EU Member States participating in the Unitary Patent system. Its uniform validity consists in the fact that the European Unitary Patent provides for a single claim for the lifting of the infringement and its omission in the future in all the participating Member States and can only be limited, transferred, revoked, or terminated in respect of all the participating Member States.[213]

The applicable law in case of an infringement is determined in accordance with the provisions of the regulation and consists of the law of the Member State in which the applicant has established their domicile or residence, and a legal person or association has its seat or the law of the Member State where the European Patent Office is situated, which is to say, German law.[214]

The point of reference for issuing a European patent with unitary effect is a European patent. As a first step, a European patent must be granted in accordance with the provisions of the EPC. Thereafter, the beneficiary shall, upon his request, acquire a European Unitary Patent with effect from the date of the granting of the European patent. The European Unitary Patent application form must be submitted, at the latest, one month after the publication of the patent in the Community Patents Bulletin.

In attempting juxtaposition, the European patent consists of a bundle of national rights. On the other hand, European Unitary Patent consists of a single Unitary Patent claim. Accordingly, the respective administrative activity of the European Unitary Patent is entrusted to a central service – the European Patent Office based in Munich – while national authorities remain competent for the European patent.

272. Greece has, moreover, ratified, by L. 2029/1992, the Luxemburg Patent Agreement[215] which has not been entered into force until now, due to lack of a sufficient number of ratifications. In view of that failure, a proposal for a Community Patent Regulation (2000) is now under examination.

---

210. CA of Athens 5111/2012, unreported, MMCFI of Athens 728/2009 DEE 2009, 1194.
211. Despotidou, *The protection of intellectual property rights in the EU after the entry into force of the Treaty of Lisbon: Interpretative contribution to the provision of art 118 TFEU*, EpiskED 2014, 21.
212. The introduction of the European Patent with unitary effect has made use of the IX part of European Patent Convention (Munich Convention 1973).
213. Article 3 Regulation 1257/2012.
214. Article 7(3) Regulation 1257/2012.
215. Th. Xatzigagios, *The Luxemburg Convention on a Community Patent*, Arm. 1983 (in Greek) 186, I. Voulgaris, *The Community Patent*, EEmpD 1993 (in Greek) 521.

II. Adherence to the Formal System

273. Despite its European orientation, the Greek system presents a significant difference comparing to the systems of the most developed countries of free market economy(US, France, Germany, UK, Japan, etc.) as well as that of the EPC. While the latter have opted for the full preliminary examination of the substantive conditions in view of the award of a patent right, Greece has adhered to the formal system. That means that, for the granting of a patent, the competent Patent Office, i.e., the Industrial Property Organization (hereinafter OBI – *Organismos Biomixanikis Idioktisias*) examines *only* whether the relevant application contains the elements required by law and whether the subject matter is, in principle, allowed to be protected by patent (the so-called negative conditions).[216] If those formal requirements are met, the OBI is obliged to grant the patent. No guarantee is, however, provided regarding the fulfilment of the substantive conditions.[217] In other words, the patent granted does not certify, in any form whatsoever, that the invention described therein is a new one, involving an inventive step, and susceptible of industrial application.[218]

274. The policy reasons underlying the above legislative option are obvious: Taking into account the relatively limited size of the Greek economy and of the national industrial production in comparison to those of the leading western countries, it would be practically unfeasible and, in any case, economically non-viable for the Greek State to afford a system involving numerous scientists and experts in various fields (from the medical sector to the air-construction and the information technology sector) as well as databases covering the human contrivances worldwide. The solution is, thus, tailored to the needs and the characteristics of the invention and innovation market of the country.

275. From a legal point of view, the consequences of the above policy option are the following:

– The patent is an administrative act which confers a private-law right.[219] Therefore, it is deemed valid and effective in a two-fold sense: Regarding the formal conditions which have been examined by the Patent Office, a presumption of legality is established, subject to the control of the competent administrative

216. *Infra*, 297.
217. Although a Search Report is established by the Patent Office (OBI) which contains all elements on existing technical level which need to be taken into account in order to evaluate whether the invention may be patented, it is clearly prescribed in the Law that this report has only an informative character (Art. 8 L. 1733/87).
218. A. Liakopoulos, *supra* n. 35 at 211–212, B. Antonopoulos, *Industrial Property*, 693–697, 758 (Athens-Thessaloniki 2005 (in Greek)), A. Argyriadis, *Patent*, 85 (Athens 1985 (in Greek)), K. Lymperopoulos, *The Nullity of Patent*, 47, 53 (Athens 1987 (in Greek)), MMCFI of Athens 10914/1996, EEmpD 1999, 146, MMCFI of Athens 5841/1995, EEmpD 1996, 592, MMCFI of Athens 729/2009, DEE 2009, 1194, CA of Athens 3676/2010, DEE 2011, 39.
219. CoS 683/2014, 1337/2010, 1346/2010, CoS 1017/2002, DEE 2003, 937, CA of Athens 1502/2010, DEE 2010, 784.

courts.[220] For the conditions of substantive validity, which are not examined by the office prior to the granting of the patent, the legal effect of the patent is reduced to a reversal of the burden of proof.[221]

- The control for the fulfilment of substantive validity conditions falls into the jurisdiction of the (civil) courts. The claimant invoking the nullity of a patent has the burden to prove that the substantive conditions justifying the grant of the patent are not satisfied. In case the civil court decides that the validity conditions are not met, the patent granted is considered as an *ab initio* null and void juridical act.[222] Under Greek law, the difference between a void and a voidable act is that the first one produces no legal effects and need not be rescinded by the court (for that reason the judgment of the civil court is of a declaratory nature), while the second produces all its legal effects, unless rescinded by a judicial decision.
- Finally, it is noted that the applicant (i.e., the person who has filed a patent application) enjoys the same protection and holds the same rights as the owner of the patent and the beneficiary of an exclusive licence.[223] This is related to the fact that, once a patent application has been filed in a complete and orderly manner, the OBI is constrained to grant the patent.

III. Scope of Protection

276. Law 1733/1987 applies only to patented inventions (and inventions for which an application has been filed). Non-patented inventions do not enter into the scope of the law. The frontier is marked by the issuance of the patent as an administrative act.

277. The patent constitutes a form of legal recognition that the invention filed is a protected good offering to its owner an exclusivity right and that this good deserves the increased legal protection granted by L. 1733/1987. The invention (non-patented) right presents some similarities with the patent one, mainly that they both have an immaterial and two-fold nature (moral and economic). However, they present also some major differences: The acquisition of the invention right is not subject to any formalities. Due to the absence of an administrative act, its protection is not provided by L. 1733/1987 but by other provisions, mainly the L. 146/1914 on unfair competition;[224] it may also be protected by the provisions of civil code, as 'product of the human mind' (Article 60 GCC) or as an 'expression of personality' (Article 57 GCC).[225] Moreover, the invention right does not confer to its holder the privilege of exclusive exploitation; eventual use of the right by third persons may be addressed only as a form of unfair competition.[226]

220.
221. Article 15 L. 1733/1987, B. Antonopoulos, *supra* n. 218 at 693, 694, 758–761.
222. A. Liakopoulos, *Industrial Property supra* n. 35 at 253, 255.
223. Article 17 L. 1733/1987.
224. AP 1192/03, EEmpD 2004, 165.
225. N. Rokas, *supra* n. 25 at 23–24.
226. N. Rokas, *supra* n. 25 at 24.

§2. Acquisition of a Patent Right

278. Patents are granted to: (a) inventions, which are (b) new, (c) involve an inventive step, (d) are capable of industrial application and do not fall within any of the categories of subject matter specifically considered as non-patentable. The first four conditions are called positive substantive conditions (I), while the last is known as negative condition (II). Finally, a number of procedural requirements have to comply with (III).

I. Substantive Conditions

A. *Invention*

279. Although the 'invention' is the basic concept of Patent Law, no definition is provided by L. 1733/1987. According to the legal doctrine,[227] the invention must be understood as a composition or a rule (contrivance) of the human mind for the resolution of a technical problem by using the principles and rules of physical science, in a manner unknown and exceeding the existing state of the art.[228] More particularly:

> The first element is the creation of a *complete rule*, which needs no further research and may be applied at any time by any third person. A vague or uncompleted idea does not suffice. The term 'invention' refers to the intellectual construction and not to the result of its application (i.e., material object).
>
> The said rule must be created by the *human mind* through the *use of the sciences of physics, chemistry, or biology*. Thus, discoveries do not enter into this definition as they result from the observation of the characteristics of the organic and/or inorganic world and not from the intervention of the human mind into the technical domain. Works of art and literature either do not fit into that definition because they are not related to the technical domain; the latter is protected by the law on copyright. On the same line, Article 5(2) clearly states that the following shall not be regarded as patentable inventions: (a) discoveries, scientific theories, and mathematical methods, (b) aesthetic creations, (c) schemes, rules and methods for performing mental acts, playing games or doing business, and programs for computers, (d) presentation of information.
>
> The rule (composition, device, process) of the human mind must result in the *resolution of a technical problem*. The sole description of the problem does not suffice.[229] The resolution may be effectuated through the creation of a new product or the improvement of an existing one, as well as through the creation

227. B. Antonopoulos, *supra* n. 218 at 667 et seq., A. Liakopoulos, *supra* n. 35 at 190, A. Argyriadis, *supra* n. 218 at 42.
228. I. Venieris, *'Legal Protection and Nullification of Patents According to art. 5 para 1 of L. 1733/1998 (novelty, inventive step, industrial application)'*, EllDni 2012, 623.
229. B. Antonopoulos, *supra* n. 218 at 669.

of a new process aiming at a certain result or the improvement of an existing process. The transfer of an already known solution to another problem may be considered as an invention[230] if such solution of the said problem was not technically expected.[231]

Finally, the resolution of the problem must be novel (i.e., unknown to the experts taking into account the available technical information) and original (in the sense that it exceeds the existing state of the art). The first element indicates the *quantitative* dimension of the invention while the second functions as a *qualitative indicator.*[232] These two components are important enough to be constructed by the law as independent substantive conditions and will, therefore, be further analysed in the relevant section.

280. Depending on the content of the invention, one may distinguish two main categories: those related to a product and those related to a process or an industrial application (Article 5(1) L. 1733/87). Moreover, the invention may consist in the modification of an existing one and may conduct to the grant of a *patent of modification* (Article 19(1)) or may be related to a previous one and may conduct to the grant of a *depending patent* (Article 13(4)).[233]

B. Novelty

281. Novelty of the invention is a substantive requirement met in all legal systems, aiming to ensure that no excessive constraints are put on the industry, without sufficient return. Greece makes no exception to that principle.

282. According to Article 5(3):

> [a]n invention shall be considered new if it does not form part of the state of the art. The state of the art shall be held to comprise anything made available to the public anywhere in the world by means of a written or oral description or in any other way, before the filing date of the patent application or the date of priority.

From the above provision, one may draw the following remarks:

283. While the previous system of L. 2527/1920 looked only at anticipations within the national territory,[234] L. 1733/87 adheres to an unconditional internationalism, by referring to *anything made available to the public anywhere.* Thus, the element of novelty is assessed, in an absolute way, on the basis of *the principle of*

230. AP 545/1996 *infra* at 277, CA of Athens 4999/2010 *infra* at 277, MMCFI of Athens 728/2009 *infra* at 277, MMCFI of Thenssaloniki 3887/2015, EEmpD 2016, 168.
231. *Ibid.*
232. A. Liakopoulos, *supra* n. 35 at 197.
233. *See infra*, 359.
234. A. Argyriadis, *supra* n. 218 at 61.

universality;[235] any anticipation made at any place worldwide affects the novelty of the invention, independently of whether the applicant was aware of the pre-existing contrivance. Novelty is also an *objective* concept. Thus, it is irrelevant what the inventor thinks about his own invention or whether he knew or used the previously available information, provided that the information was available to the public.

284. Novelty is defined in a negative way, comparing to the existing state of the art.[236] It is new if it does not form part of the state of the art. The two concepts are opposite: the larger the state of the art, the narrower the place left for innovation.[237] The state of the art comprises anything made available in the public through a written or an oral description or in any other form, by the inventor or a third person connected or unconnected to him. The written form comprises any publication or document, handwritten, typed, or recorded, appearing in a material or in an electronic form, in one or more copies (i.e., publications, reviews, recorded text, powerpoints, lists, letters, advertisements, films, photographs, etc.).[238] The number of copies is irrelevant. Even one may suffice if this document is available to the public. The language in which the document is drafted is also without importance, provided that the said language is known or used somewhere in the world. The claimant invoking the nullity of the patent does not bear the burden to prove that the inventor was in a position to understand or has indeed understood the content of the document. The oral description may consist in a lecture, public announcement, comments or exchange of views on the invention, advertising gatherings, radio–TV or Internet transmissions, etc., made by the inventor or by a third person, to the knowledge, or not, of the inventor. The anticipation may also take any other form, including the *use*[239] of the invention (i.e., trial tests), provided that such use is not a symptomatic one, allows for the content of the invention to be revealed, and is susceptible of repetition.[240]

285. The information must have been disseminated to the public. It is not clear from the text of the law how far must information have been communicated or have made available to the others. Theoretically, the information must be available to any interested person (skilled in the art) or to a definite circle of persons, each of whom may have access to the information. In reality, the availability requirement calls for an (artificial) minimum of dissemination.[241] It suffices that the information has been

235. L. Kotsiris, *The Inventive Idea as a Substantive Condition for the Novelty of the Invention*, 184 (Legal Matters 1982 (legal opinion)).L. Kotsiris, *The Novelty of the Invention and the State of the Art According to the Principle of Universality*, 254, 256 (DEE 2005 (in Greek)).

236. AP 1654/2013 EEmpD 2013, 977, AP 1588/1991 EEmpD 1992,146, AP 545/1996, EEmpD 1997,346, CA of Athens 173/2016 DEE 2016, CA of Athens 4999/2010, DEE 2011,186, CA of Thessaloniki 1908/2014, EllDni 2016, 227, CA of Thessaloniki 467/2009, EEmpD 2010, 481, MMCFI 728/2009, DEE 2009, 1194 with comments by I. Venieris, MMCFIof Athens 4581/2011, EEmpD 2012, 180 with comments by Apostolopoulos, SMCFI of Athens 3222/2013 EllDni 2014, 832, SMCFI 1060/2010, DEE 2012, 116.

237. K. Lymperopoulos, *Patent Law*, 38 (Athens 2010 (in Greek)).

238. *Ibid.*, 44–45.

239. Expressly referred to in Art. 55 EPC.

240. K. Lymperopoulos, *supra* n. 237 at 47–48.

241. Cf. Cornish, Llewelyn & Aplin, *Intellectual Property*, 5–13 (7th ed., Sweet & Maxwell 2010).

put at the disposal of a single person with the appropriate skills, even if this person did not study or take knowledge of the content of the information. It is, thus, unimportant whether the description is kept in public or private premises, or whether it was destined for private use. However, it is not considered as publicly available, the information is kept to a restraint circle of persons bound with obligations of confidence.[242]

286. The crucial time for deciding whether there has been anticipation is the filing date of the application or the date of priority. *Priority* is granted for applications covered by the *Paris Convention.*[243] According to Article 4 of the convention, if an orderly patent application has been filed to a Contracting State, the applicant is entitled to claim priority, provided that he/she shall file an application in Greece for the same invention, within a period of twelve months from the filing date. An *international priority* of the same period is also granted for an application filed abroad, beyond the scope of the convention, on the basis of reciprocity (Article 9(1)). It follows from the above that any dissemination made during the twelve-month period does not affect the novelty of the submitted invention.

287. Another issue is the way dissemination has taken place. According to the prevailing opinion in the legal doctrine,[244] the anticipation destroys the novelty of the invention, provided that the persons to whom the information has been made available or communicated were not bound by legal obligations of confidentiality or good faith to respect the secret of the invention. The novelty condition is not fulfilled only if the third person who had access to the information may use it as he/she likes. This conclusion is sustained by paragraph 9 of Article 5.

288. Paragraphs 9 and 10 of Article 5 L. 1733/1987 introduce a certain form of grace period for inventions which have been disclosed prior to the application date or the priority date, following the example of Article 55 EPC. More particularly, patents are granted for an invention which has been disclosed *not earlier than six months* preceding the filing of the patent application if the (non-prejudicial) disclosure was due to one of the following reasons:

(a) An evident abuse in relation to the applicant or his/her predecessor. The term of 'evident abuse' has to be construed according to Article 281 GCC prohibiting the exercise of the rights when it manifestly exceeds the limits dictated by good faith or morality or the social or economic purpose of the right, on the basis of objective considerations. Thus, if a third person acquires or communicates

242. K. Lymperopoulos, *supra* n. 237 at 46.
243. Ratified by L. 213/1975.
244. A. Argyriadis, *supra* n. 218 at 61, *contra* K. Lymperopoulos, according to whom the lawful or unlawful character of the dissemination does not have any influence whatsoever to the assessment of the novelty. The crucial element is whether the information has been made publicly available. Whether this has happened due to a violation of a confidentiality obligation or of similar duties may have legal consequences *inter partes* (between the employer and the employees) but does not alter the application of the Patent Law. For the same reason, he considers irrelevant whether the third person having acquired access to the information has acted in good or bad faith (48).

information in a manner violating Article 281 GCC or, more generally, the principle of good faith, to the detriment of the inventor (i.e., by violating a relationship of confidence with the inventor), such dissemination does not affect the novelty of the invention.[245]

(b) The fact that the invention was displayed at an officially recognized international exhibition falling within the terms of the convention on international exhibitions signed in Paris on 22 November 1928 and ratified by L. 5562/1932. In that case, when filing the application, the applicant should state that the invention has been so displayed and should file the relevant supporting certificate.

289. Obviously, the novelty requirement imposes a complex factual investigation, in order to assess whether the same invention has already been made public. If the invention is a synthesis of numerous elements, the novelty will be assessed for the whole and not for each of its components. Thus, novelty is not affected even if some elements are known already if the synthesis exceeds the state of the art. Moreover, the characteristics of the previously disclosed and of the second invention need not be identical; it suffices that a person skilled in the art may deduce the solution of the technical problem based on the information available to him. For the same reason, novelty is not recognized in the case of the so-called 'technically equivalent means', i.e., means which, according to the opinion of a skilled person, are tantamount or interchangeable for the solution of the concrete technical problem.[246]

C. Inventive Step

290. The second substantive condition, and by far the most important one, is that of the 'Inventive step'. Repeating the wording of Article 56 EPC, Article 5(4) provides that '*[a]n invention shall be considered as involving an inventive step if, having regard to the state of the art, it is not obvious to a person skilled in the art.*' This requirement represents the qualitative feature of the invention: in order for it to deserve legal protection, it must not constitute a simple predictable link to the chain of the technological progress but must represent a stride of progress, beyond the predictable measure of a skilled technician.[247] The line is drawn by the criterion of the inventive step.[248]

291. The test is an *objective* one. The question which needs to be answered is whether the appropriate, skilled technician, having in mind the available knowledge, would have reached the same resolution to the problem addressed by the

245. A. Liakopoulos, *supra* n. 35 at 197, B. Antonopoulos, *supra* n. 218 at. 677–678.
246. K. Lymperopoulos, *supra* n. 237 at 43.
247. AP 1654/2013 ChrID 2014, 296, CA of Thessaloniki 1908/2014 EllDni 2016, 227, CA of Thessaloniki 1816/2009 DEE 2010, 881, CA of Thessaloniki 2333/2005, EpiskED 2006, 474, with comments by K. Pamboukis, CA of Athens 9505/1999, DEE 2000, 271.
248. M.Th. Marinos, *The Notion of the Inventive Step according to the Munich Convention and the Greek Patent Law,* in memoriam of A. Argiriades, II, 1996, 591, M. Th. Marinos, Inventive Step. Some Remarks on the Vague Notion of the Law of Patents, EllDni 2012, 913.

invention.[249] Thus, the comparison takes place between the state of the art, on one hand, and the invention, on the other. The difficulties encountered by the inventor to achieve the concrete result do not play any particular role; the protection may be granted to the outcome of a long research as well as to a symptomatic or sudden contrivance.[250]

292. The state of the art is assessed *as a whole*. This is the major difference with the requirement of novelty, the latter involving a more isolated comparison between the invention into question and the prior similar one(s).[251] The crucial time for deciding whether the invention filed is obvious or not is the application date or the date of priority; the same date determines the applicable law in time, as far as the substantive conditions are concerned.[252]

293. In assessing the obviousness, the judge will use as a point of reference the notional skilled worker, working in normal conditions and supposed to have in mind the common general knowledge as well as the specific information deemed relevant to the concrete technical domain. Various factors may be taken into account as elements indicating the existence or not of an inventive step, such as:[253] (a) the long lasting need for the resolution of a technical problem; (b) eventually, the previous unfulfilled efforts of the skilled technicians; (c) the economic success, provided that such success is related to the technical value of the invention and not to other parameters (i.e., publicity, price strategies, monopoly); (d) the overcoming of technical difficulties hindering, until the relevant date, the solution of the problem; (e) the advantages achieved by the invention (i.e., increase of efficiency, cost savings, better satisfaction of consumer needs);[254] (f) the unexpected and surprising results; (h) the long research having conducted to the invention. On the contrary, the simple automation of the production, the replacement of the raw material of a product, the 'transfer' of a process to the solution of a different problem, the juxtaposition or synthesis of already known processes or devices, the modification of the size or form of a product, the verification of previous predictions, the use of alternative equivalent means for the resolution of the same problems, the use of analogous procedures, are not in principle indicative of inventive activity, unless it may be proved that the invention presents characteristics of ingenuity allowing to cross the evaluative line.

249. A. Liakopoulos, *supra* n. 35 at 198, B. Antonopoulos, *supra* n. 218 at 678.
250. K. Lymperopoulos, *supra* n. 237 at 56.
251. *Ibid.*, 58.
252. CA of Thessaloniki 2713/1998, DEE 1999, 165.
253. *See* K. Simitis, *The Invention Right*, 126 et seq. (Athens 1967 (in Greek)), K. Lymperopoulos, *supra* n. 237 at 59 et seq., I. Venieris,supra n. 228.
254. CA of Thessaloniki 1363/1997, *Arm.* 1997, 788, 2619/1989, *EllDni* 1991, 1354.

D. Industrial Application

294. The last substantive condition is the requirement of industrial application.[255] This requirement was also present, although without definition, in the previous L. 2527/1920 (Article 1). Article 5(5) of L. 1733/1987 clarifies now that '*[a]n invention shall be considered as susceptible of industrial application if its subject matter may be produced or used in any sector of industrial activity.*'

295. The scope is wide enough to cover any form of practical use or exploitation in any economic sector, including not only the industrial sector *strictosensu* but also the commercial, artisanal, professional, agricultural[256] ones and, more generally, any activity aiming at the provision of goods and services.[257] The cost, price, or profitability of the invention are irrelevant from that point of view.[258]

296. According to Article 5(6), shall not be regarded as inventions susceptible of industrial application: (a) methods for treatment of the human or animal body by surgery or therapy, and (b) diagnostic methods practised on the human or animal body (compare Article 57 EPC). The *ratio* of this provision is the protection of human and animal dignity and health, dictating that the above methods, although theoretically capable of industrial exploitation, should remain free of any exclusive right. The same reason justifies, according to the prevailing view of the Greek doctrine, a wider interpretation of the said provision in order to cover not only the surgical methods aiming at the cure of an illness but also any surgical method applied on human or animal body (i.e., aesthetic surgery).[259] In any case, this exception is considerably restricted by the provision of paragraph 7, stating the said exception does not apply to products and, in particular, to substances or compositions for use in any of these methods. Therefore, although surgical, therapeutic, and diagnostic methods are not patentable, the medical substances and other products for use in the context of those methods are considered capable of industrial application. It is clearly a pragmatic solution inspired by the need to enhance research investment in the pharmaceutical sector, mainly assumed by the private sector.

II. Negative Conditions

297. Greek Patent Law, as all Patent laws, determines, as a policy issue, the types of subject matter to which it grants exclusive rights. In designing these exceptions, the national legislator has fully complied in substance with the EPC provisions, despite the partial disparities in the drafting of the relevant provisions. Thus,

255. Cf. Arts 52 and 57 EPC.
256. Express reference to the agriculture is made in Art. 57 EPC.
257. B. Antonopoulos, *supra* n. 218 at 678. K. Lymperopoulos, excludes, however, the activity of liberal professions (*supra* n. 237 at 65).
258. A. Argyriadis, *supra* n. 218 at 63.
259. A. Liakopoulos, *supra* n. 35 at 199–200, B. Antonopoulos, *supra* n. 218 at 680. On the contrary, other ways of treating human or animal bodies not consisting in surgery, therapy or diagnostic method, must be considered as susceptible of industrial application.

the three categories of exceptions to patentability, described in Article 53 EPC, have been divided in L. 1733/1987 as follows: case (c) referring to surgical, therapeutic, and diagnostic methods, has been addressed separately under the requirement of industrial application (*see* above). The other two cases, (a) and (b), are dealt with in Article 5(8), as negative substantive conditions. More specifically, Article 5(8) provides that patents shall not be granted to:

(a) Inventions the publication or exploitation of which would be contrary to public order (‘*ordre public*’) or morality.
(b) Plant or animal varieties or biological processes for the production of plants or animals. The last provision does not apply to microbiological processes or the products thereof.

A. *Opposition to the* ‘Ordre Public’ *or the Morality*

298. The concepts of public order and morality are, by nature, vague and evolving. ‘Morality’ encompasses what is objectively considered as the social belief, prevailing at a certain place and time, and not the subjective moral opinions of one or some individuals.[260] The ‘public order’ represents the main principles underlying each legal order and aiming at the preservation of its basic values. Under this approach, the concept of public order (GCC Article 33) is wider and includes the concept of morality.[261]

299. The assessment will take place by reference to the publication (through the patent application) or the exploitation of the invention; the latter term must be understood widely, as including the subject matter of the invention and its purpose as well as its possible applications. An invention shall be considered non-patentable if its exclusive application is contrary to the public order, but not if the opposition concerns only one of its possible applications (i.e., a method for the production of synthetic drugs is not patentable, while the invention of a new gun is not excepted despite the fact that it may facilitate the commitment of criminal offences). Unlawfulness is not *ipso facto* a proof of opposition to the public order.[262] As already mentioned, the concept of public order is evolving with time; thus, products or processes that would be deemed to violate the principles of a legal order at a certain stage may be accepted at a later stage (i.e., contraceptive pills).

300. As a general guideline, patents would not, in principle, be granted under Greek law for inventions referring to the human body or using forces existing in the human body (i.e., as a means for the production of a serum). It would be the same for inventions aiming or used to damage the health or deceive the public.[263] The

260. B. Antonopoulos, *supra* n. 218 at 681.
261. A. Liakopoulos, *supra* n. 35 at 203.
262. Cf. Art. 53(a) EPC, A. Liakopoulos, *supra* n. 35 at 203, *contra* B. Antonopoulos considering that an unlawful invention does not fulfil the negative condition of public order (*supra* n. 218 at 681–682).
263. B. Antonopoulos, *supra* n. 218 at 681.

public order issue has also played an important role in the controversy (developed nationally and worldwide) regarding the patentability of biotechnological inventions and their potential dangers.

B. Biological Processes and Biotechnology

301. The second negative condition concerns the plant or animal varieties as well as the biological processes for the production of plants or animals. The said exception is repeated in Article 4(3) of Directive 98/44/EC on the legal protection of biotechnological inventions.

302. Although agriculture, horticulture, and livestock farming enter into the scope of 'industrial application', the above exception reflects the legislator's reluctance to grant patent rights on human intervention for the identification of plant and animal species. This provision, to be constructed narrowly as all exceptions, has a more limited scope of application than it appears at first sight. More particularly:

(a) Patents are, first, excluded for plant or animal *varieties*. This means that patents are available for inventions which concern plants or animals in general, provided that the claims are not confined to a particular animal or plant variety. Moreover, regarding plants, a special regime has been established at national and European level allowing for the grant of industrial property rights; thus, at national level, L. 1564/1985 *on the Organization of Production and Marketing of Propagating Material of Plant Species*[264] was designed to protect the rights of plant varieties creators. Moreover, Council Regulation 2100/94 *on Community plant variety rights*[265] establishes a regime co-existing with the national ones, providing for the possibility of granting exclusive rights, valid all across EU, on varieties of all botanical genera and species (including *inter alia* hybrids between genera or species) which are distinct, uniform, stable, and new.
(b) Patents are, second, excluded for biological processes for the production of plants or animals.[266] Although the legal wording refers to the production of plants and animals in general, it is commonly accepted that the prohibition concerns only macro-biological processes applying to the production of plant or animal *varieties*.[267] In any case, the process is patentable if it is microbiological (meaning any process involving or performed upon or resulting in microbiological material).

264. OG A 164.
265. OJ L 227/1.9.1994, 1.
266. L.Lefakis, *Myriad Genetics Case: The Case for a Definite Prohibition of Granting Patents to Genes and Gene Sequences?*, 106 (DEE 2015).
267. *See* B. Antonopoulos, *supra* n. 218 at 880, A. Liakopoulos, *supra* n. 35 at 204.

303. Article 5(8) of L. 1733/1987 has to be read in accordance with the more recent legislation on the protection of biotechnology.[268] By PD 321/2001, Greece has incorporated into its internal legal order Directive 98/44/EC *on the legal protection of biotechnological inventions*. The said Directive aims at ensuring uniformity regarding the conditions of patentability and the legal protection of biotechnological inventions and, at the same time, promoting the development of biotechnology within commonly accepted safeguards; still, the rights granted to the inventors are national. On the basis of the above texts, a patent may be granted to an invention which concerns a product consisting of or containing biological material or a process by means of which biological material is produced, processed, or used.[269] Biological material which is isolated from its natural environment or produced by means of a technical process may be the subject of an invention even if it previously occurred in nature.[270] Regarding the human body at the various stages of its formation and development, the rule is that they cannot constitute a patentable invention; however, it is provided, as an exception, that an element isolated from the human body or otherwise produced by means of a technical process, including the sequence or partial sequence of a gene, may be protected by patent, even if the structure of that element is identical to that of a natural element.[271] The well-known negative condition of public order is stressed once more: biotechnological inventions are considered unpatentable where their commercial exploitation would be contrary to *ordre public* or morality.[272]

304. It is, finally, worth mentioning that pharmaceutical products and substances were, until quite recently, not patentable in Greece,[273] as the country had deposited reservation according to Article 167(2a') EPC. The exclusion did not cover the methods aiming at the production of pharmaceutical products, for which patents could be granted. The above interdiction has been repealed on 7 October 1992.

III. Formal Conditions

305. As stated above, Greece has adhered to the *formal* or *declarative* system; that means that, for the granting of a patent, the OBI examines only whether the subject matter is, in principle, allowed to be protected by patent (the negative substantive conditions) and whether the application fulfils the formal conditions prescribed by law. More particularly:

---

268. On this debate, *see*, mainly in Greek doctrine, A. Mikroulea, *The Protection of Biotechnological Inventions by Patent*, 245–280 (EEmpD 2000 (in Greek)), L. Lefakis, *Biotechnological Inventions* (Athens 2004 (in Greek)).
269. Article 3(1) PD 321/2001 (3(1) D. 98/44/EC).
270. Article 3(2) PD 321/2001 (3(2) D. 98/44/EC).
271. Article 5(1) (2) PD 321/2001 (5 (1) (2) D. 98/44/EC).
272. Article 6 PD 321/2001 (6 D. 98/44/EC).
273. Article 1 L.D. 8.6.1926 in combination with Art. 45 L. 5607/1932 & 20 L. 27/27.6.1935. *See also* Tsironis, *Patents for Pharmaceutical Products under Greek and European Law*, 360 (EEmpD 1990 (in Greek)).

306. According to Article 7(1), the application must include: (a) personal details of the applicant, (b) description[274] of the invention and determination of one or more claims, and (c) a request for the grant of a patent. By 'claim' is meant the extent and the content of the requested protection.[275] The application must be accompanied by the drawings referred to in the claims or the description, an abstract of the invention, the relevant explanations, the documents empowering the applicant, as well as the receipts evidencing payment of the application fee and of the first annual renewal fee.[276] The claim shall be based on the description;[277] that means that the description and the drawings accompanying it shall be used for the interpretation of the claim.

307. The application is accepted for filing, provided that it fulfils the requirements of Article 7(1) and it is accompanied by the receipts of the fees' payments. In this case, the filing[278] of the application *is deemed as orderly effected by not complete.*[279] The applicant must, within a period of four months from the filing date, submit any missing drawings or other supporting documents, complete any lacking data, and correct any eventual errors in the draft of the documents and of other supporting documentation; if the above takes place, the filing of the application shall be considered *complete*[280] and *the date of the orderly filing shall be considered as the filing date of the application.*[281] On the contrary, if OBI concludes that the application was filed in an orderly but not complete manner, this shall be considered as not filed.[282]

308. The orderly filing of the application is crucial for *the priority* of the invention. No application may be filed afterwards by a third person for the same invention, as the latter will miss the element of novelty. Thus, according to Article 6(3), if two or more persons have made an intention independently of each other, the right to the patent shall belong to the person whose patent application has the earliest date of filing or to the person enjoying of an *international priority*. International priority is granted to orderly patent applications which have been filed abroad, if the applicant files an application in Greece for the same invention, within twelve months from the filing date, provided that the condition of reciprocity applies.[283] The right of priority goes back to the date of the first filing abroad.

---

274. The description of the invention must be drafted in such a way as to be sufficiently carried out by a third person skilled in art (Art. 7(4)),.
275. MMCFI of Athens 6949/2009, EEmpD 2009, 893, with comments by I. Venieris, also EllDni 2010, 270 with comments by Marinos, CA of Thessaloniki 1816/2009, DEE 2010, 881, with comments by Apostolopoulos.
276. Article 7(2).
277. Article 7(3).
278. Upon filing the patent application, the applicant may state that he wishes his application to be considered as an application for the grant of a utility model certificate, in case the application is rejected as a patent application (Art. 7 para. 7).
279. Article 7(8).
280. Article 7(9).
281. Article 7 (10).
282. Article 8(1).
283. Article 9(1).

309. The patent application, as well as the documentation attached thereto, are made available[284] to the public eighteen months following the filing date or the date of priority unless the patent has already been granted; in the latter case, they are made available to the public on the date of grant of the patent.[285] In addition, extracts of the application are published in the Industrial Property Bulletin.[286]

310. If the filing of the application is orderly and complete, OBI moves to the next step: it examines: (a) whether the prerequisite of 'industrial application' and the negative conditions are obviously not respected, and (b) whether the subject matter of the application cannot be obviously considered as an invention. If either of the above cases occurs, OBI shall reject the application, wholly or in the part, which falls under said cases.[287] If none of the above cases occurs, OBI shall grant a patent, after having drafted a (final) search report based on the description of the invention.[288]

311. The *patent is an administrative act* certifying the complete and orderly nature of the patent application and indicating its classification and its period of life.[289] Attached to the patent are: the original of the description together with the claims, the abstract and the drawings if any, the search report or the final search report, and the priority claim from an application in another country. If the legal conditions for the granting of the patent are met, the applicant has a claim towards OBI for the issuance of the administrative act.[290] Thus, if, despite the fulfilment of the legal conditions OBI rejects the patent application, the applicant is entitled to submit an application for judicial review before the Supreme Administrative Court (Council of State).[291] The patent granted is recorded in the Patents Registry, while its summary is published in the Industrial Property Bulletin. The publicity is of a declaratory nature.

---

284. As from the date on which the application is made available to the public, any third party may request information and copies of the application, of the description, of the drawings and any other relevant data (Art. 7(13)).
285. Article 7(12).
286. Article 7(14).
287. Article 8(2).
288. The search report is drafted on the basis of the description of the invention, the claims, and the attached drawings. It mentions all data of the state of the art necessary for the assessment of the novelty and the inventive step of the invention. The above report is drafted only if the applicant pays the search fee within four months from the filing date of the application. In case the fee is not timely paid, the patent application is automatically converted into an application for grant of a utility model certificate. The search report is notified to the applicant, who is entitled to submit comments within a period of three months from the date of notification. On the basis of the applicant's comments, OBI shall draft a final search report including all data of the state of the art which have to be taken into account in appraising the patentability of the invention. The search report is made available to the public along with the patent application or, if it has not yet been drawn up, following its notification to the applicant. Both the search report and the final search report have an informative character (Art. 8(3–10)).
289. Article 8(11).
290. Article 12(1).
291. N. Rokas, *supra* n. 25 at 39.

§3. PROPERTY RIGHTS AND EXPLOITATION

I. Who Is the Right Holder?

A. *The Principle of the Effective Inventor*

312. Greek law adopts the principle of the effective inventor.[292] Thus, according to Article 6(1), the right to a patent belongs to the inventor or to his/her successors in title. However, the same article introduces a presumption according to which *'[w]hoever requests the grant of the patent shall be deemed to be the inventor.'* The presumption allows accelerating the procedure, taking into account the fact that OBI does not enter into a full preliminary examination of the substantive conditions. It may be rebutted if it is proven untrue, either by an action on nullification of the patent (Article 15(1)) or by an action of ownership claim (*rei vindicatio*) (Article 6(9)).

313. The two legal remedies differ in their nature and their effects. The first (action on nullification) ends up to a court decision declaring the nullity of the patent,[293] but it presents the disadvantage of destroying the novelty of the invention, hindering, thus, the filing of a new application by the effective inventor.[294] In view of the above, the effective inventor is better protected by the second remedy provided for in Article 6(9). According to that provision, the beneficiary of the invention may, if a third party has filed without his/her consent a patent application relating to his invention or to essential constituents thereof, demand, by legal action against said third party, the recognition of his/her rights emanating from the patent application or, in case that a patent has been granted, his/her rights emanating from the patent. Thus, the latter action, instead of questioning the validity of the patent, seeks, by the court, to declare that the rights emanating from the patent application or the patent shall be granted to the claimant/effective inventor.[295] In such a case, claimant is the real inventor or the person entitled to the grant of the patent, according to the applicable law; the action is addressed against the third person who has filed the application without the consent of the real inventor or the entitled person.[296] The legal action must be brought before the court[297] within a period of two years from the date of publication of the summary of patent in the Industrial Property Bulletin.[298] This term does not apply if the patentee is aware of the right of the

292. Cf. Art. 60(1)(a) EPC.
293. *See infra* n. 393.
294. I. Venieris, *Invalidity of a European Patent – Invocation Before a Greek Court and Consequences of Its Nullification*, 1043 (DEE 2007).
295. Cf. Art. 61(1)(a) EPC.
296. The inventor himself/herself may be the defendant, i.e., if the person entitled to the patent is the employer (*see infra*, at 62).
297. The action is brought either before the MMCFI of Athens or before the same Tribunal in Thessaloniki, depending on the defendant's domicile (Arts 6, 7, and 9 L. 2943/2001).
298. Article 6(10).

claimant at the time of grant or assignment of the patent.[299] If the latter occurs, the only (indirect) term derives from the duration of the patent itself (twenty years).[300]

314. In order for the aforementioned action to be accepted, the claimant has the burden to prove that: (a) he is the effective inventor of (or the person entitled to the grant of a patent for) the invention, for which the defendant has filed an application or obtained a patent; (b) that the application was filed without his/her consent; and (c) that the application consists an usurpation of his own invention.[301] The defendant may respond on the basis of the following allegations: (a) that the claimant is not the real inventor, nor the entitled person to the grant of the patent; (b) that he/she (the defendant) has a legal right on the invention; (c) that the exercise of the legal action is abusive in the sense Article 281 GCC,[302] in case the previous behaviour of the claimant has resulted in the 'deactivation' of his rights.[303] However, the defendant may not allege that the invention is not patentable, because the aforementioned legal action does not refer to the content of the invention and the conditions of its legal protection but to the person who is entitled to the grant of the patent.

315. A summary of the *irrevocable* decision stating the acceptance of the aforementioned legal action shall be recorded in the Patents Registry.[304] Once the irrevocable decision is issued, the existing patent is revoked and a new one is granted to the claimant, for a period of twenty years as from the date of the filing of the application by the first applicant (non-effective inventor).

316. Moreover, the licences and all other rights which have been granted on the patent shall be considered null *ex nunc*, i.e., null as from the date of the recording in the Patents Registry. Thus, the validity of the legal relationships established in the past is not retroactively affected and, for that reason, the new right holder has not a claim for unjust enrichment against the previous patentee regarding the fees earned by any licences granted previously.[305]

317. Moreover, the defeated litigant and third parties, if they have exploited the invention in good faith or had proceeded with the necessary preparations for the said

299. *Ibid.*
300. K. Lymperopoulos, *supra* n. 237 at 129–130.
301. *Ibid.*, at 131.
302. *'The exercise of a right is prohibited when it manifestly exceeds the limits dictated by good faith or morality or the social or economic purpose of the right'.*
303. A right may be 'deactivated' if the right holder fails to exercise it for an inordinately long (though shorter than the applicable prescription) time, under conditions that have led the defendant reasonably to believe that the right has been renounced or would not be exercised, and if the enforcement of the right would render severely onerous the condition of the defendant. K. Kerameus & Ph. Kozyris (ed.), *Introduction to Greek Law*, 87 (3rd revised ed., Kluwer Law International 2008). *See also* P. Nikolopoulos, *The Abuse of Right in Industrial Property*, 743 et seq. (DEE 2012 (in Greek)).
304. Article 6 (11).
305. K. Lymperopoulos, *supra* n. 237 at 131.

exploitation, may request from the recognized beneficiary the grant against compensation of a non-exclusive licence for a reasonable period of time.[306] In case of dispute, the conditions shall be determined by the SMCFI in the place of the residence of the applicant.[307] This is one of the grounds on which a *compulsory licence* may be granted.[308]

B. More than One Inventors

318. An invention may belong to more than one persons for factual (i.e., co-inventors) or legal (i.e., subsequent dealings) reasons.

319. First of all, an invention may have been devised jointly by two or more inventors, i.e., as the result of collaboration between scientists or in the context of a partnership relationship. According to Article 6(2), if two or more persons have made an invention jointly, the right shall belong to all of them jointly, provided there exists no other agreement. Each co-beneficiary may freely assign his/her share and take care of the maintenance of the *joint patent.*[309]

320. Thus, in view of the above provision, the co-inventors participate in a fractionally shared community; they are entitled in equal undivided shares on the invention and the subsequent patent, as tenants in common, unless otherwise agreed.[310] Their relationship is governed by Article 6(2) and the provisions of GCC on Community (Articles 785 et seq.).

321. In order to draw the powers and duties of the co-inventors (co-beneficiaries), one must distinguish among assignment, administration, and maintenance. As mentioned above, each co-beneficiary may freely assign his/her share on the patent;[311] any agreement restricting or abolishing the right of free assignment is binding only between the contracting parties and does not affect the validity of the assignment.[312] If one co-beneficiary resigns from his share, this increases proportionally the shares of the remaining co-owners.[313]

322. Administration includes all acts of management and economic exploitation of the patent. Filing of the patent application, exploitation of the patent, production of the products protected by the patent, granting of licences, are some examples of

306. Article 6 (11).
307. In accordance with the procedure laid down in Arts 741–781 of the Greek Code of Civil Procedure, the competent court will be the EU Trademarks Court, either in Athens or Thessaloniki, as provided for by Art. 9 L. 2943/2001.
308. *See infra*, 355.
309. AP 1192/2003, EEmpD 2004, 165.
310. For example, the interested parties could agree that their relationship is subject to the provisions of the GCC governing the partnership (Arts 741 et seq. GCC).
311. Cf. Art. 743(a) GCC.
312. Article 177 GCC.
313. K. Lymperopoulos, *supra* n. 237 at 136.

this category. The power to proceed to the above acts belongs to all co-beneficiaries jointly, whereby they are liable to one another for any fault;[314] no one may act without seeking the consent of the others.[315] However, provided there is no other agreement, each co-beneficiary is entitled to use or operate under the patent,[316] insofar as the use of the other co-beneficiaries is not thereby interfered with; this possibility is rather a theoretical one, if one takes into account the particularities of the patent and, thus, the suitable conditions of use will be normally fixed by the court.[317]

323. Maintenance is an aspect of the administration of the patent. It includes all acts necessary to the preservation of the right and its legal protection (i.e., payment of annual fees, filing of a legal action, defence against an action on nullity filed by a third person). The act presupposes the existence of a danger and it must be necessary and proportionate to the objective of the maintenance. Proceeding to such maintenance acts is not only a right but also an obligation of each co-beneficiary, deriving from the good faith and the business usage. Obviously, acts relating to the exploitation of the patent may not be considered as maintenance, such as the granting of licences.

324. It may also happen that two or more persons have devised the same invention, independently of each other. In such a case, the right to the patent shall belong to the person whose patent application has the earliest date of filing[318] or the person who has a priority right against the others.[319] Although it seems somehow unfair to the second inventor, the above provision aims at encouraging early disclosure of the invention, to the benefit of the society as a whole.

C. Inventions Made by Employees

325. In the current area of technology, it is a common phenomenon that inventive activity is conducted in organized laboratories or technical departments of large corporations, requires important investments, and presupposes the collaboration of a significant number of experts. The provisions related to the inventions devised by employees reflect this reality.

326. Law 1733/1987 distinguishes three legal categories of employees' inventions: the *service inventions*, the *dependent inventions,* and the *free ones*.[320]

---

314. Article 788 I GCC.
315. By a majority vote, regulations for the proper way of normal management and exploitation of the joint patent may be adopted. The majority vote shall be reckoned according to the size of the shares (Art. 789 GCC).
316. Article 787 GCC.
317. Article 790 GCC.
318. K. Lymperopoulos, *Invention by Multiple Inventors,* volume in honour of K.N.Rokas, 1985, 497.
319. Article 6(3).
320. R. Chatzinikolaou-Aggelidou, *The New Provision regarding Inventions made by Employees,* volume in honour of N. Deloukas, 1989, 19.

327. A *service invention* is the outcome of a contractual relationship between the employer and the employee for the development of inventive activity.[321] Two conditions have to be fulfilled: (a) first, existence of an active contractual relationship, irrespectively of whether the contract is valid or not, and independently of its legal qualification or the legal regime applicable to it;[322] (b) second, the invention must be the result of the contractual obligation of the employee aiming at inventive activity;[323] the obligation may be explicitly provided for in the contract or deriving from the good faith (Article 288 GCC). It makes no difference whether the invention was devised during or outside the working time of the employee, or whether there are more than one contracts between the employer and the employee, or whether the employee is exclusively or not attached to the inventive activity.[324] A decisive criterion for the qualification of the invention as a service one is the payment of a salary for the inventive activity.

328. In case that a service invention[325] is accomplished, it entirely belongs to the employer.[326] The right of the employer is absolute, exclusive, and originally acquired.[327] The name of the inventor shall be mentioned in the patent and the inventor shall have the right vis-à-vis the applicant or the owner of the patent to demand his recognition as inventor.[328] If the invention is particularly profitable to the employer, the employee shall have the right to request an additional, reasonable recompense.[329] For the recompense to be defined one has to take into account the profit deriving for the employer, the contribution of the employee to the accomplishment of the patent, the salary or other reward received by him, etc.[330] In case of disagreement, the amount of a reasonable recompense shall be fixed by the courts.

329. A *dependent invention* is the invention made by an employee with the use of materials, means, or information of the enterprise in which he/she is employed. It is not the outcome of a contractual obligation; otherwise it would be qualified as a service invention. The dependent invention belongs by 40% to the employer and by 60% to the employee.[331] The above percentages may be modified only to the benefit of the employee. According to Article 6(7), any agreements which restrict the rights of the employee shall be considered null.

330. The right of the employer is acquired as from the moment of the invention's creation, but it is subject to a *resolutory condition* in the following sense: the

321. Article 6(5).
322. B. Antonopoulos, *supra* n. 218 at 708.
323. AP 367/05, EEmpD 2006, 142, comments by I. Venieris.
324. B. Antonopoulos, *supra* n. 218 at 708–709.
325. AP 367/2005, EEmpD 2006, 1042, *with comments by* I.Venieris, CA of Athens 3268/2001, EErgD 2002, 1293.
326. Article 6(4).
327. K. Lymperopoulos, *supra* n. 237 at 144.
328. Article 6(8).
329. Article 6(5).
330. K. Lymperopoulos, *supra* n. 237 at 144–145.
331. Article 6(4).

inventor is obliged to notify, in writing and without neglect, the employer on the accomplishment of the invention and to give all necessary data for the filling of a joint patent application.[332] If the employer does not answer in writing within four months from said notification that he is interested in jointly filing the patent application, the said application shall be filed by the employee only. In the latter case, the invention belongs entirely to the employee.[333] During the pendency of the condition, both parties must refrain from acts that would impair or destroy the right subject to the condition. If the employee breaches his obligation to notify, without neglect, the accomplishment of the invention or to provide all necessary data, he will be liable for damages (Article 904 GCC) which are collectable upon fulfilment of the condition.

331. If a joint patent is granted, the employer and the employee participate in a fractionally shared community. However, the employer is entitled to exploit the dependent invention *by priority* against compensation to the inventor, proportional to the economic value of the invention and the profits it brings.[334] The above right of the employee to receive compensation may not be contractually restricted. As in the case of the service invention, the name of the inventor shall be mentioned in the patent and the inventor shall have the right to demand his recognition as inventor.[335]

332. The last category is that of the *free inventions*. An invention which is neither a service invention nor a dependent one is qualified as free and shall belong to the employee.[336] The latter enjoys the exclusive right to file a patent application and to use and exploit the invention, regardless whether it has been devised within the premises of the employer or outside.[337]

II. Which are the Powers of the Right Holder?

A. *Extent and Limits of Powers*

333. The patent right, once granted, has both a moral and an economic dimension. The first one relates to the right of the patentee to be recognized and mentioned as inventor. The second, far more important, is the economic one and relates to the exclusive right of the patentee to productively exploit the invention, either

332. Article 6(6).
333. *Ibid.*
334. Article 6(6).
335. Article 6(8).
336. Article 6(4).
337. CA of Athens 1046/2003, EllDni 2004, 225.

directly or through the granting of licences. The economic dimension of the industrial property right is both *positive* and *negative*: positive in the sense that the patentee has the exclusive right to proceed to the exploitation of the invention; negative in the sense that all third parties are excluded from such exploitation without the consent of the patentee.[338]

334. In order to ensure maximum legal protection, Article 10 describes in detail the powers of the patent's owner. In particular, he is entitled:

(a) to produce, offer, or make available in the market, to use and to possess, for said purpose, the products protected by the patent;
(b) to apply, offer, or make available in the market the process protected by the patent;
(c) to produce, offer, or make available in the market, to use and to possess, for the said purpose, the product whose production results from the process protected by the patent;
(d) to forbid each and every third party from productively exploiting the invention, with the meaning of the above, or to import, without prior consent of the patentee, the products protected by the patent.

335. However, the exercise of the exclusive right of the patentee is not unlimited.[339] The limits are expressly provided in the L. 1733/1987, taking into account the interests of the society as a whole. The first limit is related to the *duration of the validity* of the patent; such duration is fixed to twenty years starting the date following the date of the filing of the patent application.[340]

336. The second set of limits is provided for in Article 10(2). More particularly, the patentee may not forbid the following activities:

(a) The use of the invention for non-professional or research purposes (as such use does not affect the exclusive right of economic exploitation).
(b) The use of the invention built in an automobile, railway, vessel, or aeroplane entering the Greek territory on a temporary basis.
(c) The preparation of a pharmaceutical product in a pharmacy for a specific individual, following medical prescription as well as the dispensing and use of the said pharmaceutical product.

337. In addition, the rights of the patentee shall be limited in favour of the (third) person who, at the time the application for the patent was filed or in accordance with the date of priority, has already proceeded with the preparations required for the exploitation of the contrivance or has already exploited it. The said person is entitled to go on using the said contrivance but only for his enterprise and its needs.[341] This

338. N. Rokas, *supra* n. 25 at 42.
339. AP 344/2012, ChrID 2013, 139, also at Arm. 2013, 1096.
340. Article 11(1)(2).
341. Article 10(3).

right may be only assigned along with the enterprise. This provision softens, somehow, the unfair consequences of the principle dictating that the right to the patent shall belong to the person whose patent application has the earliest date of filing.

338. To the above limits, one should add the *exhaustion theory* as developed by the European courts. According to that theory, when an authorized sale of a patented product occurs, the patentee does not have, any longer, the right to exclude others from using, selling, or *importing* the said product. This happens when the patentee has already received compensation for the use of his or her invention through the sale, in which case the purpose of Patent Law is fulfilled (with respect to that certain product).

339. The theory of exhaustion derives from EU law (Articles 34 and 36 of TFEU about the free movement of goods within the internal market) and has been vastly interpreted by case law.[342] When a product is sold within a Member State, the right of the patentee is exhausted. So the product can be imported freely in another Member State. Therefore, the possibility of parallel imports is not being restricted. Greek law does not establish explicitly the theory of exhaustion as far as patents are concerned, as it does in the case of the trademark (the exhaustion of the right on the trademark is provided for by Article 128(1) L. 4072/2012). However, this does not mean that the theory of exhaustion cannot be applied to patents according to Greek law since it has been supported[343] that the theory can be based on Article 281 GCC, relating to the abuse of right.

340. The rights of the patentee may be also limited through the granting of *compulsory licences*. This issue will be addressed in the relevant chapter.

342. The Court of Justice of the EU dealt with the theory of exhaustion at the case *Centrafarm v. Sterling* (ECJ 31.10.1974, C-15/74, *ECR* 1974, 451), where it set for the first time the two preconditions for the application of the theory. First, the patentee must consent to the sale of the product. Second, he/she must be reimbursed for this sale with any kind of compensation (thoughts 9, 11). Hereinafter, the patentee cannot claim any infringements concerning the import of the patented good in another Member State, even if the product is sold at higher prices in the second Member State where the parallel import takes place. In the following case *Merck v. Stephar* (ECJ 14.7.1981, C-187/80, *ECR* 1981, 2063), it was judged that the patentee who consents to sell his/her goods within a Member State that does not legally protect patents, he/she bears the burden of that choice and his/her right has been exhausted. In *Pharmon v. Hoerchst* (ECJ 9.7.1985, C-19/84, *ECR* 1985, 2281), the Court dealt with the case of obligatory licenses, where it was judged that no exhaustion of the right of the patentee takes place since he/she does not voluntarily give his/her consent. Finally in *Greenstar-Kanzi v. Hustin & Goosens* (ECJ 20.10.2011, C-140/10, *unpublished*) the Court concluded that, when a firm has granted another firm with a license plus the permission to sub-license under certain terms other firms to produce certain goods, the exhaustion of the right of the patentee depends on the following criterion: when the sub-license breaches an essential term of the permission granted, then no exhaustion takes place and the patentee reserves his rights, because he has not consented. If, however, the breach concerns a secondary term, the right of the patentee has been exhausted (thoughts 41–45).

343. Ch. Chrissanthis, *Exhaustion of Intellectual Property Rights and Parallel Imports*, 177 (Athens 2012 (in Greek)).

B. Assignment of the Patent Right

341. Instead of exploiting the patent himself/herself, the patentee may choose to assign the rights deriving therefrom.

342. The right on the patent itself as well as the right on a patent application may be assigned by written agreement, according to Article 12(1) and the provisions of GCC on the assignment of claims (Articles 455 et seq.). The assignment may concern the right as a whole or a share of it.[344] It may be accomplished independently of the transfer of the enterprise.[345]

343. The assignment needs to be executed in writing; the written form (either private act or notarial deed) is incumbent for the validity of the transaction. Thus, if the act is not executed in the form prescribed by law, it is absolutely null and void (Article 159(1) GCC). In order to be completed and to produce its legal effects, the assignment agreement must be registered in the Patent Registry.[346] It has to be also published in the Industrial Property Bulletin, but the latter publication is of a declaratory nature and does not affect the validity or the effects of the agreement.

344. The assignment may concern the economic powers as well as the moral content of the right. In case of doubt, only the rights related to the economic exploitation of the patent and/or the invention are assigned. The moral rights may be assigned in the sense that the assignor consents to accept acts or omissions, which would otherwise violate the moral content of the right.[347] The so-called *honour of the inventor*, i.e., the right of the patentee to be referred as the inventor, may not be transferred.[348]

345. The rights and obligations of the assignor and the assignee are governed by the relevant provisions of the GCC. Thus, the assignor-patentee is liable towards the assignee only for the existence of the right and not for its commercial or industrial value, unless otherwise agreed (Articles 467, 468). If the patent is not valid, the patentee is bound to pay back the whole or part of the price paid, taking into account the benefits gained by the assignee until the recognition of the patent's nullity. If the assignment is made gratuitously, the patentee is not even liable for the validity of the patent (Articles 467(2), 470).

346. The right on the patent application and the right on the patent itself may also be transferred by inheritance. In such a case, the formalities prescribed for the assignment (registration of the inheritance certificate in the Patent Registry, publication in the Industrial Property Bulletin) have to be equally fulfilled.

---

344. According to Art. 12(2), the joint owners of a patent may assign, each one separately, following written agreement, their share of the patent. The same applies to the right in common for granting a patent.
345. B. Antonopoulos, *supra* n. 218 at 724.
346. Article 12(1).
347. B. Antonopoulos, *supra* n. 218 at 726.
348. A. Liakopoulos, *supra* n. 35 at 242.

C. Patent Licences

347. Greek law provides for two categories of licences: the contractual and the non-contractual or compulsory ones.[349]

1. Contractual Licences

348. Through the method of licences and on the basis of the freedom of contract, the parties may define the scope and extent of their respective powers and obligations in various ways. That means that in real business life, the terms of the licences vary greatly, depending on the ingenuity, the needs, and the economic power of the parties. As a matter of law, there is only one distinction of importance in the category of contractual licences: The exclusive one by which the licensor undertakes voluntarily not only to grant no other licences but also to not exploit (manufacture or sell) within the licensee's territory; the non-exclusive or simple one by which the licensor reserves the right to grant other licences and to exploit the patent by himself. Both types are further analysed below.

a. Non-exclusive (Simple) Licence

349. When granting a licence without exclusivity (simple), the patentee also reserves the right to exploit the invention, as well as to grant other licences to third persons. The licence may be unlimited or limited; the limits may concern the duration and the geographical scope of the agreement and/or the form, the amount and the sector of exploitation.[350] Some of the above restrictions (duration, geographical limits, etc.) are inherent to the content of the patent right and, therefore, in case of breach of the agreement the patentee is protected by the provisions of the Patent Law. Other restrictions (i.e., price-fixing, commission, use of trademarks) are indirectly related to the patent right and may only be addressed on the basis of the general provisions of Contract Law.[351]

350. The simple licence agreement is a *promissory* contract, *bilateral* in the majority of cases (in the sense that compensation is normally agreed upon) and including an obligation of long-term performance. The agreement is executed in writing,[352] as well as any contract modifying the first one. No registration is needed. Its legal qualification (whether it belongs to the regulated contracts of the civil code or it is a sui generis non-typical contract) depends largely on the content of the agreement. Basically, it presents the characteristics of a *usufructuary lease of*

---

349. CA of Thessaloniki 1032/2009, EEmpD 2009, 721.
350. B. Antonopoulos, *supra* n. 218 at 731–732.
351. *Ibid.*, 732–733.
352. Article 12(3).

income producing objects (Article 638 GCC),[353] although it may also acquire elements from other specific contracts (i.e., provision of services) and being, thus, qualified as a *mixed contract.*[354]

351. The rights and obligations of the parties vary according to the type of the licence and the specific content of each agreement.[355] Generally speaking, the main obligation of the patentee (and the corresponding right of the licensee) is to give, during the term of the agreement, the use of the patent and the fruits deriving thereof. Some additional secondary obligations accompany the above principal one, such as the obligation to provide technical guidance and all necessary information to the licensee, the obligation to preserve the patent and the rights arising thereof (i.e., payment of annual fees, obligation not to resign from the patent until the expiration of the licence), and the obligation to take all necessary actions for the legal protection of the right. The latter is of importance for the licensee, given the fact that, he is not legally entitled to directly sue infringers of the right on the patent; only the patentee may invoke the protective and efficient provisions of L. 1733/1987, while the licensee (without exclusivity) may base his claims only on the L. 146/1914 relating to unfair competition and to Articles 914, 919 GCC on tort liability.

352. The main obligation of the licensee is to pay the *royalties* or any other form of reward or compensation agreed with the patentee; however, the compensation is not a constitutive element of the licence agreement. Among the secondary obligations of the licensee deriving from the good faith and the business usages, one may mention the obligation to exploit the patent (the extent of which depends on the content of the contract), the obligation to provide information and accountability to the patentee, and the non-competition obligation towards the patentee.

353. According to Article 12(4), the licence is neither exclusive nor assignable nor inheritable, unless otherwise agreed. It results from the above provision that the licensee may not transfer the rights of the licence to a third person without the express consent of the licensor. If the transfer is allowed, the third person enters into the agreement, in the place of the licensee, and exercises all rights belonging to his assignor. The granting of sub-licences is not expressly addressed in the law. According to the prevailing opinion, the licensee without exclusivity is not entitled to grant sub-licences, although such power is recognized to the licences with exclusivity.[356]

354. The duration of the licence is normally agreed upon by the parties. If no reference is made in the contract or the licence is described as of undefined duration, the expiration coincides with the expiration of the patent itself.

---

353. By a contract of usufructuary lease the lessor is bound to give to the lessee during the term of the lease not only the use of the thing or right leased but also the enjoyment of its fruits, insofar as they are to be considered as products (*Ph. Christodoulou*, in K. Kerameus/Ph. Kozyris, *supra* n. 304 at 124-125).
354. B. Antonopoulos, *supra* n. 218 at 735.
355. *See* analysis by B. Antonopoulos, *supra* n. 218 at 737–741.
356. B. Antonopoulos, *supra* n. 218 at 741.

b. Exclusive Licence

355. By the exclusive licence, the licensor voluntarily undertakes not only to grant no other licences but also not to exploit (manufacture or sell) within the licensee's territory. The powers and the legal position of the exclusive licensee are far stronger than that of any other licensee and, for that reason, the exclusivity has to be expressly agreed upon or clearly deduced from the content of the agreement. In case of doubt, the licence is deemed non-exclusive.[357]

356. The agreement is a *dispositional* and not a *promissory* contract (as the simple licence one), in the sense that the licensee acquires a position of some independence from his licensor and may exercise his rights against third parties. The exclusive licence is executed *in writing*. Although there is no statutory obligation to register the transaction, the prevailing opinion in legal theory accepts that the exclusive licence (in contrary to what applies to licence without exclusivity) has to be registered in the Patent Registry and published in the Industrial Property Bulletin, by analogy to statutory provisions for the assignment of patent rights.[358]

357. The exclusive licence may contain various restrictions (geographical, temporal, commercial, etc.); if geographical limits are agreed, the licensee gets the exclusivity on his own territory. That means that the granting of more than one exclusive licence is not only legally possible but also common in practice. If only one exclusive licence is granted, the position of the licensor is very much alike to that resulting from an assignment of the patent right. The obligations and the rights of the parties may vary according to the content of the agreement; the main obligations described above in the context of licences without exclusivity are also applicable here, although the extent differs considerably. For example, the obligation of the exclusive licensor to exploit the patent is much more pronounced here, given the fact the patentee is excluded from the said exploitation (the number of licences granted and the method of calculation of royalties, i.e., percentage on the sales, are parameters to be also taken into account).

358. The extent and the degree of exclusivity granted to the licensee and, in general, the content of a licence agreement may raise concerns from the competition law point of view.[359] Indeed, it is in the essence of the licence that third persons are excluded from the exploitation of the patent, giving the licensee a great competitive advantage against his or her competitors. Concerns may also relate to the design of the internal relations between patentee and licensee since the contractual licences usually incorporate various clauses restricting competition. However, these doubtful clauses may be necessary in order for the licensee to sign for such a contract. This happens because the patentee, despite possessing the inventive idea, frequently misses the capital to commercially exploit his or her patent, so the licensee undertakes the venture to invest in the said patent and to produce and/or distribute the

357. Article 12(4).
358. Article 12(1).
359. For an analysis on that issue *see* E. Mastromanolis, *supra* n. 50 at 377 et seq.

relative products to the market. Therefore he/she assumes a certain economic risk to promote the novel product and, to that end, he/she demands a level of exclusivity in his/her favour.

359. The Commission Regulation 772/2004 on the application of Article 81(3) of the Treaty to categories of technology transfer agreements tries to balance the conflicting interests, by offering an exemption from Article 81(1) (now Article 101(1) TFEU) to technology transfer agreements permitting the production of contract products, provided that the market shares of the undertakings involved do not exceed a certain limit (20% for both sides if they are competitors, 30% for each one if they are not). So, even if the agreement between the patentee and the licensee contains (permitted) restrictions of competition, the agreement will still be valid and legal.

360. The regulation, however, contains a list of illegal hardcore restrictions, the presence of which deprives the parties of the benefit of the exemption. The treatment is more severe when the undertaking-parties to the agreement are also competitors. Qualified as hardcore restrictions are: the price-fixing, the limitation of output, the allocation of markets, the obligation to produce with the licensed technology, the restriction of active or passive sales, etc. However, the distribution of geographical territories (by granting an exclusive licence) is allowed.

361. With the reserve of the application of EU Competition Rules, the exclusive licensor is entitled to claim protection of his rights not only against his contracting party-patentee but also against third parties; indeed, Article 17(3) puts the licensee in the special semi-independent position of being able to sue infringers of patent and, consequently, of his rights on the basis of the protective provisions of Patent Law and to claim lifting of the infringement, omission in the future as well as restitution of damage.[360]

2. Compulsory Licences

362. Greek law, as the majority of the patent systems, endeavours to establish a fair balance between the protection of the monopoly powers of the patentee and some public policy objectives, such as the local working of the invention, the satisfaction of the consumer needs, and the interest of the society as a whole to enjoy the results of the technical progress. Taking into account the above, L. 1733/1987 establishes an exhaustive list of grounds for the granting of compulsory licences. More particularly:

(1) *Licence to the public sector*: For imperative reason of serving public health and national defence, following justified decision of the Minister of Industry, Energy and Technology, and according to the case, any competent Minister, a

360. *See infra*, 377.

licence for exploitation for an invention can be granted to bodies of the public sector, provided that the relevant invention has not been productively exploited in Greece or the production of products thereof is insufficient to cover local needs.[361] Prior to the issue of the above decision, the patentee and anyone who is in a position to give useful advice are called upon to express their views.[362] This provision refers to the so-called public interest inventions.

The MD determines, following the opinion of OBI, the amount and the terms of compensation to the owner of the patent. The amount of the compensation is determined in accordance with the extent of the industrial exploitation of the invention. In case of disagreement of the patentee regarding the amount of the compensation, the said amount is determined by the competent SMCFI, following the injunctions proceedings.

(2) *Compulsory licence due to insufficient exploitation*:[363] A second ground for granting a licence without the consent of the patentee is that of the insufficient production. For the compulsory licensing to be allowed, the following conditions have to be met accumulatively:[364] (a) A period of three years must have elapsed since the grant of the patent or a period of four years since the filing date of the patent application; (b) The relevant invention has not been exploited in Greece or, in case it has, the production of the products thereof is insufficient to cover local demand; (c) the third party requesting the licence is in a position to exploit productively the invention covered by the patent; (d) the third party must have notified the patentee, one month prior to the initiation of the judicial proceedings, regarding his intention to request a non-contractual licence.

The competent court will decide upon petition of the interested party[365] whether, and under which terms, a compulsory licence should be granted. The petition is accompanied by the opinion of the OBI regarding the fulfilment of the above conditions, the amount and the terms of the compensation to be given to the owner of the patent, and the exclusive or non-exclusive character of the exploitation of the invention. OBI states its opinion following the petition of the party interested in exploiting the patent. The said opinion is granted within one month from the date the relevant petition is filed and it is not binding for the court.[366]

The court will not accept the petition and will not grant the licence if the patentee justifies, on the basis of good faith, the lack of exploitation or the insufficient exploitation in the country. In any case, the importation of the product does not constitute a satisfactory excuse, unless the products are imported from Member States of the European Union and the Member States

361. Article 14(1).
362. Article 14(2).
363. Cf. Art. 31 TRIPS.
364. Article 13(1).
365. Article 13(5).
366. Copy of the application for granting a compulsory license along with the opinion of OBI and the note fixing the date of the trial must be notified to the owner of the patent and to the beneficiaries of other contractual or non-contractual licenses (Art. 13(5)).

of the WTO.[367] If the court approves the petition, it grants the compulsory licence and determines its terms and conditions (extent of the exploitation rights, duration, date of commencement of the productive exploitation of the invention in Greece, and the amount and terms of compensation to be paid to the patentee by the beneficiary of the licence).[368] The amount and the terms of the compensation are determined in accordance with the extent of the industrial exploitation of the protected invention.[369] The decision of the court must be recorded in the Patents Registry of OBI, published in the Industrial Property Bulletin, and notified to the patentee and the interested third parties.[370]

(3) *Compulsory licence on an earlier patent*: Another legal ground for compulsory licensing is that concerning the exploitation of a *dependent patent.*[371] The owner of the said patent may request from the competent court the grant of a non-contractual licence on an earlier patent, under three cumulative conditions: (a) that his/her invention relates to the invention of the earlier patent; (b) that the productive exploitation of said patent is not possible without offending the rights of the owners of the earlier patent; and (c) that his/her invention constitutes a significant progress in comparison with the invention of the prior patent.[372] The procedure described above under (b) applies also to the present compulsory licensing. When the licence has been granted by the court, the owner of the earlier patent may request, in a form of reciprocity, the granting of a non-contractual licence for the subsequent invention.

(4) The last ground for compulsory licensing is provided for in Article 6(11) and concerns the case when the real inventor has been recognized, by judicial decision, as owner of the patent right.[373] The defeated litigant and third parties, if they have exploited the invention in good faith or had proceeded with the necessary preparations for the said exploitation, may request from the recognized beneficiary the grant against compensation of a non-exclusive licence for a reasonable period of time.[374] In case of dispute, the conditions shall be determined by the competent EU Trademarks Court.

In the above (2), (3), and (4) cases, the grant of a compulsory licence does not exclude other contractual or non-contractual licences. The non-contractual licence may be assigned only along with the part of the enterprise which exploits the invention.[375]

---

367. Article 13(2). The non-contractual license does not grant the right for importation of the products covered by the invention (Art. 13(9)).
368. Article 13(6).
369. Article 13(6) 2.
370. Article 13(7).
371. Although the terminology may be confusing, a clear distinction has to be established between the dependent invention of an employee and the dependent invention which is related to an earlier main patent.
372. Article 13(4).
373. *Supra*, at paras314-318
374. Article 6(11).
375. Article 13(3).

363. The court which had competence to grant the compulsory licence and to determine its terms is also competent to amend such terms, upon petition of the patentee, if new data justify the amendment, or even to revoke the compulsory licence if the beneficiary does not respect the terms of the licence or if the prerequisites for its granting have ceased existing. If the immediate revocation of the licence brings about a significant damage to the beneficiary of the said licence, the court may allow the continuation of the exploitation for a reasonable period of time.[376]

§4. Legal Protection and Remedies

I. Infringement of a Patent Right

364. The right on a patent may be infringed in its moral content (i.e., a third person contests the identity of the inventor) or, more frequently, in its economic content (i.e., a third person proceeds to preparatory works or to advertisement regarding the patent, or imitates the product or the method protected by the patent).

365. The most difficult task here is to define the boundaries of the legal protection reserved to the monopoly rights of the patent owner, especially when the third person acts on the periphery of the patent claims; such task inevitably involves a balance between the need of fair protection for the patentee and the long-term public interest.

366. In order to define the field of protection, one has to take into account the technical problem addressed by the invention, the solution submitted by the inventor, and the proposed industrial application, as the above are disclosed in the *description and drawings of the patent* and *the scope of its claims*. Although the extent of protection must not be strictly linked to the literal meaning of the wording used in the claims the scope of such claims, in combination with the purpose of the invention, serve as a guideline to that end.[377]

367. In view of the above, the technical solutions must be compared on the basis of the *essential elements* of the invention, as they derive from its description.[378] Considered essential or material are the elements, the existence of which is necessary for the achievement of the technical solution. If the same essential elements are met in another technical solution but they serve a different purpose, no identity can be ascertained. In addition, if one or more of the essential elements is omitted or replaced by something different (not falling in the description used in the claim) then no infringement may be ascertained. In contrary, an article with the attributes

376. Article 13(8).
377. K. Simitis, *supra* n. 253 at 190–191, I. Venieris, '*The Protection of the Inventor by L. 1733/1987 against Infringement from Equivalent Technical Rule*', EEmpD 2006 (in Greek), 500, 514, CA of Thessaloniki 1586/2012, DEE 2012, 1020.
378. B. Antonopoulos, *supra* n. 218 at 768–769.

described in the claim remains an infringement, even if further insubstantial elements are added to it and, independently, whether such elements make the article more or less successful. Likewise, it remains an infringement when the infringer selects the best version of all the alternatives covered by the claim or he uses *technical equivalents* (i.e., similar means that can be identified by a person skilled in the art) to achieve the same solution to the technical problem.

II. Remedies in Case of Infringement

A. *Civil Remedies*

1. Action for Lifting of the Infringement

368. The main legal basis for civil remedies in case of infringement of patent rights is provided for in Article 17 of L. 1733/1987. If the moral content of the right is also violated, Articles 57 et seq. GCC on the protection of personality may receive application. Furthermore, L. 146/1914 on unfair competition offers an additional ground of action, although less effective than the Patent Law.[379]

369. The first civil remedy is the legal action aiming at the lifting of the infringement and its omission in the future. According to Article 17(1), in case of an infringement or *threatened* infringement of a patent right, the patentee may request the lifting of the infringement and its omission in the future. No fault from the part of the infringer is required. The action must refer to concrete and existent violation acts (i.e., manufacture and/or sale of patent products) and must request all necessary measures for the cease of the infringement. Such measures may include, on application by the patentee, indicatively and not restrictively the following: (a) the recall of the goods that were found to be infringing a patent right and, as in appropriate cases, materials principally used in the creation or manufacture of these goods from the channels or the commerce; (b) the definitive removal of these goods and materials from the channels of commerce; or (c) the destruction of these goods or materials. The law provides that, in considering the application of the patentee, the need for proportionality between the seriousness of the infringement and the remedies ordered, as well as the interests of third parties, shall be taken into account. The above measures are carried out at the expense of the infringer unless particular reasons are invoked for not doing so.

370. The patentee is also entitled to exercise the above action against intermediaries whose services are used by a third party to infringe the rights provided by law. In order to facilitate proof of infringement, Article 17(6) establishes the presumption according to which if the invention relates to a process for the manufacture of a product, each product of the same nature is presumed to have been manufactured according to the protected process.

379. AP 1344/2012 ChrID 2013, 139, also at Arm. 2013, 1096, CA of Athens 1502/2010, DEE 2010, 784, CA of Athens 3676/2010, DEE 2011, 39.

371. The demand *for omission of infringement in the future* may be brought before the court if there is a real and serious threat of repetition of such infringement; the existence of threat must be assessed objectively, although the intention of the infringer is seriously taken into account. The fact that the infringement has already occurred once constitutes, by itself, a presumption of a 'repetition threat'. The patentee requests the omission not only of the infringement suffered but also of any other related or similar act capable of negatively affecting its rights. For each act of omission contributing to an infringement, the court may impose a monetary penalty of up to EUR 10,000 in favour of the patentee.[380]

372. The action for lifting and omission of the infringement may be also exercised by the beneficiary of an exclusive licence to the person who has a right on the invention and to the person who has filed a patent application. In the latter case, the court may postpone the trial procedure of the case until the said patent has been granted.[381]

373. The defendant may allege against such action:[382] (a) that he/she has a legal right on the invention; (b) that the exercise of the legal action is abusive in the sense of Article 281 GCC, in case the previous behaviour of the patentee has resulted in the deactivation of his rights; or (c) the objection of the absolute nullity of the patent according to Article 15.[383]

374. When a person is entitled to exercise the above action, the most efficient means of protection is *the procedure of injunction measures*. Until 2011, such measures could have only been ordered according to the procedure provided for in the Code of Civil Procedure (Articles 683 et seq.).[384] However, Article 53 of L. 3966/2011 (incorporating Directive 2004/48/EC into the Greek legal order) has introduced into L. 1733/1987 the new Article 17B dealing with precautionary evidence and other injunction measures. The said Article 17B corresponds to Articles 7 and 9 of Directive 2004/48/EC. It provides that the SMCFI may, in case of alleged infringement of a right protected under the Patent Law, order – as an injunction measure – the precautionary seizure of items in the possession of the alleged infringer that constitute means of commitment or product or evidence of the infringement.[385] The court may order, instead, the detailed description of such items, including taking of photographs.[386] In any case, the court may issue against the

380. Article 17(1) *in fine*.
381. Article 17(3).
382. B. Antonopoulos, *supra* n. 218 at 772.
383. According to Art. 15(1), the patent shall be declared null by Court decision if: (a) the owner of the patent is not the inventor or his assignee or beneficiary according to Art. 6(4), (5), and (6); (b) the invention is not patentable in accordance with Art. 5; (c) the description attached to the patent is insufficient for the invention to be carried out by a person skilled in the art.
384. MMCFI of Athens 5249/2005 EEmpD 2006, 154, SMCFF of Athens 4286/2012 DEE 2012, 655, SMCFI of Thessaloniki 14372/2004 ChrID 2004, 1010, SMCFI of Athens 3791/2007 EEmpD 2007, 717, SMCFI of Thessaloniki 3744/2013 EEmpD 2014, 486.
385. P. Kolotouros, *The Proof of Infringement of Intellectual Property Rights*, 458 (EPolD 2013).
386. Article 17B(1).

alleged infringer injunction measures intended to prevent any imminent infringement or to forbid, on a provisional basis and subject where appropriate, to a penalty payment, the continuation of the infringement.[387] In the case of an infringement committed on a commercial scale, the court may order the precautionary seizure of the property of the alleged infringer, including the blocking of his/her bank accounts.

2. Action for Damages

375. The patentee (as well as the inventor, the exclusive licensee, and the person who has filed a patent application) is also entitled, in case of infringement, to exercise an action for damages. The claimant has to invoke and prove the occurrence of four elements: (a) the infringement; (b) the fault of the infringer, malice, or negligence;[388] (c) the amount of damage; and (d) the causal link between the damage and the illegal behaviour of the infringer.

376. The most difficult item in this context is the definition of the damage suffered. According to Greek Private Law, only the concrete damage (*damnunemergens* and *lucrumcensans*) is indemnified; however, when a patent right and, in general, an industrial property right, is violated, it is difficult, if not impossible, to quantify with exactitude the extent of the damage suffered (it is possible, e.g., that the invention protected by the patent has not yet been commercialized and has not acquired a 'price' in the market). In order to overpass the above obstacles, the avant-garde provision of Article 17(2) provided, long before the Directive 2004/48/EC, for three alternative methods of definition of the damage suffered, the first being a *concrete* one, the two others are being qualified as *abstract* methods.[389] More particularly, the patent owner is entitled to demand: (a) restitution of the damage, or (b) return of the benefits derived from the unfair exploitation of the invention, or (c) the payment of an amount equal to the value of the licence of the said exploitation.

377. The first method reflects the compensatory function of the indemnification, as adopted by the general private law and necessitates the proof of the exact positive damage and loss of profit suffered by the claimant; the evidentiary difficulties render its use very rare in practice.

378. The second method consists in the return of the benefits derived from the unfair exploitation of the invention. The benefits are those causally linked to the infringement and correspond to the net earnings of the infringer (if one deduces the expenses related to the exploitation and the eventual additional earnings solely

387. Article 17B(2).
388. The existence of fault is not a prerequisite for the exercise of the action for lifting and omission of the infringement.
389. A. Liakopoulos, *supra* n. 35 at 141.

related to the exceptional capacities of the infringer).[390] If no earnings have been derived, the claimant may choose one of the two other available methods of calculation.

379. The third method of definition of the damage consists in the payment of an amount equal to the value of the licence for said exploitation. The value is calculated at the end of the infringement, on the basis of the market conditions; the question is which royalties a third person would pay, reasonably and objectively, under the same circumstances in order to get a licence on that patent right. It is irrelevant whether the said patent has already been on the market or not, or whether a licence has already been granted or not.

380. According to Article 17(5), in case of condemnation of the defendant, the court may order the destruction of the products manufactured in violation of the dispositions of the present law. The court may also, instead of the destruction, order that the products or a part thereof be rendered to the plaintiff for his total or partial compensation, upon request of the latter. This presupposes that the court has determined the value of the products to be rendered.

381. In addition to the restitution of the economic damage, the patentee may claim a reasonable compensation for moral prejudice (Article 932 GCC).

382. It has to be noted that, following the incorporation of Directive 2004/48/EC into Greek legal order by L. 3966/2011, new Articles 17B–17Z have been introduced to L. 1733/1987. Article 17D,[391] corresponding to Article 13 of the Directive, deals more specifically with the question of damages and, in fact, duplicates, to a great extent, the pre-existing and still applicable provision of Article 17(2). This overlapping was a conscious choice of the legislator, in order to achieve systematic coherence in the regulation of intellectual property rights.[392] The new article repeats

390. *Ibid.*, 144–145.

391. Article 17D (1) '*On application by the injured party, the court may order the infringer who knowingly, or with reasonable grounds to know, engaged in an infringing activity, to pay the right holder damages appropriate to the actual prejudice suffered by him as a result of the infringement of his right. In setting the compensation the court (a) shall take into account all appropriate aspects, such as the negative economic consequences, including lost profits, which the injured party has suffered, any unfair profits made by the infringer and, in appropriate cases, elements other than economic factors, such as the moral prejudice caused to the right holder by the infringement, or (b) as an alternative to clause (a), may, in appropriate cases, set the compensation as a lump sum on the basis of elements such as at least the amount of royalties or fees which would have been due if the infringer had requested authorization to use the infringed right*'.

392. According to the Introductory Report of L. 3966/2011, Art. 53, with which Greek law complied with Arts 13, 14, and 15 of Directive 2004/48/EC, it is mentioned that the said Directive regulates, *in a uniform manner, all intellectual property rights*. The international term 'intellectual property', in Greek language, actually includes copyright and industrial property (meaning trademarks and patents). In Greek law, however, protection of industrial property rights is fragmented in separate special laws, depending on the right protected. Thus, Art. 17D L. 1733/1987 was established in order for this special law of patent rights to comply, systematically, with the more general scope

the above alternative methods of 'the definition of damages, with the only difference that it includes the 'unfair profits' among the elements to take into account when assessing the actual damage of the patentee.

383. One has to also mention the new Article 17A, corresponding to Articles 6 and 8 of the Directive, which deals with evidence and the right of information; this provision greatly facilitates access of the patentee-claimant, by judicial order, to the evidence which lies in the control of the opposing party[393] as well as to the information in possession of any involved person, on the origin and distribution networks of the goods or services which infringe a right protected by the Patent Law.[394] The above provisions are expected to reduce evidentiary difficulties hindering the legal actions for damages.

B. Penal Remedies

384. Article 17(7) is the only provision of L. 1733/1987 stating penal remedies; it supplements and completes the civil protection of the same law and aims at the establishment of transparency and integrity in commercial transactions.[395] It provides that:

> whoever places on products or on their wrapping, or on any kind of commercial documents destined for the public or on other relevant means of publicizing and advertising a false statement that the objects in question are protected by patent, shall be punished by up to one year imprisonment or by fine amounting to at least fifty thousand drachmas or by both penalties.

385. It is doubtful though if this provision is set in order to protect the general public (meaning the consumers of the product in question) or the owner of the patent himself/herself. In any case it is required, of course, that the product in question is protected with a valid patent. Although the prevailing view accepts that the purpose of the said article is the protection of the patentee, it is more consistent[396] to consider that this provision aims at the protection of consumers from misleading impressions that could influence their judgment and buying options. This could happen if a false label upon a product mentioning that it is protected with a patent, pushes the consumer public (as an undefined number of people) to make a buying choice that they would not have made should they have known the truth about the product not being protected with such an industrial property right; or if they would have offered a lower price for the product, it should also be considered that they are misled. This happens because the assurance, via advertisement, that the product is

---

and wording of the Directive. In the same line, the respective laws protecting topographies of semiconductor products (PD 45/1991) and industrial designs (PD 259/1997) also included similar provisions, in compliance with the said Directive.

393. Article 17A(1)(2).

394. Article 17A(4)(5).

395. K. Lymperopoulos, *The Law of Inventions, supra*, at 217.

396. According to N. Rokas, *supra* n. 25 at 56.

protected by a patent creates a certain level of expectation for the consumer public. For instance, the incentive for a consumer in order to make a buying choice could be the requirement of novelty that exists when a patent is granted.

386. However, the absence of a more specific penal protection for the owner of the patent within L. 1733/1987 does not mean that he/she cannot be protected through means of the general provisions, meaning the Penal Code or other laws of the penal legislation. For example, Article 386 PC could have effect if the requirements for *fraud* are met.

III. End of Protection: The Loss of a Patent Right

387. The loss of patent rights may be due to a reason already existent when the patent is granted (so the loss dates back to that time), or due to a subsequent reason (so the loss takes place henceforth). The reasons leading to such a loss of the patent rights are basically three:

(1) *Duration of the validity.* First of all, the duration of the patent is limited. This limitation by time derives from the social character of the invention protected with the patent. Indeed, the inventor using his creative way of thinking actually teaches society, taking advantage, though, of the pre-existing level of technique. This means that the new invention has been based upon countless older inventions and that it pushes the technological evolution one step beyond. Subsequently, the law must not prevent any further evolution but ensure that the general public will benefit from it. Despite the loss of the patent right, the inventor keeps his moral right (protected by Articles 57, 60 GCC).
According to Article 11 paragraph 1, the validity of the patent lasts for twenty years, starting the day following the date of the filing of the patent application. Article 11(2) points out that in case there is a claim of priority on the basis of filing abroad, the duration of the validity is calculated from the day following its filing in Greece. Therefore, after twenty years have passed the right on the patent is lost and anyone can make use of the invention, presupposed that such use is neither illegal nor illicit. Apart from the main patent, any patent of modification shall also follow the same fate and expire therewith (Article 18(2)). Finally, no extension or renewal of the patent can be made.

(2) *Forfeiture.* As far as forfeiture is concerned (Article 16), the owner of the patent loses his right in two cases:
   (a) when he/she files a statement of waiver with OBI; or
   (b) when he or she does not pay the protection fee in the due term (as described in Article 24).

   In both cases, the patentee declines from the rights derived from the patent as soon as OBI issues an act for the forfeiture (also published in the Industrial Property Bulletin). Until the issue of this act, the patent normally generates every right associated. The person entitled to file for the statement of waiver is the patentee or his authorized representative. The statement is a unilateral declaration addressed to OBI. If the patentees are more than one, then the statement must be made by all of them. Partial loss of the patent rights is possible if the patentee wishes so and declares it in his statement. Then OBI replaces the initial patent with the modified content. According to Article 18(4), the statement of waiver includes the patent of modification, unless the latter is converted into the main patent.

The payment of the protection fee aims at the demonstration of interest on behalf of the patentee to commercially exploit his or her invention. If such interest is not shown, then the invention must be freely given to the general public.

(3) *Nullification.* Unlike the case of forfeiture where the patentee himself declares his waiver, the nullification requires a court decision that is issued only if certain reasons exist. These reasons are described in Article 15(1) in a restrictive way and are the following:
   (a) The patentee is not the inventor or his/her assignee or beneficiary according to Article 6(4), (5), and (6).
   (b) The invention is not patentable in accordance with Article 5.
   (c) The description attached to the patent is insufficient for the invention to be carried out by a person skilled in the art.
   (d) The subject matter of the granted patent extends beyond the content of the protection, as requested in the application.

   Article 15(2) indicates that the person entitled to bring action against the owner of the patent in front of the court is one of the persons mentioned in passage (a) of paragraph 1, and whoever has legal interest in every other case (passages (b), (c), or (d)). The consequences of the nullification run back and it is considered that the patent has never been granted.[397]

388. The ratio for the existence of such a drastic measure, such as the nullification of the patent, is explained as follows: For the reason under passage (a): The purpose for the granting of the patent is to protect the inventor and reward him or her with the exclusive (for a limited period of time) enjoyment of the fruits of his/her accomplishment. The true inventor is already protected by Articles 57, 60 GCC; however, the legal protection is not complete and becomes fully activated only with the granting of the patent. Therefore, if the patent is granted to the wrong person, meaning someone who is not the true inventor (due to the weaknesses of the declaratory system), he/she must be excluded from the further exploitation of the invention. In this case, the patent granted is just an empty outer shell with no true content, although the legal procedure has been followed. For the reason under passage (b): If the patent is granted for a creation that does not meet the criteria of 'invention' as described in Article 5, then the patent must be nulled. For the reason under passage (c): Likewise, the patent must be nulled if the description attached to the patent is insufficient for the invention to be carried out by a person skilled in the art because such description must be precise, complete and accurate. For the reason

397. AP 2214/2013 EEmpD 2014, 223, CA of Athens 4999/2010, DEE 2011,188, CA of Athens 1852/1997, EEmpD 1997, 992, CA of Thessaloniki 348/2010, EEmpD 2011,166, MMCFI of Athens 2800/2011, ChrID 2011, 746, MMCFI of Athens 6228/2010, EEmpD 2010, 1214.

under passage (d): This reason of nullification is related to the extent of legal protection that the inventor wishes to have; if the patent extends beyond his or her request, then the patent must be partially nulled.[398]

§5. DRUG PATENTS

I. Regulatory Framework

389. Under the previous regulatory framework (Article 1 paragraph 1 of Decree 8/17 June 1926) the granting of patents for pharmaceutical packaging was prohibited unless the said drug had been licensed by the competent ministry. In effect, there were no legal provisions for patents concerning pharmaceutical products but only patents granted for methods of producing drugs.[399]

390. The EPC[400] provides that Contracting States may make a reservation that European patents, insofar as they provide protection for medicinal products, are invalid or can be invalidated in accordance with the provisions in force for national patents. The Greek legislator made use of this reservation under Article 23(7) of L. 1733/1987.[401] In 1992, this provision was abolished, thus permitting the granting of patents for pharmaceutical products.[402, 403]

II. Generics

391. A generic drug is the equivalent of an originator medicinal product whose patent protection has either expired or which was never patented. Generic drugs contain the same active pharmaceutical ingredients as the original medicinal products. The term generic drug refers to a medicinal product with the same qualitative and quantitative composition in terms of active substances and the same pharmaceutical form as the originator medicinal product, whose equivalence with the originator medicinal product has been formally certified. Regarded under the prism of

398. L. Kotsiris, *European patent. Invalidation and revocation by the Prosecutor's Department of the SAD Office. Impact on the Greek legal order*, 852 (DEE 2017).
399. AP 1263/1974, NoB 1975, 362, CA of Athens 2559/1977, Arm. 1979, 714, MMCFI of Athens 15746/1983, EEmpD 1984, 504.
400. Article 167(2).
401. MMCFI 2800/2011, ChrID 2011, 746 with comments by Apostolopoulos, MMCFI of Athens 3971/2007, EEmpD 2007, 718 with comments by I.Venieris, MMCFI of Athens 10342/1995, EEmpD 1995, 696.
402. Tsironis, *Patents for Medicinal Products under Greek and European Law*, EEmpD 1990, 381, Antonopoulos, *'Patents for medicinal products and their methods of production'*, (legal opinion) EEmpD 2009, 700, Chrysanthis, *Drug Patents (the Swiss patent claims, the reservation on pharmaceutical patents, the retroactivity of the TRIPS agreement and the Supplementary Protection Certificate)*, volume in honour of Kousoulis, 2012, 699, G. Alexaki, *The TRIPS Agreement and the Protection of Drugs Granted a Patent and a Supplementary Protection Certificate*, 107 (DEE 2014), Tsimikalis, *The Scope of Protection for Patented Drugs*, EEmpD 2013, 1017.
403. AP 548/2011, NOMOS Database,, MMCFI of Athens 728/2009 DEE 2009, 1194, with comments by I. Venieris, MMCFI of Athens 6105/2011, NOMOS Database.

Patent Law, generic drugs raise no issues of patent infringement as they are marketed and licensed after the expiration of the protected drug invention.[404] Another case in which generic drugs may be produced and marketed is if the manufacturer considers the patent of a medicinal product to be invalid or if the patented medicinal product is marketed in a country where the patent is not valid (in accordance with the principle of territoriality).

III. Supplementary Protection Certificate

392. The regulatory framework on the status of supplementary protection certificate (SPC) is contained in Regulation 469/2009 codifying EU legislation on the issue. According to its provisions, any product that is patented in the territory of a Member State and submitted as a pre-market medicinal product to an administrative authorization procedure under Directive 2001/83 EC may, under the conditions and in accordance with the procedures laid down in the said regulation, be the subject of a certificate.

393. A Supplementary Protection Certificate shall be issued if the following cumulative conditions are met: (a) the medicinal product must be granted a valid patent; (b) the proprietary medicinal product must have been subject to a marketing authorization procedure in accordance with Directive 2001/83 EC or Directive 2001/82 EC; (c) the same product cannot have been granted an SPC in the past; (d) the marketing authorization for the medicinal product should be the first authorization issued for the said product.

394. The SPC confers the same rights and protective scope as the basic patent and is subject to the same limitations and obligations. As regards the duration of the protection, the SPC takes effect from the moment of the expiration of the basic patent and is valid for a period equal to the period between the filing date of the original patent application and the issuing date of its first marketing authorization in the Union market, reduced by five years.

404. MMCFI of Athens 668/2016 EllDni 2016, 519 with comments by M. Th. Marinos, SMCFI of Athens 295/2016, EEmpD 2016, 708, SMCFI of Athens 984/2010, EEmpD 2010, 486.

Chapter 3. Utility Models

L.I. Athanassiou

§1. General Backgroung

395. The utility model certificate is an intellectual property right that protects inventions. Though similar to the patent, it has a shorter term and less stringent patentability requirements. It is established in many different countries to protect what is considered as 'incremental inventions', thus, also being called 'petty patent' or 'small patent'. The utility model certificate is a statutory monopoly like the patent, meaning that it provides its owner with the absolute right to exploit his or her invention commercially for a certain period of time, excluding all others from any use. This exclusive exploitation comes as a reward to the inventor's efforts and struggles to create something that is new and useful. It also acts as an incentive for new inventors to try and improve the level of technique since they will be compensated in a way, as well as an incentive for companies to invest and support new creations.

396. It has been made clear that in countries that are not industrialized at a high level, like Greece, the importance of the 'small invention' is great and also necessary for a middle-scale industrial development. However, due to the declaratory system in Greece that does not thoroughly examine the substantial requirements for the granting of the patent, OBI has not made extensive use of the utility model certificates and usually grants patents instead, even for the so-called small inventions.

397. Greek law first established and protected the utility model certificate with Article 19 L. 1733/1987, and this is the statute applicable on this intellectual property right to date.

§2. Definition and Requirements

398. According to Article 19(1):

> the utility model certificate shall be granted for each novel and industrially applicable three-dimensional object with definite shape and form, such as a tool, an instrument, a device, an apparatus or even parts thereof, proposed as novel and industrially applicable and capable of giving a solution to a technical problem.

399. This definition sets the requirements in order for a creation to be able to be protected with a utility model certificate. These substantial preconditions are the following:

(a) The creation must be an *invention.*[405] Though not explicitly mentioned in Article 19, from the combined application of Article 19(6) and Article 5(2) it is concluded that a utility model certificate may not be granted for discoveries, aesthetic creations, etc. It is, equally, considered[406] that the creation as an object should *facilitate human labour and use*; this precondition could be implied by the capability of the creation to give a solution to a technical problem.
(b) The creation must be a *three-dimensional object with definite shape and form* (like a tool, device, or apparatus), thus, excluding methods, chemical compounds, medication, alimentary products, etc. Of course, the protection of Article 19 does not cover the material vehicle itself where the invention is incorporated (the three-dimensional object), but *the rule for the solution of the technical problem.* This solution should need a material vehicle in order to be incorporated though. The three-dimensional aspect is not required for the patent, and it was established for the utility model certificate due to the influence of the Greek legislator by the German. Theory has criticized this precondition as unnecessary, and it has been supported that the utility model should be granted for two-dimensional objects as well.[407]
(c) From the above general description of the 'small invention' protected by the utility model certificate, it is made understood that unlike the patent, the utility model can be granted even if the creation in question does not bear what is called the 'inventive idea'. This means that it is not required for this creation to contribute a remarkable progress to technology, or be distinguished because of its inventive originality. It is necessary but also sufficient for the creation to *solve a certain technical problem,*[408] as mentioned above. Nevertheless, it has been supported that the invention in question should make at least a small contribution to technological progress.[409] It has also been judged[410] that the technical rule protected with the utility model should lead to an improvement of the object's outer form, thus, helping the purpose for which the object was constructed.
(d) The requirement of *novelty* is the same as in the patent (as described in Article 5(3)).
(e) The requirement of the *industrial application* is the same as in the patent (as described in Article 5(5)).

§3. Procedure

400. According to Article 19(4) the application for the granting of the utility model certificate is submitted to OBI. The requirements for filing the application,

405. CA of Thessaloniki 467/2009, EEmpD 2010, 481, CA of Thessaloniki 2333/2005, EEmpD 2006, 747.
406. A. Liakopoulos, *supra* n. 35 at 270.
407. N. Rokas, *supra* n. 25 at 62.
408. SMCFI 5725/2007, EEmpD 2008, 688 with comments by I. Venieris.
409. *Ibid.*
410. SMCFI of Thessaloniki 5725/07, EEmpD 2008, 688 comments by I. Venieris.

the relevant supporting documentation, and all other pertinent details are determined by Decision 15928/E Φ A 1253/87 of the Minister of Industry, Energy and Technology. OBI checks the typical requirements as well as the down payment of the submitting and protection fee. OBI also checks if the application regards a three-dimensional object, but the substantial requirements of the protection regarding novelty and industrial applicability are not examined, as Greece has adhered – for utility models as well as for patents – to the formal system. Therefore the granting of the utility model certificate does not mean that the creation in question meets the established requirements, as described above. The applicant bears the responsibility for the existence of these requirements (thus he runs the risk of having his utility model certificate declared null).[411]

401. The granting of the utility model certificate by OBI to the inventor offers the latter an absolute, exclusive, and limited by time industrial property right over the utility model. Hence the inventor can make full use of his or her creation while being protected against each and every one who tries to benefit from it. According to Article 19(6), the respective provisions of L. 1733/1987 about assignment, contractual licences, etc., also apply to the utility models.

§4. Conversion from Patent Application

402. According to Article 19(2) whoever files a patent application may request, up to the date of grant of the patent, the conversion of his patent application into application for a utility model certificate. This is allowed practically because the person who files a patent application cannot really know if his creation meets the high requirements for the protection of a patent.[412] The conversion of the application can include changes in the extent of the protection requested. Article 7(7) also mentions that upon filing the patent application, the applicant may state that he or she wishes his or her application to be considered, in accordance with Article 19, as an application for the grant of a utility model certificate if the application shall be rejected as a patent application. Therefore the request for the conversion can be made from the beginning of the filing of the application or subsequently.

403. Apart from the above facilitation, the inventor can go the other way round: file for a utility model certificate at first and, once this has been granted and the inventor gets some protection, then he or she can also file for a patent. This choice enjoys the extra advantage that the procedure for the granting of a utility model certificate is much faster and simpler.

---

411. CA of Thessaloniki 3100/1995, EpiskED 1997, 401, SMCFI of Athens 2004/2007, DIMEE 2007, 257.
412. Al. Mikroulea, *Utility Models*, 196 (Athens 1999 (in Greek)).

§5. Duration of Validity and Other Issues

404. According to Article 19(3) the duration of validity of the utility model certificate is seven years from the day following the application for the grant of a utility model certificate or for the grant of a patent, in case of conversion in accordance with paragraph 2. Therefore the protection here is shorter than in case of a patent, which is protected for twenty years. Every year the owner of the utility model certificate must prepay for the protection fee of the following year.

405. As far as any other aspect of the utility model certificate is concerned, the same rules as in the patent application. These rules include the determination of the persons who are entitled to file for an application (beneficiaries), the contents of the right, the exploitation of the certificate, the loss of rights, and the available civil remedies.

Chapter 4. Trademarks

Ch. Chrissanthis

§1. Sources of Law and International Conventions

406. The Greek law on trademarks is set by L. 4072/2012, Articles 121–183. This law has been published in the OG A 86/11.4.2012 and came into force on the date of its publication, save for certain provisions, which became effective six months after the publication of the law in the OG. It replaced L. 2239/1994. L. 4072/2012 has been further amended by L. 4155/2013. At the time of writing (March 2018) this law was under revision, in order to implement the new EU trademarks harmonization Directive 2015/2436.

407. It is interesting that L. 4072/2012, in addition to trademarks, legislates also on several other matters of commercial law, such as commercial partnerships and company law in general, investments, real estate brokers, rehabilitation of companies, etc. So, as the law currently stands (January 2013) the Greek law on trademarks is set by L. 4072/2012. The law on unfair competition is L. 146/1914. Non-registered marks, company names, and distinctive titles are protected under the unfair competition legal regime.

408. The Greek law on trademarks implements the EU harmonization Directive 2008/95, as well as the EU intellectual property rights enforcement Directive 2004/48. With effect from 15 January 2019, Directive 2008/95 will be repealed and replaced by Directive 2015/2436. This Directive has to be implemented into Greek law by 14 January 2019. The EU unfair trade practices (also dealing with advertisement) Directive 2005/29 is implemented into Greek law by virtue of L. 2251/1994, as amended and currently in force. False advertisement is also considered to qualify as unfair competition and is governed by Article 3 of L. 146/1914, which applies together with Articles 9 et seq. of L. 2251/1994.

409. Since Greece has implemented the EU trademarks harmonization Directive 2008/95, most of the provisions of L. 4072/2012 copy the respective provisions of the Directive. Hence, the provisions regarding the types of signs which may qualify as trademarks (i.e., words, letters, etc.), the provisions regarding the prerequisites for registration (i.e., distinctiveness and graphical representation), the provisions on absolute and relative grounds for rejection of trademark applications, the provisions regarding likelihood of confusion and dilution, the provisions regarding trademark licensing, limitation of trademark rights, cancellation, parallel imports, etc., copy the respective provisions of the Directive. As a matter of historical record, the first EU trademarks harmonization Directive 89/104 was implemented into Greek law by virtue of PD 317/1992, later replaced by L. 2239/1994. Greek courts and the Trademarks Committee also follow up the ECJ (now Court of the European Union) and the CFI (now General Court) jurisprudence, as well as the jurisprudence of the European Union Intellectual Property Office (EUIPO). In addition, one could argue that the EUIPO Trademark Guidelines (now called The Trademark Manual) can prove very influential upon Greek courts and should be considered of great value in terms of legal interpretation, although it is true that Greek courts and the Trademarks Committee do not expressly refer to them.

410. One of the more important consequences of the implementation of the EU law was that Greece abandoned the concepts of imitation and falsification (equivalent to the French concept of *contrefaçon*) and adhered to the concept of likelihood of confusion. Moreover, before the implementation of the EU law, the test for trademark infringement (or the test for likelihood of confusion) was a rather simplistic one and was based on a comparison of the marks (in terms of visual, aural, and conceptual similarity) as well as a comparison of the respective goods or services. Under the EU law and because of the influence of the ECJ jurisprudence, the test for likelihood of confusion became more complex (a multifactor test) and more factors were added, such as the channels of distribution for the respective goods, the level of awareness of consumers about the marks involved, the reputation of each mark, etc. Another consequence of the implementation of EU law was the introduction of the concept of dilution, as an alternative ground for trademark infringement in addition to likelihood of confusion. Famous marks were protected under Greek law even before the implementation of the EU Directive 1989/104, as per the provisions of the Paris Convention. However, in practice, the protection of famous marks was deduced only to the administrative procedure for trademark registration. In this context protection was afforded to famous marks in the sense that an application of a national to register a famous mark that its foreign owner had not yet arranged to register in Greece was considered to be an application in bad faith and was open to opposition or cancellation. After the implementation of the EU law, famous marks were granted greater legal protection before civil courts as well as in case of trademark infringement. It is true, though, that the first judgments of Greek civil courts raising the issue of dilution appeared only in 2010, that is about twenty years after the implementation of the Directive. A final point regarding dilution and famous marks is that under the EU law protection of famous marks against dilution is a matter of trademark law, while before the implementation of the Directive protection of famous marks against dilution was considered to be a matter for the law of unfair competition. Finally, another consequence of the implementation of EU law relates to parallel imports. It is because of this implementation that Greece moved from national exhaustion of trademark rights to Community exhaustion, as per the express provisions of the Directive. It is true that the first judgments of Greek courts on parallel imports from the point of view of trademark law appeared only after the implementation of the Directive; however, before this implementation, national exhaustion seemed to be a natural and predictable consequence of the general principles of trademarks law, such as the principle of territoriality.

411. Greece has also ratified and implemented four major multinational conventions regarding trademark law: (a) The Paris Convention (1883), implemented by L. 213/1975 (Greece has implemented the Stockholm version of the Paris Convention); (b) The TRIPS Agreement, implemented by L. 2290/1995; (c) The Madrid Protocol (1989) regarding international registration of trademarks through WIPO, implemented by L. 2783/2000; and (d) The Nice Classification Agreement (1957), implemented by L. 2505/1997 which provide for forty-five classes of goods/ services. The EU Regulation on the Community Trademark 207/2009 is also applicable in Greece. The following international conventions have not been implemented into Greek law: (a) The Madrid Agreement (1891) on international registration of trademarks, (b) The Vienna (1973) Trademark Registration Treaty, (c) The Vienna Convention (1973) on the classification of figurative elements of marks, (d) The Geneva (1994) Trademark Law Treaty.

412. Regarding foreign applicants, until recently, Greece required proof of reciprocity for applicants originating from countries which were not members of the Paris Convention (1883). However, since the implementation of L. 4072/2012 the reciprocity requirement has been abolished for all foreign applicants.

§2. Registered Trademarks and Non-registered Distinctive Signs

413. Trademarks are acquired through registration and are used in connection to goods or services. They have an origin function, a quality guarantee function and an advertisement function. In addition to trademarks there are other intellectual property rights, which have the same functions as above and are used in connection to either goods or services, or the legal entity or the person carrying on a certain commercial activity, or the business establishment through which goods or services are offered. These include company names, distinctive titles, and other distinctive signs. Sometimes, such rights are called brand names. With the exception of trademarks, all other rights over such distinctive signs, in general, are acquired, not through registration, but through use in the course of trade; advertisement and promotion also qualify as such use.

414. So, what are the main differences among registered and non-registered rights? One difference relates to the way of acquisition, i.e., trademarks are acquired through registration, even in the absence of any use, while non-registered marks and distinctive signs are acquired through use in the course of trade. Furthermore, trademarks grant legal rights which cover all the jurisdiction of Greece, while non-registered marks and signs are territorial rights; the legal rights granted apply only in the geographical area where use is situated. In addition, each time the owner of a non-registered right applies to the court for legal protection against infringement, he/she has to prove adequate use in the course of trade that leads to the creation (acquisition) of the respective right. This means that he/she has to produce massive evidence of prior use. The owner of a registered trademark, on the contrary, needs only to invoke and produce a registration certificate. Another important difference, which is a peculiarity of Greek trademark law and is discussed elsewhere in this text, is that registered trademarks cannot be challenged before civil courts. For example, a trademark may have achieved registration even though it is evidently descriptive. A civil court, still, cannot review its validity. Such validity can be challenged only through cancellation proceedings; such proceedings may lead to the deletion of the registration, but this requires a final court judgment and the cancellation occurs only after the issue of this judgment and does not have any retrospective effects. So, trademark rights are accompanied by increased legal certainty; this is not the case on non-registered rights, though. Finally, trademarks are protected under the trademark law, while non-registered marks and distinctive signs are protected under the law of unfair competition (Article 13 of L. 146/1914 in particular); this means one of the prerequisites for the protection of non-registered marks, according to established principles regarding unfair competition, is that the claimant has a business establishment in Greece or has made use of the non-registered mark in Greece. Trademarks, on the contrary, are protected irrespective of any business establishment of the owner in Greece and irrespective of any use in Greece.

§3. Trademarks Systems

415. A foreign applicant may acquire trademark rights in Greece in three different ways:

(a) National registration: A foreigner may apply for national trademark registration in Greece, under the same conditions and according to the same procedure as a Greek national. Establishment in Greece is not required. Trademark applications submitted by foreigners enjoy protection under the Paris Convention (1883). As a result, foreigners may claim international priority for their applications on the basis of a mark applied for in their country of origin. They can also invoke the *tellequelle* principle established by the Paris Convention. As a matter of statistics, national applications submitted by foreigners in Greece amounted to about 500 in 2017, while applications submitted by nationals amounted to about 4,500.

The national trademark system employs an ex officio search of prior rights. Actually the search covers only prior national trademarks, prior Community Trademarks, and prior International Registrations with WIPO which have been forwarded to Greece as well. An important peculiarity of the Greek trademark system is that a trademark, after its registration, cannot be challenged before civil courts in the context of infringement proceedings. Instead, it can only be challenged through cancellation proceedings before the Trademark Committee and, on appeal, before the administrative courts. This means that in Greece a trademark registration grants very strong legal rights. cancellation proceedings may last for more than ten years and, in the meantime, civil courts are obliged not to challenge the validity of the registration of the trademark.

(b) International Registration through WIPO, according to the Madrid Protocol: Trademark rights can be acquired in Greece through the WIPO system based on the Madrid Protocol. So, on the basis of a trademark application in another Member State a foreigner may, through WIPO, request that his/her International Registration with WIPO be extended to Greece. According to the Madrid Protocol, in order to make use of the WIPO system, it suffices if the applicant has made an application in his home country and it is not necessary that this application has also been registered. The benefits of the WIPO systems is that it reduces costs and expenses dramatically, as it is not necessary to employ a local trademark agent or attorney-at-law. International applications forwarded into Greece through WIPO enjoy priority as from the date of their respective registration with the WIPO registry. The number of WIPO International Registrations is progressively increasing in Greece since the implementation of the Madrid Protocol in 2000. In 2017 the number of such international registrations forwarded from WIPO into Greece amounted at about 1,600. When an international registration is forwarded from WIPO into the Greek trademark registry, it is adjudicated with respect to absolute and relative grounds, in the same way as a national application. If it is finally accepted and registered with the Greek registry, it grants the same rights as a national registration.

(c) European Union Trademark (EUTM): Previously called Community Trademark, EUTM rights acquired through the European Union Intellectual Property Office (EUIPO) registry, apply in Greece as well. Disputes regarding infringements of EUTMs are referred to special divisions of local civil courts and hence enjoy earlier hearing dates than cases regarding infringement of national trademarks. Moreover, the judges appointed to such special divisions have a greater level of specialization on trademark law and intellectual property law in general.

It is to be noted that the Greek Trademarks Committee may refuse to register an application for a national trademark if the applicant already possesses an EUTM registration (or has filed an EUTM application) for the same mark. Moreover, an application for a national trademark will also be refused if the applicant already possesses a national registration (or has filed a prior national application) for the same mark.

§4. Types of Marks

416. Marks are registrable if they are distinctive and can be represented graphically. In this context, all types of traditional, two-dimensional marks are available for registration. This includes words, drawings, figurative elements, slogans, abbreviations, colour combinations, or even colours as such, etc. Three-dimensional marks are also registrable if they can be represented graphically. Non-traditional marks, such as sounds, smells, or the feeling of touch are not registrable, as they cannot be represented graphically and there are no technical specifications set for their reproduction and representation for the purpose of application to the trademark registry.

The new Directive 2015/2436 EU on the approximation of national laws on trademarks has abandoned the requirement of graphical representation and Greek law will do the same when the process of the implementation of the new Directive will be finalized, that is, until 14 January 2019. Under the new Directive it suffices that a mark is capable of being represented in the registry in a manner which enables the competent authorities and the public to determine the clear and precise subject matter of the protection afforded to its proprietor. This new requirement that the mark should be sufficiently clear and precise is expected to facilitate the registration of non-traditional marks, like sounds, smells, tastes, etc. Still, the registration of such non-traditional marks is not expected to become an automatic process. On the one hand, such marks should be distinctive. Consumers only rarely conceive sounds, smells, or tastes of products as distinctive features. This means that consumers usually do not attribute to sounds, smells, or tastes an origin function. On the other hand, the local Trademark Office should establish specific technical specifications relating to the representation of non-traditional marks.

417. Collective trademarks are also recognized and protected under Greek law. Certification marks are currently considered to fall within the category of collective marks. However, the new Directive clearly distinguishes among collective marks on the one hand and certification marks on the other. Hence, Greek law is expected to introduce the concept of certification marks, in addition to collective marks.

§5. Registration Process

418. The Greek registration process is similar to the process used by the EUIPO, with the main difference that in Greece there is an ex officio search of prior rights and earlier trademark registrations, or applications, will lead to rejection of an application, even in the absence of an opposition by the owner of the earlier rights.

419. Each application is adjudicated by an Examiner with respect to absolute and relative grounds. If the Examiner is satisfied that there are no grounds for rejection, the application is published and remains open for opposition for a three-month period. If the decision of the Examiner is negative, it can be challenged before the Trademark Committee, which is a three-member administrative body. The judgment of the Trademark Committee can be appealed before the administrative courts. Registration occurs if no opposition is filed within the three-month period, or when the judgment on the opposition becomes final.

420. A peculiarity of the Greek trademark law is that there is a distinction between competence of the administrative and civil court in trademark cases. Cases regarding the registration process, i.e., cases relating to relative or absolute grounds, as well as oppositions and cancellations are referred to administrative courts where proceedings are extremely time-consuming (it takes about seven years to obtain a judgment from the First Instance Administrative Court). Cases regarding infringements are referred to civil courts. Civil courts are not allowed to challenge the validity of a registered trademark. A registered trademark is subject only to cancellation, which is referred to the Trademark Committee and, on appeal, to the administrative courts. This is another very important peculiarity of Greek trademark law, i.e., as long as a mark has been registered with the trademark registry, civil courts dealing with infringements are bound by this registration and are not allowed to challenge or review it, even in the case of an evidently descriptive mark that has been registered in violation of the provisions on absolute grounds. This makes the trademark a very strong title under Greek law. Greek law provides for a long and complicated process for trademark registration, which it requires, among other, a prior publication of the mark in the OG, in order to inform third parties and give them the opportunity to lodge an opposition, i.e., a third party appeal against the registration sought by the applicant. However, in exchange for granting such an opportunity to third parties to object to trademark registration, Greek law grants extensive protection to the trademark proprietor by providing that cancellation (i.e., deregistration of a trademark) requires: (a) a prior final judgment, and (b) such cancellation is enforceable and occurs only after the publication of such a judgment and not beforehand, i.e., the judgment has no retrospective effect. Hence, Greek law ensures that every application for a trademark registration is scrutinized before its acceptance and that any third party interested therein is entitled and has the opportunity to object to the registration of a particular trademark. At the same time, a trademark, which has been successfully registered and has been assessed as complying with all legal requirements, enjoys legal recognition and protection of the highest standards, such as that: (a) cancellation (i.e., deregistration) takes place only on certain grounds and upon a final court judgment ordering such deregistration, with no retrospective effects; and (b) before a particular trademark has been officially cancelled (i.e., deregistered) from the registry by virtue of a final court judgment, full legal protection in every aspect provided under the law is granted to the trademark's proprietor and the civil courts are not allowed to question into whether the respective trademark has been properly registered, i.e., on whether such registration has been carried out in accordance with the requirements of law on absolute grounds. This enhanced legal protection and legal certainty serve market needs because the trademark proprietor invests large amounts of funds for advertising his products on an annual basis; these are usually higher (or even multiple) than the value of the fixed assets of the respective undertaking. Hence, the legal regime applicable to trademarks should be absolutely certain.[413]

421. Registration occurs only after the trademark application has been published, provided that an opposition has not been filed. Publication is considered to give to owners of earlier rights a fair chance to take notice of new applications and file an opposition to defend their earlier rights. If an opposition is not filed, then the trademark registration can be challenged through cancellation proceedings.

422. Use or intent to use is not a prerequisite for application or registration. However, in exceptional cases, if it is self-evident that intent to use is absent, and that the only purpose of an application is to prevent third parties from using the mark, then such an application is considered to be in bad faith and can be rejected; if it passes the examination process and is registered, the trademark can be cancelled on the basis of bad faith. Non-use for five consecutive years is a ground for cancellation.

---

413. Ch. Chrissanthis, *Lack of Distinctiveness, Descriptive Marks and Marks in Common Use in Trademark Law*, 469 (EEmpD 2008 (in Greek)).

§6. Absolute Grounds

423. The absolute grounds for rejection of an application are those mentioned in Article 4 of EU Directive 2015/2436, which is implemented into Greek law by Article 123 of L. 4072/2012. The more important absolute grounds are those relating to lack of distinctiveness, descriptiveness, deceptiveness, and the mark applied for being commonplace. In addition to the above, Article 123 expressly mentions that the following marks are not registrable: (a) functional marks, (b) marks used in connection to wines or alcoholic beverages which include an appellation of origin or geographical indication protected under EU law, (c) marks consisting of protected appellations of origin or geographical indications used in connection to foodstuffs, (d) the names of the States and national emblems, (e) any mark whose filing for registration is made in bad faith. The reasoning behind absolute grounds is mainly freedom of competition; in this sense, absolute grounds are justified because of the concern to protect freedom of competition. The law would not bear to grant trademark rights (i.e., exclusive rights amounting to a legal monopoly) in respect to mark that should be free for use by all traders.

424. Legal issues relating to absolute grounds are very common in the Greek trademark practice. The reason is that most of the marks applied for trademark registration contain some descriptive or generic elements or elements that are commonplace in trade while, at the same time, also contain some unique, genuine, and novel elements. Only a few of the trademarks applied for are totally unique and novel. Most of them bear only a number of distinctive features and at the same time contain elements commonly used in common parlance. This stems from the fact that a totally fictitious, genuine, and novel mark may comply with the legal conditions required for trademark registration, but it is not so useful from a marketing and advertising perspective, nor does it adequately help a manufacturer to make his good easily recognizable by consumers. On the contrary, a mark can only rarely serve as a means of communication between its proprietor and consumers, unless it contains a particular (direct or indirect) meaning and can transmit information about the respective goods. A totally fictitious and novel mark cannot easily serve this objective unless (and until) consumers have already become familiar with it; however, the latter cannot be achieved without long (persistent) and expensive advertising campaigns. However, it is less expensive to promote a mark which already contains, in itself, some specific information about the goods to which it is attached to and, thus, is able to transmit some feedback about such goods to consumers. This, however, means that the mark needs to contain some descriptive or generic elements, or elements that are commonplace and in common use in the market. As a result, trademark proprietors choose between various marks according to advertising and investing criteria instead of purely legal criteria.

425. On absolute grounds the Greek Trademark Committee and courts usually apply the jurisprudence of the Court of Justice of the European Union (CJEU, ex ECJ) and the General Court of the European Union(GCEU, ex Court of First Instance, CFI), as well as that of the European Union Intellectual Property Office (EUIPO, ex OHIM). The legislative provisions, on absolute grounds, are destined to strike a balance between the granting of exclusive trademark rights on the one hand and the need to protect free competition on the other. It is to be mentioned, however, that trademarks are an integral part of free competition,[414] for without trademarks it would be impossible to achieve market differentiation (i.e., differentiation among similar goods which are competing with one another) and it is this market differentiation which is the quintessence of free competition. In this context, it is to be noted that according to the legislative provisions on absolute grounds it is only marks devoid of *any* distinctive character that are barred from trademark registration. This means that absolute grounds prohibiting registration apply only when it is amply evident that a mark is merely descriptive, generic, commonplace, etc. A theory that very much assists us to clarify the types of marks that are eligible for trademark registration is the following: Marks used in the course of trade in connection to goods or services may be classified into five classes depending on the degree and level of descriptiveness:

(a) Imaginary marks: These are purely imaginary, i.e., creatures of our imagination and, accordingly, do not have any particular meaning or concept; hence, they cannot be descriptive at all, e.g., KODAK, POLAROID, XEROX, ADIDAS, etc. Their distinctive character (i.e., their ability to distinguish between goods and services) is not contested and they may be registered as trademarks.
(b) Common marks that are used in an unusual way: These are not imaginary. They do have a certain meaning and concept. However, because they are not used according to their customary usage, they are not used in a descriptive way. This means that such marks are not used with their usual concept. So, the unusual manner in which they are used does not directly describe the goods or services to which they are affixed. Such marks are, e.g., BLACK & WHITE or WHITE HORSE for alcoholic beverages, RED BULL for non-alcoholic beverages, PAPAGALOS (meaning parrot) for coffee, CAMEL for tobacco products, etc. These marks are regarded to be distinctive and eligible for registration as they escape absolute grounds since there is no relevance between them and the goods thereby distinguished.
(c) Laudatory marks: These are marks and terms that are not directly or totally descriptive of the goods that they distinguish, but contain an indirect laudatory ('flattering') message about the goods thereby distinguished. This class includes also marks and terms that cannot be classified as 'laudatory per se', but distinguish some products by providing a description of a particular characteristic or a particular quality of such products, but such description is not made directly (i.e., by means of the conceptual meaning of these terms), but only indirectly and subconsciously through symbolisms and parallelisms, e.g., BEAR for warm (heavy) clothing, ASPROS SIFOUNAS (meaning WHITE HURRICANE) for cleaning products, NEW LOOK for tobacco products and cigarettes, PLAYBOY for adult entertainment magazines, POLYCOPY for photocopying machines. These marks and terms bear a distinctive character and may be registered as trademarks because they transmit information about the goods distinguished, thereby, only in an indirect way, that is by means of symbolisms,

414. Thus held by the ECJ in Case C-228/2003, Gillette at para. 25.

inferences, implications, etc. These symbolisms, inferences, implications, etc. are in themselves novel and unique and, hence, must be legally protected by being registered as trademarks. This kind of indirect information about a particular product does not need to be classified as part of the public domain. The GCEU has ruled that laudatory signs, such as VITALITE and ULTRAPLUS, are eligible for trademark registration.[415]

(d) Descriptive marks: These marks describe *directly* (neither indirectly, nor by means of symbolisms or metaphorical representations, etc.) the kind, origin, quality, destination of the respective goods. The use of such descriptive signs or indications should be free and accessible to all prospective market competitors, since they provide directly to the public feedback about the characteristics, functions or quality of the goods, thereby, distinguished. The case law of the CJEU has confirmed in the DOUBLEMINT[416] case that protection of freedom of competition (i.e., the objective to achieve and ensure free competition) justifies the introduction of legal provisions that descriptive signs are ineligible for trademark registration. Competitors need to use marks and terms that contain and provide feedback directly about the goods or services thereby distinguished. On the contrary, indirect information derived from symbolisms, inferences, and metaphorical expressions is based on novelty and human innovation and it is not necessary to ensure that everybody has a free access to it, in order to protect freedom of competition. It is important to mention that descriptive marks can be registered as trademarks only on the grounds of acquired distinctiveness (or, in other words, acquired secondary, i.e., ancillary, meaning). So, a descriptive mark that conveys direct information through its common conceptual meaning about the products to which it is affixed can still be registered, as long as it has obtained through long used in the course of trade a distinctive character (i.e., is able to perform a distinctive function and differentiate the products of one manufacturer from those of other manufacturers). In this case, such secondary non-descriptive meaning excludes the mark at issue from public use and the public domain, since it does not provide any direct feedback to consumers anymore and, as a result, competitors do not need to use it. Some examples from case law may be illuminating and instructive: The Greek Council of State *(Conseil d' Etat)*, which is the Supreme Administrative Court, has found the term 'REFLEX' for steam generating engines to be distinctive and accepted its registration;[417] the Trademarks Committee has found the mark 'WORLD ACADEMY OF SPORTS' to be indistinctive and rejected its registration,[418] but this decision was reversed by the First Instance Administrative Court of Athens;[419] the mark 'WALKMAN' for audio apparatus was found to be distinctive, although it is a combination of two common vocabulary words.[420]

415. T-24/2000, 31.1.2001, VITALITE, and T-360/2000, 9.10.2002, ULTRAPLUS.
416. C-191/2001 P, 23.10.2003.
417. Council of State (*Conseil d' Etat*) 3617/2007.
418. Greek Trademark Committee Decision 2481/2008.
419. First Instance Administrative Court of Athens 383/2016.
420. Second Instance Administrative Court of Athens 2505/2008.

(e) Generic marks that declare a particular class of products: These marks define the name of a whole class of products and convey to consumers direct information about the products to which they are affixed. Hence, they are regarded to be devoid of any distinctive character and are not eligible for registration. Moreover, the acquired distinctiveness exception cannot apply to such marks and terms. Marks falling within this class (i.e., VIDEO GUIDE) are generic terms. So, if a mark is generic, the argument of acquired distinctiveness cannot be invoked to allow registration.

426. The conclusion to be drawn from the above classification of marks is that what is important in terms of absolute grounds is whether the mark conveys a direct, or an indirect, information about the goods or services in connection to which it is used. If the mark conveys direct information it is considered to be descriptive and, in principle, it cannot be registered,[421] unless acquired distinctiveness can be proved. If the mark is generic, acquired distinctiveness cannot assist us to overcome absolute grounds. Finally, if the mark does not convey any information at all about the goods distinguished, or if it conveys only indirect information, then the mark is eligible for registration.

427. Distinctiveness, descriptiveness, and other absolute grounds are always examined and appreciated in view of the particular goods or services for which the mark is applied for.[422] So, e.g., the mark DIESEL may lack distinctiveness and may be descriptive with respect to fuel, motor engines, and similar products but, at the same time, may be distinctive with respect to fashion goods and clothing. In addition, court judgments usually hold that whether a particular mark lacks distinctiveness, or is descriptive, etc., is assessed in view of the particular circumstances of each case and the peculiarities of the products at issue.[423] In case of marks which consist of combinations of more than one element (i.e., combinations of words, or combinations of words with drawings and colours, etc.) distinctiveness, descriptiveness, and other absolute grounds are appreciated on the basis of the overall impression of the mark. If one part of the mark is prevailing over others, the overall impression is determined mainly by that prevailing element.

428. Common vocabulary words will most probably be commonplace widely used in the course of trade and, hence, not registrable. However, such common vocabulary words can be registered, if used in connection to goods/services with which they cannot reasonably be associated, that is, if used in connection to goods/services which are not denoted or implied by such words. For example, the term

---

421. *See* the following precedents of the ECJ and CFI: C-517/1999 Mertz & Krell GmbH of 4 Oct. 2001 paras 27, 29, 31, 33; T-360/2000 ULTRAPLUS case of 9 Oct. 2002 para. 43 allowing the registration of the mark ULTRAPLUS, although the terms ULTRA and PLUS are laudatory; T-163/1998 BABY DRY case of 8 Jul. 1999 paras 20, 21.

422. First Instance Administrative Court of Athens 13939/1998, *DEE* 1998, 871.

423. First Instance Administrative Court of Athens 13939/1998, *DEE* 1998, 871. N. Vozenberg, *The Concept of Trademarks and Marks Non Eligible for Registration*, 47 (Athens 1969 (in Greek)).

PAPAGALOS (meaning 'parrot') has been registered for coffee, the term FANTASIA (meaning 'imagination') has been registered for olive oil, and the term THALASSA (meaning 'sea') has been registered for spa services.[424]

429. Foreign vocabulary words may be distinctive and registrable in Greece if the average Greek consumer is not familiar with them.[425] For example, the English word CLUSTERS, which is considered descriptive of a particular type of cereals for an English speaking consumer, has been registered as a trademark in Greece, on the ground that Greek consumers are not familiar with the term CLUSTERS as a common English vocabulary word. It should be noted, however, than, in principle, English vocabulary words are deemed to be well-known to Greek consumers as well. This is not, however, the same with French, German and other foreign languages vocabulary terms.

430. Laudatory marks, like SUPRA, EXTRA, GOLD, SILVER, PLATINUM, PLUS, ULTRA are usually found to be registrable by the majority of court authorities, on the ground that they do not make any direct implication to the qualities of the respective goods/services and, hence, they do not describe goods/services as such. So, e.g., the marks VELVET DE LUXE and MASTER SOUND have been found to be registrable.[426]

431. The Trademark Committee and the courts are particularly suspicious with applications consisting of geographical terms. Geographical terms are usually rejected either as descriptive or as deceptive terms. There are, however, geographical terms which cannot reasonably be associated with certain products, such as the term EVEREST for foodstuffs. Such geographical terms are registrable, because the average consumer cannot reasonably believe that foodstuffs originate from an area like the Everest.

432. Colour combinations are usually found to be distinctive and registrable. So, the well-known Gucci colour combination (three horizontal stripes of green, red and again green) has been considered to be registrable by the Greek Trademark Committee.[427] However, a mark consisting of two curved colour ribbons, one red and one blue, which was filed for toothpastes was found to be indistinctive.[428] This situation is more difficult with respect to single colours as such. There are some, rather old, court rulings that colours as such are not registrable, because the number of the basic colours available for use is limited and, hence, grant of trademark (exclusive)

424. First Instance Administrative Court of Athens 1686/1998, *EEmpD* vol. 49, 860 and SMCFI of Rhodes, 1066/2003, *DEE* 2004, 47.

425. Greek Council of State (*Conseil d' Etat*) 190/1984, unreported, accepting the mark LIGNE INTEGRALE D' ORLANE for perfumes. *See also* Council of State 191/1984 accepting the mark BUBBLE GUM for gums, 648/1984 accepting the mark ROSSO ANTICO for alcoholic beverages.

426. First Instance Administrative Court of Athens 5404/1993, unreported, and 8196/1996, unreported; while 16722/1996 of the same Court rejected the mark COTTON DE LUXE.

427. Greek Trademark Committee 855/1987, unreported.

428. Council of State (*Conseil d' Etat*) 886/2009.

rights with respect to colours would inevitably lead to a restraint of competition.[429] Another line of authority submits that single colours as such are not registrable for lack of distinctiveness.[430] For example, a mark consisting of the colour pink, which was filed in class seventeen for insulating materials, was rejected registration on the ground that it was not distinctive.[431] However, there are many cases where single colours have been registered as such, particularly when acquired distinctiveness can be established, such as in cases of famous trademarks consisting of single colours.

433. Three-dimensional marks, usually consisting in the shape of the product, are also registrable, provided that this shape is not functional, i.e., it is not necessary to achieve a certain technical result. Usually, three-dimensional trademarks consist of the shape of bottles for beverages or fragrances.[432]

Slogans are deemed to be registrable if they enjoy a minimum level of originality. The slogan 'WITH US YOU CAN DO EVERYTHING' was considered to enjoy such a minimum level of originality and was accepted for registration.[433]

434. Greek trademark law has adopted the concept of acquired distinctiveness. Hence, marks that lack distinctiveness as such, or are descriptive as such, or are commonplace as such, can be registered if the applicant can prove acquired distinctiveness through use in the course of trade. The time by which distinctiveness must have been acquired is not the date of the filing of the application but the date of its examination. However, acquired distinctiveness cannot be invoked in favour of marks that are deceptive.

435. According to case law, a mark is distinctive as long as it performs the origin function and the quality guarantee function. These functions are performed if the mark allows consumers to identify that the goods, thereby distinguished, originate from a particular undertaking, and to identify the particular qualities of such goods that differentiate them from goods originating from other competing products. There are no further requirements for distinctiveness. The case law of the CJEU and the GCEU adopts the above position and it has been ruled that:

> The signs referred to in Article 7(1)(b) of Regulation No 40/94 are signs which are regarded as incapable of performing the essential function of a trade mark, namely that of identifying the origin of the goods or services, thus enabling the consumer who acquired them to repeat the experience, if it proves to be positive, or to avoid it, if it proves to be negative, on the occasion of a subsequent acquisition.[434]

429. AP 399/1989, *EEmpD* vol. 41, 145. SMCFI of Athens 8567/1988, *EEmpD* vol. 39, 696.
430. First Instance Administrative Court of Athens 3964/1998, *EEmpD* 1999, 817.
431. Second Instance Administrative Court of Athens 1346/2010.
432. First Instance Administrative Court of Athens 3694/1998, *EEmpD* vol. 50, 817 allowing registration of the shape of a bottle for beverages.
433. Council of State *(Conseil d' Etat)* 1240/2008.
434. T-79/2000, *Rewe-Zentral v. LITE*, at [26]; T-128/2001 DAIMLER-CHRYSLER case of 6 Mar. 2003 at [31]; similarly the ECJ case law: e.g., C-383/1998 P, PROCTER & GAMBLE (BABY DRY) case of 20 Sep. 2001, at [38]; C-136/2002 P MAG INSTRUMENT INC. of 7 Oct. 2004, at [29].

Hence, in order to confirm that a particular mark is distinctive, it must perform the quality guarantee function and the origin function in connection to the respective goods, but (as it has been ruled in the above cases) it is not required that the mark at issue assists consumers to identify the name of the manufacturer of the respective goods. It is adequate that consumers are able to identify that the respective goods (that bear a particular mark) originate from a particular undertaking, regardless of whether they (consumers) can identify the name and identity of such an undertaking or not. What is important is that consumers identify a particular trademark and infer that the respective product originates from a particular undertaking and that all products bearing the same trademark have identical qualities and features; hence, every time they purchase products bearing the same trademark, they expect that the products they choose shall bear the same qualities and features as those that they had purchased the previous time. As a result, contemporary legal literature accepts that the origin function somehow approaches the quality guarantee function. The fact that the particular goods originate from a particular undertaking is important from the perspective of consumers only insofar as the goods meet certain quality standards.[435]

436. It is the perception and understanding of consumers and not that of competitors that is important to assess distinctiveness and absolute grounds in general.[436] This view is also supported by the case law of the CJEU. The CJEU has reasoned that:

> There are purely legal considerations which justify taking into account the actual perception which the public has of a mark in order to assess its distinctiveness *ab initio*. First of all, according to the seventh recital in the preamble to Regulation No 40/94, the function of the protection afforded by a Community trade mark is to guarantee the trade mark as an indication of origin; the only way in which it can be established with certainty whether the role of the mark as an indication of origin is guaranteed is to rely on the actual perception of the mark by the relevant public. Next, it follows from the wording itself of Article 7 of Regulation No 40/94 – and particularly from the use of the words 'in trade' in Article 7(1)(c) and 'the public' in Article 7(1)(g) – that each of the absolute grounds for refusal referred to in Article 7(1) must be considered in the light of the opinion of the relevant public. Lastly, that interpretation has been confirmed on a number of occasions by the Court of Justice (Baby-dry, paragraph 42) and by the Court of First Instance (Case T-135/99 Taurus-Film v. OHIM(Cine Action) [2001] ECR II-379, paragraph 27, and Case T-331/99

435. Ch. Chrissanthis, *Likelihood of Confusion under the Law of Distinctive Marks*, 339, 342 (EpiskED 2003 (in Greek)); N. Rokas, *Exploitation and Protection of Advertising Value*, 2 (EEmpD 1999 (in Greek)) and by the same author, *Functional Amendments and Variations of a Right on a Registered Trademark*, 446 (EEmpD 1997 (in Greek)); A. Liakopoulos, *supra* n. 35 at 316; B. Antonopoulos, *supra* n. 218 at 234, 367 (2002).

436. N. Vozemberg, *The Concept of Trademarks and Marks Non Eligible for Registration*, *supra*, at 47.

Mitsubishi HiTec Paper Bielefeld v. OHIM (Giroform) [2001] ECR II-433, paragraph 24), and it is also the interpretation which has been adopted by the German courts.[437]

It is apparent that third parties (competitors) are eager to replicate and imitate a famous and well-established trademark; hence, their assessment with respect to the distinctive character and with respect to whether such trademark comprises terms that have become customary in common parlance is neither impartial nor reliable. Similarly, the assessment of intermediaries (e.g., distributors) is not reliable, because they are equally eager to trade goods bearing trademarks that are either similar to famous trademarks or which imitate/replicate them.

437. It is generally established that a combination of descriptive, common terms may be regarded as totally original and may be registered as a trademark, especially where such combination results in the creation of a new word or term.[438] Such combinations are assessed depending on the impression that their conceptual meaning creates as a whole (the so-called overall impression) and not according to the impression that is created from each individual component of the combination.[439] Hence, even descriptive or common terms that are combined with each other may culminate in an original outcome, especially where the latter is uncommon and unusual. As a result, trademarks comprising a combination of multiple terms and elements (i.e., combination of word terms, or combination of a word term and a figurative element and artistic device) are eligible for trademark registration, even if only one of their comprising elements possesses some kind of originality and bears a distinctive character. By applying the above considerations, case law has accepted for registration the mark SAT 2 (SAT deriving from the term 'satellite') in connection to satellite transmission and satellite communication services, on the grounds that even though its components (SAT & 2) constitute common terms, their combination into a single multiple-term is unusual and uncommon and the outcome possesses some kind of originality that attributes to such trademark a distinctive character.[440] Based on similar grounds, case law has reasoned that the mark CELLTECH is eligible for registration as a trademark in connection to cell research.[441]

438. Complex marks (i.e., marks that contain both word terms and figurative elements) are eligible for trademark registration, as long as at least one of their components is original and distinctive. For instance, a common and customary term, which is combined with an original and novel artistic indication, or artistic device, may produce a distinctive mark which is eligible for registration. Such artistic elements may be a special design, or a particular colour, or a combination of colours,

437. C-136/2002 P, Mag Instrument of 7 Oct. 2004 para. 43; C-383/1999 P BABY DRY case of 20 Sept. 2001, para. 42.
438. B. Antonopoulos, *supra* n. 218 at 419.
439. The ECJ case C-383/1998, BABY DRY, dated 20 Sept. 2001 at paras 39–41.
440. ECJ C-329/2002 P of 16 Sep. 2004 especially at para. 28 with further references in C-265/2000 of 12 Feb. 2004 at paras 40–41 and C-363/1999 of 12 Feb. 2004 at paras 99–100.
441. T-260/2003 (upheld by ECJ, C-273/2005 P).

or even a particular formation the format style and the lettering of a word term, by means of which the common or customary word term is presented. Hence, the following trademarks have been considered to be eligible for registration as EUTMs by the EUIPO: EUTM 657627 GLOBAL INTERNET (with a combined word indication and a representation of terrestrial globe) and EUTM 788455 NATIONAL CAR RENTAL (with a combined word indication and a representation of three parallel lines in a colour context).

439. Other examples from case law with marks which were found to be eligible for registration include the following: 'NEW BORN BABY' for children dolls: GCEU, T-140/2000. 'DAS PRINZIP DER BEQUEMLICHKEIT' for furniture: GCEU, T-138/2000. 'VITALITE' for children foods and sparkling water: GCEU, T-24/2000. 'BABY DRY' for baby diapers: CJEU, C-383/1999. Greek case law has ruled that the mark CLUB SWISS is also eligible for registration.[442]

§7. Relative Grounds

440. Relative grounds are dealt with by Article 124 of Greek L. 4072/2012, which is similar to Article 5 of EU Directive 2015/2436. Relative grounds refer to earlier rights, and the reasons justifying rejection on relative grounds are associated with the protection of owners of such earlier rights. The appreciation of relative grounds requires an assessment of likelihood of confusion between the mark applied for and earlier rights. Such earlier rights may consist in national trademark rights, European Union trademark rights, or rights relating to other non-registered marks and distinctive signs, such as corporate names, distinctive signs, brand names, distinctive titles, etc. They may even include copyright, or the right to personality (i.e., the name of a trader, or the name of a celebrity, etc.). However, under the practice of the Greek Trademark Committee the ex officio search carried out relates only to applications and registrations with the Greek trademark registry and the Community trademark registry, as well as International Registrations with the WIPO registry, which have already been forwarded to the Greek registry and are already filed, or registered with it.

441. Earlier rights may also be invoked by their respective proprietors through opposition, or cancellation proceedings.

442. The central issue on relative grounds is likelihood of confusion and, in case of famous marks, dilution. Likelihood of confusion and dilution are also the grounds for trademark infringement invoked before civil courts. The concept of likelihood of confusion and dilution are discussed below.

443. Another general principle which is innate to relative grounds is the priority principle. In case there are more rights (belonging to different proprietors) over identical or similar signs used in connection with identical or similar products, it is

442. First Instance Administrative Court of Athens 2946/1992, *DDik* 1993, 1355.

the earlier right that prevails. For example, a trademark application may relate to a mark, which is used by somebody else as a company name, or as a distinctive title, etc.; it is the earlier rights which will prevail. The priority principle implies that all intellectual property rights (i.e., trademarks, company names, distinctive titles, distinctive signs, etc.) are equal and none of them is by itself more important or more powerful over the other. So, rights acquired through registration are equal with rights acquired through use, and it is only the factor of time that is decisive. The comparison as to the time the right was created is not easy, because although the acquisition of registered rights such as trademarks is rather straightforward and dates back to the date of filing, the acquisition of non-registered rights is more complicated. Non-registered rights are acquired through use in the course of trade. This means that the creation of the right occurs when the use has been so strong that the average consumer associates the respective sign with a particular trader. So, rights over company names, distinctive titles, distinctive signs, and other non-registered distinctive signs are acquired through use in the course of trade. The volume of use does not need to be that strong leading to high reputation and fame; however, there has to be some actual use and not a fictitious one. Preparatory acts are not sufficient and do not qualify as use. Advertisement and promotional activities qualify as use in the course of trade.

444. Although trademarks and other non-registered rights are, in principle, equal there seems to be an exception to this in favour of trademarks. Under Greek law, a registered trademark is valid until it is cancelled by way of a final court judgment. The legal consequences of such a judgment (i.e., deletion of the registration) do not have retrospective effects and appear only after the issue of the judgment. At the same time, civil courts cannot challenge the validity of the registration, which can be challenged only through cancellation proceedings. It follows that in a situation where a registered trademark coexists with an earlier non-registered right, the trademark owner does not automatically lose his rights and can continue using the registered trademark until cancellation. From this point of view a trademark registration seems to be more powerful than a non-registered distinctive sign, which is acquired through use.

445. According to Article 124(4) the applicant can produce a letter of consent from the owner of earlier rights in order to facilitate registration. According to the letter of this provision the Trademarks Committee and the Registry cannot challenge the merits or the validity of a letter of consent and are bound by it.

§8. Opposition

446. If the application passes successfully the examination of absolute and relative grounds, then it is published (uploaded with) on the website of the registry. An opposition can be filed either on absolute or on relative grounds by third parties within a period of three months, commencing from the publication of the application. An opposition based on relative grounds can be filed only by the owners of the respective earlier rights. An opposition based on absolute grounds can be filed by anyone who can prove a personal and legitimate interest, including associations of consumers and chambers of commerce.

447. The opposition is adjudicated by the Trademarks Committee. Its judgments are appealed before the First Instance Administrative Court of Athens within a period of sixty days for nationals and ninety days for foreigners. This period commences on the next day after the judgment is served to the party wishing to appeal.

448. Under Greek law (Article 143 of L. 4072/2012) the party that files an opposition, on the ground of earlier rights arising from an earlier registration, may be required to prove that he/she has used his/her earlier trademarks on which the opposition is based, within a period of five years before the publication of the opposed application.

§9. Cancellation and Revocation

449. Cancellation and revocation of registered trademarks are dealt with by Articles 159–161 of L. 4072/2012, as amended by L. 4155/2013. The ground for revocation are: (a) non-use for a period of five consecutive years; however the owner of the trademark is not obliged to commence using it before the lapse of five years as from registration, (b) the trademark becoming commonplace due to conduct of its owner; this is discussed in more detail below, (c) if the use of the trademark by its owner is such that there is a likelihood that the public may be deceived, particularly with respect to the geographical origin of the goods or their quality. It is to be noted that this latter ground – (c) – can be invoked by associations of consumers and chambers of commerce, as well as by anyone who can prove a legitimate interest. Revocation becomes effective by way of a final court judgment and only after such a judgment is issued (i.e., the judgment does not have retrospective effects).

450. The grounds for cancellation are the same as absolute and relative grounds for refusal. A registered trademark can be cancelled if it has been registered in violation of the provisions regarding absolute and relative grounds. Again, cancellation is made by a final court judgment and does not have any retrospective effects. Chambers of commerce and associations of consumers, as well as any person who can establish a legitimate interest, can invoke grounds of cancellation due to violation of absolute or relative grounds.

451. Article 162(4) of L. 4072/2012 provided that an application for cancellation should be filed within five years as from registration, save for cancellation on the grounds of bad faith, which could be filed at any time. However, this time limit was amended and abolished with L. 4155/2013. So, under the new law, a registration can be challenged at any time and the lapse of the five years period from registration does not provide a 'safe harbour' any more.

The owner of a trademark registration attacked in the context of cancellation proceedings may invoke the 'proof of use defense'. That is, the owner of the attacked registration may request the owner of the trademark on which the cancellation is based to prove that he/she has used his/her earlier trademark within a period of five years preceding the filing of the cancellation.

452. Applications for cancellation and revocation are filed with the registry and dealt with by the Trademark Committee. An appeal can be filed with the administrative courts. A major characteristic of Greek trademark practice is that cancellation and revocation proceedings can be extremely long. Bear in mind that a final court judgment is required, which means a judgment from the Administrative CA. The time required to complete judicial proceedings up to this court may well be ten years or more. So, because of this, cancellation and revocation is quite difficult in Greece.

§10. Trademarks Becoming Commonplace after Registration

453. Sometimes famous trademarks are so successful and influential that they are almost matching with specific products, in the sense that consumers use the trademark to identify with the product. This represents a great risk to trademark owners because in such a case the trademark becomes commonplace; that is, the trademark, instead of being the name of one product, becomes a generic term describing the whole class of this product. Recently the mark WALKMAN owned by Sony was tested before Greek courts for becoming a commonplace, describing portable audio devices, but escaped being cancelled on this ground. If a registered trademark becomes commonplace, it can be cancelled (deregistered). However, cancellation is not automatic; instead, it requires someone to file an application for cancellation, which is reviewed by the Trademarks Committee, and on appeal by the administrative courts, and has to lead to a final court judgment.

454. The following should be noted in connection to the prerequisites that must be fulfilled for a trademark to become commonplace and be open to cancellation on this ground:

(a) Passive conduct on the part of the proprietor: Objective conditions need to be fulfilled so that the above-mentioned ground of cancellation will apply. In particular, the law requires evidence that the respective trademark has become a mark commonly used; however, in addition to this, there must be some passive or pathetic conduct on the part of the trademark owner. This means that such common use of the mark should be attributed to the inactive and pathetic conduct of the proprietor himself. Hence, common use of a trademark cannot be substantiated where there is evidence that the proprietor has exercised his rights under the law and has lodged the available legal remedies against third parties who infringed his right upon his registered trademark.[443]

(b) In case of doubt, the registered trademark shall remain registered and the proprietor shall retain his rights: It is quite rare and uncommon for a registered trademark to become degraded into a mark of common use. This also amounts to an exceptional restriction to freedom of competition, because an absolute right upon a trademark becomes degraded into a common term and, as a result, prejudices one of the fundamental principles of freedom of competition, i.e., the origin function and the ability to distinguish between goods that originate from different undertakings. In practice, when a registered trademark is rendered a term available for common use, third parties (i.e., competitors with no authorization to use such trademark) are allowed to use it and to capitalize on its reputation despite such reputation being built up by the original trademark proprietor, who had invested in long-term and expensive advertising campaigns and had undertaken effective marketing efforts and strategy. Consequently, legal literature concludes that cancellation of a registered trademark due to falling into common use must be substantiated by strong evidence beyond any reasonable doubt. In case of doubt, the respective trademark should not be cancelled and the proprietor should retain his/her legal rights upon such.[444] In this respect, indirect or hypothetical conclusions and inferences cannot be regarded as adequate evidence. The trademark owner does not bear the burden to prove that his/her registered trademark has not become commonplace.

(c) Indications of performing an advertising function having not fallen into common use: When a registered trademark has fallen into common use, this means that consumers are not able to describe the respective class of products without making use of the trademark. However, if consumers make use of the trademark for the ease of reference only and not because it is impossible to them to otherwise describe the class of the respective products, this does not render the trademark commonplace or a term of common use. For the same reasons, trademarks which perform a strong advertising function and possess a high advertising value are only rarely and exceptionally cancelled on this ground. In many cases, a trademark enjoys a very strong appeal to and recognition by consumers, because either other manufacturers do not produce equally competent products (i.e., products of equally high quality) or products originating from other competitors fail to take any considerable market share by reason of the excellent quality of the products that the respective trademark proprietor trades with, or the production of the respective goods, thereby distinguished, is based on the commercial exploitation of a registered patent, which the respective trademark proprietor is entitled to use exclusively and, hence, no competing products may exist due to legal reasons, or the trademark proprietor was the first to introduce into the market a new product that did not exist and was not available in the

443. Administrative Trademarks Committee 4213/1972, *EEmpD* 1973, 442; First Instance Administrative Court of Athens 3224/1990, *EEmpD* 1990, 520; First Instance Administrative Court of Athens 13939/1998, *DEE* 1998, 871; M. Moumouris, *Trademark Cancellation,* 190 (Athens 1967 (in Greek)).

444. N. Rokas, *Trademarks Law* (Athens 1978 (in Greek)).

market beforehand. In all these cases, it is difficult to identify whether a trademark has fallen into becoming commonplace since consumers continue to identify the respective trademark with the particular product thereby distinguished and its features and qualities. In other words, in all these cases 'common use' of a trademark must be attributed to its wide recognition, market establishment, and huge success. The following trademarks are indicative examples of this: WALKMAN (used by Sony for portable audio devices), NESCAFE (used for instant coffee), JEEP (used for SUV vehicles), ASPIRIN (used for paracetamol pain alleviators), MICKEY MOUSE (used for comics addressed to children), CELLOFAN (used for a thin, transparent sheet made of regenerated cellulose used to food packaging), TEFAL and TEFLON (used for glass non-stick cookware equipment) or PYREX (used for thermal shock resistant borosilicate glass cooking equipment). Especially in the field of electric appliances, technological developments allowed the production of totally innovative products and devices, which are, however, manufactured and produced by a single producer, such as the IPOD device of Apple Inc., or the BLACKBERRY device. It is totally clear that all the above indications cannot be classified as marks of common usage, despite their huge success in the market. The fact that consumers use such trademark for the ease of reference in common parlance and in order to describe a particular product or class of products is not sufficient for rendering such trademark into a mark of common use, since it is not evident that consumers fail to identify such trademark as the trademark owned by a particular undertaking that distinguishes the latter's products. On the contrary, a trademark is degraded into commonplace where consumers use this particular trademark (term or indication) in order to describe (or refer to) a particular class of products because there is no other available term bearing the same conceptual meaning as the mark that they use and not by reason of the excellent quality of the goods originating from the respective manufacturer.

(d) Common use must be general and absolute by reference to the totality of consumers: A high percentage of consumers may identify a particular trademark with a particular class of products and may have been using this particular trademark in order to describe (or refer to) a particular class of products, because there are not able to identify and use any other available term or indication bearing the same conceptual meaning. However, this is not sufficient to render such trademark into commonplace if an equally high and important percentage of consumers is able to distinguish the general trade name of the respective product from the respective trademark and perceives the trademark as an indication that declares that specific products originate from a particular undertaking and bears a number of qualities and features.[445]

(e) It is the consumers' perception that is crucial: The perception of consumers is far more important than the one of competitors or distributors or other retailers; after all, the fall of a trademark into commonplace and its cancellation on this ground would perfectly serve the interests of such competitors.

---

445. N. Rokas, *supra* n. 445 at 62; B. Antonopoulos, *supra* n. 218 at 412.

455. The Greek courts have rejected applications to cancel the following trademarks on the ground of becoming commonplace: CHLORINE,[446] ASPIRIN,[447] OLYMPIAKOS (a popular Greek football club),[448] BLANCO for correction fluid.[449]

§11. Likelihood of Confusion

456. Likelihood of confusion can be described as the very basic concept of trademark law. Likelihood of confusion is the criterion for providing two different types of legal protection to trademark owners: (a) protection against subsequent trademark applications in the context of the administrative procedure for trademark registrations, and (b) protection against trademark infringement (i.e., imitation or falsification) before the civil courts. At the same time, likelihood of confusion is one of the more confused and diversified legal concept. For example, courts and legal literature are struggling to draw a clear line among the concepts of likelihood of confusion, likelihood of association, and dilution. A theory trying to explain this complexity and diversification is the following: trademark infringement appears in very many different forms; counterfeit goods are a classic form of trademark infringement. However, with the lapse of time trademark infringement has developed into many, very different and more sophisticated forms; one example is 'look alike' products copying the colour combinations of a well-known product with different word elements. As the types of trademark infringement became more diversified and sophisticated, courts and legal literature attempted to adapt the concept of likelihood of confusion to such new types of infringements. As a result, the concept of likelihood of confusion was interpreted broadly and was supplemented with similar concepts, such as likelihood of association, after sales confusion, dilution, etc. Hence, sometimes one cannot draw a clear and straightforward line among likelihood of confusion, likelihood of association, and dilution. This diversification and confusion can be explained only on the basis of historical developments of the law and any attempt to develop more concrete and clear conceptual criteria to describe the differences among the various types of likelihood of confusion and the various expressions used to describe it.

457. The following principles are usually applied in connection to likelihood of confusion:

446. SMCFI of Athens 8784/2003, *DEE* 2004, 273.
447. Trademarks Committee 4213/1972, *EEmpD* 1972, p442.
448. First Instance Administrative Court of Athens 13939/1998, *DEE* 1999, 871; according to this judgment, a registered trademark is degraded and becomes an indication of common usage not only where third parties use it but also where the trademark proprietor has abandoned it permanently and has stopped using it long ago.
449. First Instance Administrative Court of Athens 3224/1990, *EEmpD* 1990, 520; according to this judgment, a registered trademark is degraded and becomes a common place when the trademark proprietor does not take legal action against third parties who infringe his rights by making unauthorized use of such trademark.

(1) Tests for likelihood of confusion: The traditional test for likelihood of confusion is one comprising of a comparison at two levels, i.e., comparison of the marks and comparison of the respective goods or services in connection to which the marks are used. The EU law introduced a so-called multifactor test, which takes into account various other factors. Among these factors, those that seem to be more important in practice are the channels of distribution, the expertise of consumers to which the respective goods or services are addressed, the level of use and advertisement of a mark and the time of prior use and advertisement, the intent of the party using the subsequent mark (i.e., whether the intent was to copy the earlier mark, or whether there are other reasons to use the particular mark which are justified on an objective basis), etc. Greek courts usually apply, in practice, the traditional test; however, the multifactor test is not expressly rejected. Usually, courts come to a satisfying conclusion by applying the traditional test and do not feel it necessary to examine and take into account factors other than the comparison of goods and services. However, it is true that there is one factor which is usually applied by the courts and proves to be decisive in court practice: this is the 'expert consumers' factor.

(2) Expert consumers: According to long-established case law, likelihood of confusion is remote or impossible in case of goods or services addressed to expert or sophisticated consumers, such as enterprises making use of commercial banking services (i.e., not including retail banking which is addressed to consumers). The same may apply those pharmaceuticals which are obtained only on the basis of a medical prescription issued by a doctor.[450]

(3) Average consumer: Another established principle is that likelihood of confusion is appreciated in view of the average consumer. It is usually reported in court judgments that the average consumer is someone who does not have the two marks readily available before him/her, so as to be able to make a direct comparison. Instead, consumers usually only recall to their minds the earlier mark; so, what is decisive is the memory of the average consumer about the characteristics of the earlier mark and such memory is considered to be inaccurate.[451] This view makes it easier to establish a likelihood of confusion.

It is true that due to influence by EU law, it was recently submitted that the average consumer is 'reasonably well informed and circumvent'. This would seem to suggest that consumers are aware even of slight differences among marks and are able to perceive the original marks from those imitating them. If the above phrase is to be applied literally, there will simply be no place for likelihood of confusion. It is true that sometimes Greek courts have applied this concept about the average consumer; however, these cases are related to facts where it was evident that likelihood of confusion could not be established for other reasons. In most cases where this concept of 'well informed and circumvent consumer' was adopted the main problem was that the registered trademark that sought legal protection was a rather descriptive one and

450. AP 1780/1999, *EEmpD* 2000, 804, SMCFI of Athens 10126/2001, *EEmpD* 2002, 161.
451. CA of Athens 2461/2006, *EEmpD* 2006, 740, 1088/2010, vol. 2010, 1057, Council of State 1180/2010, *EEmpD* 2010, 737.

there were many concerns whether it should have been registered in the first place. So, it seems that the idea of a 'well informed and circumvent consumer' is an attempt to strike a balance of fairness in cases where marks that are rather descriptive or generic have achieved registration. Finally, it is to be mentioned that it is also submitted that the term 'reasonably' in the above phrase means 'to a limited extent'. However, it is also true that the level of attention of an average consumer is usually higher in connection to pharmaceuticals, or very expensive goods, like, i.e., cars, furniture, etc. so, consumers' attentiveness depends on the specific products in question on each case.

(4) Overall impression: The conclusion as to whether likelihood of confusion is established in each particular case should be based on the 'overall impression' created by the respective mark.[452] The 'overall impression' principle can be used either to establish or to reject likelihood of confusion. So, in some cases courts conclude that although there are certain similarities among the marks, the overall impression is, though, different and likelihood of confusion is not established; while, in other cases the judgments hold that the differences noticed among the marks are not adequate to deter and exclude the confusion created by their overall impression. So, it can be argued that the 'overall impression' principle is not really of much assistance as it does not provide a safe and useful criterion to determine whether likelihood of confusion is established or not in each case.

(5) The double identity principle. As per recital 16 of EU Directive 2015/2436 (ex recital 11 of EU Directive 2008/95):

> The protection afforded by the registered trade mark, the function of which is in particular to guarantee the trademark as an indication of origin, should be absolute in the event of there being identity between the mark and the corresponding sign and the goods or services. The protection should apply also in the case of similarity between the mark and the sign and the goods or services. It is indispensable to give an interpretation of the concept of similarity in relation to the likelihood of confusion. The likelihood of confusion, the appreciation of which depends on numerous elements and, in particular, on the recognition of the trademark on the market, the association which can be made with the used or registered sign, the degree of similarity between the trade mark and the sign and between the goods or services identified, should constitute the specific condition for such protection.

According to this recital, in case of identity of both the respective marks and the respective goods or services (double identity), trademarks are granted absolute protection, i.e., they are considered to be absolute rights (something like the right of property over land). So, anyone occupying himself in any way with the trademark of another commits an infringement, even in the absence of any likelihood of confusion caused to consumers. According to Greek legal literature, in such cases there is a presumption in favour of likelihood of confusion, which cannot be rebutted, or, according to another view, in such cases

452. AP 751/1995, *DEE* 1996, 255, and 1123/2002, *EEmpD* 2002, 87.

the law concludes that there is likelihood of confusion and does not permit the parties involved to challenge this conclusion.[453] This view is supported by the letter of the law in Article 5(1)a of EU Directive 2015/2436 as well as by Article 16(1)2 of the TRIPS Agreement. However, save for this exception of double identity cases, in all other circumstances likelihood of confusion depends on the facts of each case and has to be proved by the claimant (i.e., the trademark owner).

(6) Comparison of marks is assessed on the basis of their visual, oral, and conceptual similarity. That is, one examines, how marks look like, how they are pronounced, and what is their respective meaning (if they have a certain conceptual meaning and are not purely imaginary). Although in past decades it was usually argued that oral similarity is more important than visual, because consumers usually ask for the products by their respective names (orally), it seems that this is ante dated nowadays; in modern markets consumers usually pick up products by themselves from the shelves of a supermarket and make a choice based on the visual characteristics of products. There is no doubt, though, that conceptual similarity is of primary importance. If there are two-word terms that have the same meaning (e.g., TORNADO and TYFOON) they should be regarded as confusingly similar, even though they look quite different and are pronounced differently.[454] For example, the following marks were found to be confusingly similar in cases where the respective goods were also found to be either identical, or similar: (a) 'LIXIDON' and 'LIXIN',[455] (b) 'WONDERBRA' and 'WONDERBODY', (c) 'FITMAXX' and 'MAXFIT'.[456] On the contrary, the following marks were found not to be confusingly similar, although the respective goods were identical: (a) 'JET OIL & device' and 'JET GAS',[457] (b) 'CLEAR GUARD' and 'ON GUARD',[458] (c) a mark consisting of a three-dimensional device representing a spruce-fir tree accompanied by the term AIR ALPINO and a device mark representing a spruce-fir tree.[459]

(7) Comparison of goods or services is mainly based on the respective circle of consumers to which the respective goods or services are addressed. For example, fashion clothing, cosmetics, jewellery are not directly competitive but they are addressed to the same consumers and they are confusingly similar in this sense. The circle of consumers is the more important criterion in determining the similarity of goods and services. Another factor that can be taken into account is whether the goods are directly competitive or not (i.e., whether increase of sales of one product could reasonably lead to reduction of sales of

453. M. Marinos, *Trademark Law*, 170 (Athens 2007 (in Greek)), N. Rokas, *supra* n. 25 at 120 (163 in 2004 edition), B. Antonopoulos, *supra* n. 218 at 437.

454. AP 1254/1994, *EEmpD* 1995, 703 found the terms BACARDI and BRICANTI to be confusingly similar. MMCFI 585/2010, *EEmpD* 2010, 180 found confusingly similar the word mark GIANT and a figurative mark consisting of the picture of a giant.

455. Council of State *(Conseil d' Etat)* 620/1982.

456. First Instance Administrative Court of Athens 5112/2012.

457. Council of State *(Conseil d' Etat)* 535/1981.

458. Council of State *(Conseil d' Etat)* 1964/1980.

459. Council of State *(Conseil d' Etat)* 1710/2006.

another). From this point of view coffee and tea are regarded to be confusingly similar in this sense. The main substance from which the products are made in may also be material. For example, cheese, milk, yoghurt, and ice cream are all made from milk and are confusingly similar because of this, although not directly competitive (i.e., someone who is willing to buy milk will never be confused so as to buy yoghurt). The consumer needs that products or services satisfy may also be taken into account; for example, chocolates, biscuits, ice creams, cereals are all foodstuffs and are confusingly similar. Furthermore, foodstuffs and non-alcoholic beverages are all nutritional goods and are again confusingly similar.

(8) In case of marks combined by multiple elements, i.e., words and figurative elements, courts usually attempt to find out if there is one element which is prevailing and material. If there is, the comparison is based mainly on the prevailing elements of each mark. In similar cases, elements which by themselves alone are only descriptive, generic, or commonly used are not taken into consideration. Finally, according to one view, in case of marks consisting of both figurative and word elements, word elements are more important and prevailing from the point of view of likelihood of confusion. This view, however, should be applied very cautiously, because the prevailing importance of word elements against figurative elements does not seem to be always the case in modern markets.

(9) Lookalike products, protection of colour, and trade dress: A great number of cases relate to the situation of the so-called 'lookalike' products. 'Lookalike' products are products which copy the colour combinations and the drawing and artistic elements of the packaging of one another but use different word elements. The legal issues arising in connection to 'lookalike' products are protection of colours and colour combinations as well as protection of trade dress. As a general remark, it should be emphasized that Greek jurisprudence on both protection of colours and trade dress protection should not be regarded as a reliable precedent that could make predictable the final outcome of a prospective future litigation. This is mainly because such cases have been decided on the basis of the 'overall impression doctrine' and on the basis of their respective facts, which are always particular to each case. On the issue of protection of colours, there seems to be no positive precedent from Greek civil courts in favour of protection of colour as such (i.e., not taking into account other figurative and pictorial elements or words) under either trademark or unfair competition law. On the contrary, the only case that seems to have dealt with this issue has been decided against the protection of colour alone. This was the case of 'Petro gas' liquid gas for home use, which was traded in blue cylinders and whose colour was copied by 'Vitom gas'. The plaintiff's legal action was rejected in both the first instance and the appeal court. The Supreme Court reasoned that copying of colour should be assessed in the context of the 'overall impression' doctrine;[460] in other words, the other figurative or word elements, as well as the overall packaging and appearance, should also be taken into account in order to determine whether there is any likelihood of

460. 399/1989, *EEmpD* 1990, 144.

confusion or association, unfair resemblance, or dilution. The Court, however, noted that copying of the colour alone could suffice to establish likelihood of confusion if, on the evidence, it was found that it is the colour which is the prevailing element of the whole packaging and appearance of the product and if it could be proved that copying of the colour alone could attract the attention of consumers.

There are numerous judgments in favour of trade dress protection under both trademark and unfair competition law. As a matter of fact, there is a strong recent trend in favour of trade dress protection and protection of the shape and the packaging of products. One important court precedent is the 'sliced toast bread case'. The case related to products (i.e., sliced toast bread) with similar packaging. In this case the court emphasized that one of the main elements copied by the defendant was the basic overall colour of the packaging. The court found that the basic overall colour was prevailing in the overall impression of the packaging. However, in this case, the defendant had also copied the colour combination as well as other figurative and word elements used by the plaintiff, and this may reasonably have had an impact on the final ruling of the court.[461] In the case of Camper Twins Shoes[462] the court granted trade dress protection under unfair competition law to the red packaging and design of 'Camper twins shoes'. It is important that the court emphasized that the red packaging of the shoes was characteristic for 'Camper twin shoes' and was therefore protected as such. Another important point in this judgment was that the court found that the red Camper packaging had become distinctive, due to intense advertisement, although it circulated in the market only for a short period of time (two years). However, in this case, again, the defendant had copied the Camper shoes design as well, and this may reasonably have had an impact on the final court's judgment. In the Toblerone case,[463] protection was granted to Toblerone's chocolate shape and packaging. Although the word elements were different in the products compared and although certain pictorial elements were different as well, the court found that likelihood of confusion was established mainly due to the copying of the triangle shape of the product, which was found to be characteristic to Toblerone chocolate. In Judgment 1687/2004, issued by the CA of Athens,[464] (the Nescafe case) the court granted protection to the NESCAFE CLASSIC overall packaging and colour combination that were copied by another manufacturer.

Recently, in a very important case, Bayer, the well-known pharmaceutical failed to obtain trade dress protection for the green and white colour combination of the packaging of ASPIRIN.[465] Bayer had registered a number of European Trademarks for the green and white colour combination and invoked both trademark law and unfair competition. In particular, they alleged likelihood of confusion and dilution of the green and white colours of the ASPIRIN

461. SMCFI of Athens 1265/2005, *EEmpD* 2005, 628.
462. SMCFI of Athens 6778/2004, *EEmpD* 2005, 634.
463. SMCFI of Athens 1478/2005, unreported.
464. *EEmpD* 2005, 623.
465. Athens CA 1702/2016.

packaging. However, on the basis of scientific literature, the court found that the green colour caused certain emotions to consumers and that it was mentally associated with the idea of relief from pain. Moreover, that it is a colour which, to the mind of consumers, is closely associated with the medical science. Hence, that it should not be monopolized by solely one manufacturer, because it is functional. In this respect, the court was very much influenced by numerous scientific articles regarding consumers' psychology and behaviour, which supported the argument that certain colours, under certain circumstances, may subconsciously cause particular sentimental reactions. The court also paid particular attention to the fact that consumers usually do not perceive colours as indications of origin. On the contrary, it is word marks that basically perform the origin function. The court further considered that the dominant component of the packaging was the word mark and not the green colour. Finally the court was of the view that the level of attention of consumers is particularly increased in the case of pharmaceuticals. The court was reluctant to accept the argument that the alleged reputation of the word mark ASPIRIN was reflected in and passed to the green and white colour packaging also; instead, it considered that an allegation on the fame of the packaging's colours should be supported by evidence specifically associated to the alleged reputation of the colours and that evidence on the fame of the word mark was not sufficient. *The aftermath of the judgment is that it may be particularly difficult to establish that a particular colour, or colour combination, is distinctive in itself and that enjoys reputation as such (i.e., irrespective of the word marks accompanying it). One has to prove that consumers would recognize the particular product from the colours of the packaging alone, even in the absence of any word mark. In simple terms, this would mean that anyone, who comes across a green and white packaging without any other word indications, has no doubt that it cannot be anything else other than ASPIRIN. Establishing something like this is particularly difficult as, in principle, consumers are not accustomed to perceive colours as indications of origin. Establishing distinctiveness on this basis may be impossible in cases where certain colours cause particular mental associations, or emotions, and are generic of particular sectors.*

(10) Another well-established rule which is much applied by the courts is that there is likelihood of confusion when the earlier mark is reproduced as such in the later mark. The situation is well illustrated by the GCEU judgment[466] in the case of the mark ARTHRUR and ARTHRUR ET FELICIE, which were found to be confusingly similar.

(11) Comparison of marks is based on their respective dominant and distinctive elements, while elements that are descriptive or commonplace are not taken into account in assessing likelihood of confusion, indeed, many trademark cases are due to the fact that the respective marks share similar, or identical elements, which are, though, descriptive and indistinctive. So, the GCEU has held that likelihood of confusion is not established between the marks 'EASY

466. T-346/04. In this context *see also* Council of State 2394/1994, unreported finding that the marks PINOCIDE and DELTA PINOCIDE are confusingly similar.

AIR-TOURS' and 'AIRTOURS' in a case where both marks were filed for transport services.[467] The common elements among the two marks were descriptive and, hence, insufficient to cause likelihood of confusion.

(12) 'After sale' confusion: According to traditional legal theory, the likelihood of confusion is relevant to a consumer who buys falsified or imitating (counterfeit) goods; this is – after all – the type of likelihood of confusion most commonly encountered. However, a trademark may be also infringed where the purchaser of a product is aware that it is a counterfeit one but other people, who shall see the particular item, are likely to be confused and deceived as to its quality and are likely to be discouraged from purchasing it themselves. As a result, according to modern legal theory, in order to assess the existence of likelihood of confusion, one should take account the positive or negative impression that the respective product makes to prospective buyers/customers, who are likely to come across the particular product bearing the conflicting indications (which the particular buyer purchased knowing that it is a counterfeit one). The latter constitutes what is usually called 'after-sale confusion'. Hence, it is important to identify not only whether the purchaser himself could possibly be confused at the time of purchase but also whether confusion may also affect other consumers, who encounter such product at a later stage in time. After sales confusion is also actionable.

§12. Famous Marks and Dilution

458. A peculiarity of some Greek court judgments is that they require additional prerequisites for a trademark to be considered as a famous one. In particular, although famous trademarks are usually considered to be those enjoying an increased awareness by consumers, i.e., those that are easily recognizable by consumers, some Greek courts require, in addition to increased awareness, that the mark is a unique one, that consumers share a positive attitude in connection to it, and that the mark does not consist of a sign which is commonly used in the course of trade. In this context, the mark APPLE was considered not to be a famous one by Greek courts, on the ground that it was not unique and that it consisted of a common vocabulary word.[468] However, other judgments suggest that the only prerequisite of fame is brand awareness by consumers.[469] This view is actually supported by Article 16 paragraph 2 of the TRIPS Agreement, as well as by the judgment of the ECJ in the case of *General Motors v. Yplon*.[470]

459. For many decades protection of famous marks in Greece was deduced only to the administrative procedure for obtaining trademark registration. Famous foreign marks were protected on the basis that should a local party apply in his name for a mark that was already famous abroad, this was considered to be a trademark

467. GCEU T-608/13, 13.05.2015.
468. SMCFI of Athens 9077/1992, *EEmpD* 1992, 661.
469. AP 1030/2008.
470. ECJ, C-375/97, 14.09.99, *General Motors v. Yplon*, paras 22–27.

application in bad faith and legal protection was granted through opposition or cancellation proceedings. Such protection was granted according to Article 6*bis* of the Paris Convention (1883).

460. It was only until around 2010 that the Greek civil courts began to issue judgments granting legal protection against infringement on the grounds of dilution. So, during the past years there are judgments from the first instance courts applying the doctrine of dilution as set by Articles 5(3)a and 10(2)c of the EU Directive 2015/2436.[471] As a matter of fact, these judgments are inspired by recent ECJ case law, such as the cases of ADIDAS/FITNESSWORLD,[472] INTEL,[473] L'OREAL,[474] and TDK.[475] These cases developed very much the concept of free riding, which is now considered to be a characteristic case of trademark dilution.

461. In order to establish fame and reputation, one has to produce evidence of long and strong use and advertisement, as well as evidence in connection to market shares. This would include published advertisements in the press, invoices evidencing transactions, and even market survey reports which are also an acceptable means of evidence under the rules of Greek civil procedure. Currently, there is a recent trend of increased use of market survey reports in Greek court practice.

In order to succeed in a dilution claim, one has to establish the following: (a) similarity between the earlier and the latter mark, (b) likelihood of a link in consumers' minds between the earlier and the latter mark, (c) unfair advantage in favour of the latter mark from the reputation of the earlier mark, or detriment to the reputation of the earlier mark. Even if the above are sufficiently established, the defendant may counter-argue that there is some due cause justifying such unfair advantage or detriment. Dilution may consist in that: (a) the latter mark becomes recognizable by consumers faster and with less advertising expenses (free riding), or (b) the latter mark is affixed to products of inferior quality, or there is some other negative publicity or negative implications against the earlier mark, or (c) there is a lessening of the distinctive value of the earlier mark.

The Greek court upheld a dilution claim by Adidas relating to their three parallel stripes against a manufacturer of athletic footwear who was using four parallel stripes.[476] In another case, the cylinder shape of a chocolate wafer that looked like a cigar was found to enjoy reputation and to be diluted by a manufacturer who was also producing wafers in a similar cigar-like shape.[477] The mark ELEMENT accompanied by the device of a tree of the well-known clothing company was also found

471. *See* MMCFI of Athens 585/2010, *EEmpD* 2010, 180 and 5610/2010, *EEmpD* 2010, 978, which both adhered to the conclusion on free riding drawn by the ECJ judgments in the cases of INTEL and L'OREAL.
472. CJEU, 23 Oct. 2003, C-408/01 which has been followed by the judgment of AP 1030/2008, *EEmpD* 2008, 891. These cases clarifies that the test for dilution is not the same as for likelihood of confusion, but a more loose and relaxed one, allowing a greater level of protection for famous marks.
473. CJEU, 27 Nov. 08, C-252/07.
474. CJEU, 18 Jun. 09, C-487/07.
475. CJEU, 12 Dec. 08, C-197/07.
476. AP 1030/2008.
477. MMCFI of Athens 585/2010.

to be diluted by a retailer selling clothing under similar marks.[478] The mark CHAMPION of the well-known manufacturer of athletic clothing was found to be diluted by a manufacturer of similar products who was using the same mark in different lettering.[479]

§13. Parallel Imports, Exhaustion and Protection of Distribution Networks

462. Regarding parallel imports Greece applies Article 15 of EU Directive 2015/2436, which is reproduced by Article 128 of Greek L. 4072/2012. Parallel imports qualify as a trademark infringement if the imported goods have not been put in the market of a Member State of the European Economic Area (EEA)[480] by the trademark owner, or with his consent. Greek courts strictly apply the jurisprudence of the CJEU on all aspects of parallel imports and particularly in connection to what qualifies as 'consent' on the part of the trademark owner and allocation of burden of proof. The judgments usually support the view that one of the powers arising from trademarks is the power of the owner to be the first who will place the goods bearing the mark within the market of the EEA.[481] Once the trademark owner has exercised this power, the respective trademark rights are exhausted; Greece applies strictly the Community exhaustion theory introduced by the CJEU in the *Silhouette* case.[482] As a result, goods imported from non-Member States of the EEA are, in principle, suspect of qualifying as illegitimate parallel imports.

463. In certain cases Greek courts have also applied Article 15(2) of the EU Directive 2008/95, which is reproduced by Article 128(2) of L. 4072/2012. According to this provision, it may be possible that parallel imports originating from Member States of the EEA qualify as trademark infringement if there are legitimate reasons for the proprietor to oppose further commercialization of the goods, especially where the condition of the goods is changed or impaired after they have been put on the market. Greek courts applied this provision in cases where the imported goods were of different quality and different characteristics than those traded in Greece. Sometimes the goods traded in one country are of different quality and characteristics than those traded in other countries, because they are adapted to the particularities of each market in terms of climatological conditions, or in terms of consumers' tastes.[483]

464. In another class of cases, trademark rights have been successfully used by trademark owners in order to protect their distribution networks against independent traders and parallel importers in particular. In these cases trademark owners

478. CA of Athens 840/2012.
479. MMCFI of Athens 5610/2010.
480. EEA consists of the EU and Iceland, Norway and Lichtenstein.
481. MMCFI of Thessaloniki 699/2011, *EEmpD* 2012, 168, CA of Patrae 1058/1998, *DEE* 1999, 860.
482. CJEU, 16 Jul. 98, C-355/96, *Silhouette v. Hartlauer*.
483. SMCFI of Chania 2410/2003, *EEmpD* 2004, 628, MMCFI of Piraeus 1735/2012, *DEE* 2012, 750, MMCFI of Thessaloniki, 8031/2005, *EEmpD* 2005, 390.

alleged that independent traders have been infringing their trademarks in making use of their advertising power and their reputation. In such cases, an independent trader, who was usually a parallel importer of goods from another EU Member State (i.e., legitimate parallel imports) was using the trademark of the imported goods in advertisements, promotional materials, or in its premises, in order to let the public know that he is offering the respective goods for sale. Most of the Greek court judgments dealing with such circumstances apply Article 14(1) of EU Directive 2015/2436 (i.e., Article 126 of L. 4072/2012) and the CJEU jurisprudence in the BMW[484] or the Dior/Evora[485] cases. The position of the CJEU in these and other similar cases is that an independent trader can make use of the advertising power of a trademark in order to let the public know that he is offering certain goods for sale, so long as the type of advertisement is not detrimental to the reputation of the trademark; the latter depends on whether the type of advertisement in each case is similar to the advertisement customarily made by other traders in this market. For example, for foodstuffs or detergents and other products usually traded in large supermarkets, it is customary to advertise through printed materials, like leaflets, etc.; this is not customary, however, for jewellery, watches, or other similar products. Unfortunately, the jurisprudence of Greek courts is not that sophisticated and does not really concentrate on the customary type of advertisement in each market. Instead, Greek courts usually conclude that an independent trader is allowed to make a limited use of the advertising power of the trademark, but not an aggressive, or even a very impressive use of its reputation. So, in most cases Greek courts conclude that an independent trader cannot really use the trademark as an advertisement tool and that such an advertising use of the trademark qualifies as an infringement and as an act of unfair competition.[486]

§14. ASSIGNMENT

465. Trademark assignment is governed by Article 131 of L. 4072/2012, as amended by L. 4155/2013. Trademark applications and trademark registrations can be assigned. Such assignment can be independent of the assignment of the business undertaking that is the owner of the mark; so, transfer of business is not a prerequisite for trademark assignment and, hence, it is possible for a business entity to assign its trademarks to another entity and continue to carry on its business under another mark.[487] Since transfer of business is not a prerequisite for trademark assignment, it follows that such assignment can lead to deception of the public, in the sense that consumers who come across products bearing the transferred trademark may believe that such products originate from the assignor and may be unaware of the assignment. The law tolerates this likelihood of deception, because

484. CJEU, 23 Feb. 99, C-63/97.
485. CJEU, 4 Nov. 97, C-337/95.
486. CA of Athens 4273/2010, *DEE* 2011, 183, MMCFI of Athens 6989/2003, *DEE* 2004, 653.
487. AP 606/2005, *EEN* 2005, 739.

it is assumed that it is only a matter of time for consumers to notice any modifications that the assignee may bring about in the quality and other characteristics of the product. So, consumers are supposed to adapt themselves to changes of quality caused by trademark assignment.

466. A trademark (application or registration) can be assigned even if it consists in the name of a natural person or the corporate name of a legal entity.

467. Trademark assignment can be for all or only part of the goods or services in connection to which the mark is applied for or registered.[488]

468. Unlike the old law (i.e., L. 2239/1994), the new law (i.e., L. 4072/2012, Article 131(3)) provides that the assignment should be in the form of a written deed. Hence, an oral agreement to assign a trademark is not enforceable.

469. Trademark assignment should be recorded with the trademark' registry. This registration of the assignment is not a legal prerequisite for its effects and legal consequences between the assignor and the assignee. Between the parties (i.e., assignor and assignee) the assignment occurs when a written agreement is executed, that is, the legal effects of the assignment occur even before its registration with the trademark registry. However, registration of the assignment is a prerequisite, so that the assignment brings about legal effects towards third parties. So, unless the assignment is recorded with the trademark registry, it cannot be invoked by either the assignor or the assignee against third parties.

470. So long as the law permits the assignment of a trademark, it is derived that it is also possible to pledge it. Moreover, a creditor may arrest a trademark application or registration and cause a public auction by way of enforcement proceedings.

§15. Licensing

471. Trademark licensing is governed by Article 132 of L. 4072/2012, as amended by L. 4155/2013. Licensing can be for all or only part of the goods or services specified in the trademark registration. In addition, the licence may refer to either the whole of Greece or only a part of the country and may be of an indefinite duration or for a fixed term. It can be an exclusive or non-exclusive one. It is also possible to grant the right to a sub-licence, but this has to be started expressly in the licence agreement.

472. The law provides that trademark licences should be recorded with the trademark registry. It is the owner of the trademark (licensor) who is responsible to arrange for the registration of the licence, but the licensee can also take action on his own initiative, if properly and specifically authorized to do so by the licensor.

488. Trademarks Committee 13360/2003, *EEmpD* 2004, 168.

473. Licences that are not registered are not invalid or unenforceable. They bring about legal effects between the contracting parties; however, they cannot be invoked towards third parties and have no legal consequences vis-à-vis third parties. As a result, if a licence is not registered and the licensor does not make any use of the mark on its own (i.e., it is only the licensee using the mark), then a third party may seek the cancellation of the mark for non-use. The licensor will be unable to prove use of the mark through licensing, since an unregistered licence cannot be invoked towards third parties. On the contrary, a non-registered licence qualifies as use of the mark in the relationship between the licensor and the licensee. Greek courts have dealt with applications by third parties to cancel trademarks that were used under a non-registered licence several times; in such cases the licensor is unable to prove use through licensing and most of these cases finally lead to cancellation for non-use. However, a registered licence qualifies as use of the mark and prevents cancellation for non-use.

474. The registration of the licence is carried on by the registry; there are no substantive law prerequisites, such as that the licence cannot lead to deception of the public, or that the licensor should retain quality control over the products, etc.

475. It is usually submitted that under Greek law only trademark registrations (not trademark applications) are subject to licensing. This is true and correct so long as it is possible to register with the trademark registry a licence for a registered trademark, while it is not possible to register a licence for a trademark application, which has not been registered yet. However, a trademark application is not a trademark and has the status of a non-registered distinctive sign, if used in the course of trade. Such a non-registered mark which is used can be either assigned or licensed under common civil law, according to the principle of freedom of contract. So, licensing of a trademark application is equal to licensing of a non-registered mark, which is legally possible, but it is a transaction which is not registered with the trademark registry.

476. If a licence is registered, the licensee can invoke, by himself/herself, trademark rights (i.e., seek legal protection against trademark infringement) against third parties, even in the absence of the licensor, if this has been expressly agreed in the licence. In case of an exclusive licence, however, the licensee is entitled to seek legal protection against third parties, even if the licence is silent on this matter and it is only if the licence expressly provides otherwise that the licensee of an exclusive licence cannot invoke trademark rights against third parties.

477. The law provides that a licence is cancelled and deleted from the registry if the licensor submits an application to this effect. Although this is a much disputed and unsettled matter, the correct interpretation of this provision seems to be that it is compulsory law that cannot be derogated by contract that the licensor can always terminate the licence at any time, without the need to invoke any serious cause. The justification for this is that the trademark owner has the responsibility to secure the quality of the products towards consumers. In case of a termination which is not justified on its merits, the licensor will bear liability for damages towards the licensee.

478. The old L. 2239/1994 also allowed parallel registration. Parallel registration was of similar effects to licensing. The new L. 4072/2012 considered that parallel registration was not different from licensing, and abandoned and abolished the respective provisions on the assumption that it was not necessary to have both parallel registration and licensing.

§16. Remedies and Evidence

479. The main remedies in case of trademark infringement under Greek law are a court cease-and-desist order and damages. A cease-and-desist order can be issued even in the absence of fault on the part of the defendant. This means that the defendant may be obliged to suffer a cease-and-desist order even if he/she was not aware that the goods he/she was trading were infringing goods. Damages, however, are awarded always only if fault (i.e., either negligence or intent) can be established. In addition to damages, courts are allowed to award moral (i.e., psychological) damages, because trademark infringement qualifies as a tort, and torts can always invoke moral damages. In the past, damages were only rarely awarded or even invoked by claimants, because of the difficulty to prove the volume of the loss suffered and to make a proper and convincing quantification of it. However, the EU Directive 2004/48 on the enforcement of intellectual property rights has dealt with the difficulty to prove the actual volume of damages in trademark infringement cases. Article 11(1) of the Directive provides that damages may be quantified on the basis of either: (a) the loss of profit suffered by the trademark owner, or (b) the volume of the unfair profits made by the infringer, or (c) the volume of the royalties that the infringer would have paid, should he/she had requested and obtained a licence. The Greek law expressly adopts these three criteria as a basis on which the court may determine the quantum of damages. Usually, trademark owners prefer to refer to the royalties that are due in case of a licence in a similar case, because it is relatively easier to prove such anticipated royalties rather than loss of profits of the trademark owner, or the unfair profits gained by the infringer. Moral damages are also usually awarded by courts in case of trademark infringement. Courts have discretion as to the volume of moral damages they award. Usually, the judgments range around EUR 10,000, or less, depending on the financial position of the defendant and on whether intent for infringement can be established. As per Article 8 of Directive 2004/48, Greek courts may also order the infringer to disclose information about distributors, suppliers, or manufacturers of infringing goods, as well as information on the quantities of infringing goods that have been traded.

480. It is to be mentioned that a cease-and-desist court order may also include an order to seize counterfeit goods and the machinery used to produce them, or an order for their destruction. In addition, a cease-and-desist order is usually accompanied by an ancillary order compelling the defendant to a civil fine in case that he/she violates the court order. The volume of this fine ranges between EUR 3,000 and EUR 10,000. Moreover, the court, in case of violation of the cease-and-desist order, may issue a judgment for the imprisonment of the defendant up to one year.

481. Since ordinary judicial proceedings are quite long in Greece (i.e., it may take about three years to obtain a judgment from the first instance court), trademark protection is usually sought on the ground of provisional court measures and summary judgment. Such proceedings can lead to a cease-and-desist court order; they cannot, however, lead to an award for damages or moral damages.

482. Greece has also implemented and applies the EU enforcement Directive 2004/48. This has very much facilitated proving infringement and obtaining provisional court orders. However, the provisions of the Directive are applied taking into account the factor of proportionality to which Greek courts pay much attention.

Chapter 5. Company Names and Distinctive Signs

Ch. Chrissanthis

§1. Legislative Provisions

483. In addition to trademarks, other distinctive signs are also used by merchants in the course of trade. Such distinctive signs may consist in company names, distinctive titles, and other non-registered marks. Unlike trademarks, where rights are acquired through registration and irrespective of use, rights over distinctive signs are acquired through use only and irrespective of registration.

484. It is usually stated that distinctive signs are protected under the law of unfair competition and that there is no specific legislation. It can be argued that this is only half true. In Greece, the law on unfair competition is L. 146/1914. Article 1 of the law contains a general clause on unfair competition. Article 1 prohibits any competitive behaviour which is contrary to good faith, it is carried out in the course of trade and it is destined to have an impact on competition. So, under Article 1 there are four prerequisites that need to be fulfilled in order to establish the tort of unfair competition: (a) competitive behaviour, (b) conflict with good faith, (c) behaviour in the course of trade, and (d) intent to affect competition. However, Article 13 of the same law provides for a special tort of infringing non-registered distinctive signs. The prerequisites of this tort are different from those of Article 1. In particular, the prerequisites of Article 13 are: (a) that there must be a right over a distinctive sign, and (b) that there must be likelihood of confusion; dilution is also regarded to be covered under Article 13 of L. 146/1914 according to a broad interpretation of the concept of likelihood of confusion.

485. The main difference among Articles 1 and 13 is that the former is interpreted to include a prerequisite of a competitive relationship, that is, that the parties in litigation are in some sort of competition. Under Article 13 this prerequisite does not exist, although, of course, in assessing likelihood of confusion among distinctive signs, one has to take into account if there is a competitive relationship or not. Still, however, the prevailing view is that Article 13 provides a better ground for protection of distinctive signs than Article 1. In this sense, it can be argued that Article 13 forms a special legislative regime for the protection of distinctive signs, which deviates from the general principles of the law on unfair competition.[489]

486. Other legislative provisions on company names, in particular, are Articles 4 et seq. of L. 1089/1980, as well as Article 8 of the Paris Convention. Articles 4 et seq. of L. 1089/1980 refers to the registry for company names. Although there is a registry for company names, company names are truly only filed and not registered.

489. N. Rokas, *supra* n. 25 at 168.

This means that the examination process that the registry for company names carries in order to allow filing is much more relaxed than that of the trademark registry. The target of the company names registry is to provide for a fast process for obtaining a company name filing; hence the examination is restricted only to identical prior company names and there is no real and full search for prior rights on the basis of a likelihood of confusion criterion. Article 8 of the Paris Convention provides that company names used abroad by foreigners are protected in Greece also in the same way as national company names.

487. Greek civil law also provides for an absolute right on personality. This is legislated in Article 68 of the GCC. Company names and other distinctive signs may consist of the name of a natural person. In such cases, infringement of the company name or other distinctive signs triggers into application Article 68 of the GCC also.

§2. Formation of Company Names

488. A company name is defined to be an indication of the entity carrying on a business enterprise. From this point of view, company names are distinguished from trademarks that indicate specific goods or services manufactured or distributed by a business enterprise. So, a business enterprise is allowed to have many trademarks, at least as many as the products it produces. It can have only one company name though. So, the rule is that only one company name is allowed per business entity. Company names are further distinguished from distinctive titles. Distinctive titles were originally supposed to operate, and continue to operate till today, as indications and identifications of branches of the same enterprise; a business enterprise can have five or more different distinctive titles, one for each of its branches. For example, a business entity active in the restaurant business, operating five restaurants, can have five different distinctive titles, one for each restaurant. Of course, from the marketing point of view, today's marketing trends are oriented towards having one single distinctive title for all branches, that is, to operate a large chain of stores under the same distinctive title, which is of course permissible and legitimate. In modern times, distinctive titles have a different operation; instead of acting as an indications and identifications for branches, they act as alternatives or substitutions of company names. Company names were traditionally formed according to strict rules and due to this they are not always commercially appealing. Hence, business entities prefer to use in their unofficial and non-formal commercial communications a distinctive title, instead of their company names. So, distinctive titles appear as substitutes for company names in various non-formal commercial communications, such as advertisements, etc.; they cannot be used, though, instead of company names in formal communications, such as contractual documents, tax statements, etc.

489. Merchants trading as natural persons are obliged to use their own names in their commercial transactions and enjoy no other alternatives. They can use, of course, a distinctive title in non-formal communications. There are various types of business entities, which are not natural persons. Under Greek law, there are legal entities of limited and unlimited liability. Until recently, the name of unlimited liability companies consisted exclusively of the name of one or more partners of unlimited liability, while the name of limited liability companies could consist of either the name of one or more of the founders, or of a word descriptive of the business activity of the company, or from an imaginary term, or from combination of the above. The justification for this was that in connection to unlimited liability companies third parties had a legitimate interest to know who the unlimited partners were and this had an impact on the formation of the company name. In 2012 there has been a substantive legislative amendment to the law of unlimited liability companies by virtue of L. 4072/2012. As a result, now, in all types of companies the company name is formed by either the name of one or more of the founders, or of a word descriptive of the business activity of the company, or from an imaginary term, or from combination of the above. So, there has been a vital liberalization of the rules on the formation of company names. As a result, it is expected that the use of distinctive titles, as more appealing substitutes for company names, is likely to retreat in the future.

490. The formation of company names is also governed by some additional general principles, which are not legislated by specific provisions, but derive mainly from good faith and good commercial practices. So, a company name should not be deceptive in any way. For example, a company name including anything that could stand for some type of an illusive implication about association with a foreign entity could be regarded to be deceptive. Further, a company name has to differ from other prior company names, so as to avoid confusion. In addition, a company name remains the same even if the partners or shareholders of the company change. Finally, each entity can have only one company name.

§3. Acquisition, Transfer and Loss of Rights

491. Acquisition of rights over company names and other non-registered distinctive signs is through use in the course of trade only; filing with a particular registry (i.e., the registry for company names) is for information purposes only and does not by itself grant any legal rights.[490] In other words, there is a prior use requirement. The justification for this, as far as company names are concerned, is rather obvious; the purpose of the filing system for company names is to make it quicker and easier to form a company, and part of this process is to file a name for the company to be formed. So, the filing system serves practical needs to avoid conflicts such as two or more companies using the same name. It is not destined, however, to carry on a thorough search for prior rights, or to grant rights which courts cannot review in the context of the judicial process; the latter applies to trademarks, where a registered trademark cannot be reviewed by the civil courts and can only be cancelled, following proceedings before the Trademarks Committee. With respect to company names, however, it is usual that one files a company name and forms a company, which never commences its business operations, though; in such

490. AP 1529/2008, unreported.

cases, there is no acquisition of rights, so long as the company has never traded and this is reasonable, because it would amount to an unnecessary restriction of free competition to grant exclusive rights over a company name that has never been used before.

492. Acquisition of rights is dealt with by Article 13 of L. 146/1914. This provision deals with acquisition of rights over both company names, distinctive titles, and other non-registered distinctive signs such as marks affixed to products, the shape of a product, trade dress, etc. The way the provision deals with acquisition of rights is indirect and rather vague. Actually, what the law provides is that a person using, in the course of trade, the company name or any other distinctive sign of someone else thus creating a likelihood of confusion may be ordered by the courts to cease doing so. There are much and conflicting court jurisprudence and views expressed by legal commentators as to which are the specific requirements for acquisition of rights set by Article 13. The prevailing view is the following: With respect to company names and other signs identifying the business entity itself, or its branches (i.e., distinctive titles of branches) there are two prerequisites, namely (a) distinctiveness[491] and (b) use in the course of trade. With respect to any other distinctive sign, i.e., non-registered distinctive signs, identifying goods or services, or the shape of a product, or trade dress, the requirement is that the respective sign must have prevailed in the course of trade and must have become established as a distinctive sign identifying the products of a particular manufacturer. This requirement refers to a level of use which is higher than mere and simple use in the course of trade. So, the essence of the law is that acquisition of rights over company names and distinctive titles are easier than acquisition of rights over signs identifying goods or services themselves. Use in the course of trade is usually defined to be any use which is genuine and actual, even if the level of such use is not high and even it has not resulted to a high degree of cognizance or awareness of the respective company name. It suffices in that it is not a merely immaterial, or spontaneous use, or a use which is not real and actual, but is only veiled, i.e., someone is only creating a false impression of use and is only pretending that he/she is using it, e.g., by making a spontaneous advertisement or so. However, the requirement of becoming established in the course of trade does not amount to reputation or fame. The level of awareness required is substantially lower than this.

493. Loss of rights over company names and other non-registered distinctive signs normally occurs when the business enterprises cease trading, that is when use in the course of trade ceases. This is a factual matter. In many cases interruption of trading is only temporary; if it can be proved that there is a serious intent to resume

491. For example, the term 'MOTOR OIL' has been considered to lack distinctiveness and hence not to be able to enjoy protection as a company name: SMCFI of Athens 3213/1988, *EEmpD* 1988, 353. Moreover, the term 'THE SHEEPFOLD OF PELOPONESE' has also been regarded to lack distinctiveness and not to be able to be protected under Art. 13: CA of Athens 799/1988, *EEmpD* 1989, 502. Similarly, AP 1529/2008, unreported, which held that the term 'LASER' is not distinctive as a company name used in connection to beauty parlour services.

business, rights are not lost. Similarly, in some cases, company names and other distinctive signs have developed a certain level of reputation (fame). So long as reputation remains, even after the use has ceased, rights are not lost. Again, this is a factual matter.

494. Transfer of rights over company names and other non-registered distinctive signs can take place only in combination with transfer of the respective business. This is one of the major differences among registered trademarks and other non-registered distinctive signs. This requirement is not expressly provided in the law but is introduced by legal theory and interpretation of Article 13 of L. 146/1914. Save this requirement, the assignment is not subject to any particular formalities and does not need to be in writing.

§4. Remedies and Defences

495. The remedies in case of infringement of non-registered distinctive signs are: (a) a cease-and-desist order and (b) compensation for any damages incurred. Proof of damage or loss of profits is particularly difficult and due to this it is only rarely sought in practice. Instead of this, usually psychological (moral) damages are sought. However, in such a case one has to prove that the legal entity whose rights have been infringed has suffered some frustration in respect of its reputation toward its clientele and potential customers. A cease-and-desist order is granted irrespective of any fault on the part of the defendant; so, good faith on the part of the defendant is not a proper and valid defence, because what is more important is to avoid confusion, which is to the detriment of consumers. In connection to damages (or psychological damages) though, fault, at least in the form of negligence, is required. The law provides that the defendant is liable for damages if he was aware, or could be aware, that use on his/her part could possibly result in confusion. Infringement under Article 13 also qualifies as a criminal offence; so the defendant will also be exposed to criminal liability. Finally, the law provides that the court has discretion to order the arrest of infringing goods and their destruction, as well as a public announcement of the judicial order in the press at the expense of the defendant. With the exception of damages, all the above remedies can be sought under ordinary proceedings, or under summary proceedings by way of an injunction. The latter is more common in practice.

496. All defences available against an unfair competition claim are also available against a claim for infringement of non-registered marks, i.e., company names, distinctive titles, etc. Such defences include the absence of use in the course of trade. This means that the claimant must have goodwill within the jurisdiction. This is of particular importance to foreign claimants. The requirement of goodwill in the jurisdiction applies to foreign company names as well, even under Article 8 of the Paris Convention. That is, Article 8 is not interoperated to do away with the goodwill in the jurisdiction requirement.

497. Another proper defence is the 'use of own name defence'. This may prove particularly important in case of distinctive signs, or company names, consisting of or including names of natural persons. If a company name consists of the name of a natural person, any other person with the same name will also be allowed to use it, save that it will be obliged to use it in a way that does not cause confusion. In practice, this usually means that he/she will have to supplement it by some additional term or other element that leads to adequate differentiation.

§5. Conflicts among Company Names and Trademarks

498. One of the major issues that repeatedly come up with the courts is conflicts among company names and trademarks.[492] The judgments of Greek courts on this matter are conflicting and it is difficult to identify a single line of reasoning among them. The main problem, on which courts have adopted different views, is whether, in assessing likelihood of confusion, one should take into account, or not, the comparison among the respective goods or services identified by the company name and trademark in question. Certain judgments[493] hold, in effect, that when company names are involved the respective goods or services identified by them are not taken into account in assessing likelihood of confusion with conflicting trademarks, other company names, or non-registered distinctive signs. One of the results to which this view leads is that, when a company name is used, which is identical or similar to an earlier registered trademark, there is always a trademark infringement, even if the company name is used in a type of business which is totally different from the goods or services identified by the earlier trademark. Moreover, a later trademark will always infringe an earlier company name, in the same way. The justification for this is that Article 13 of L. 146/1914, which is the legal ground for the protection of non-registered distinctive signs, differs from Article 1 of the same law in that it does not included a requirement that a competitive relationship should exist among the claimant and the defendant in an unfair competition claim. It is submitted that this line of argumentation is wrong. Although, Article 13 does not include an express requirement for a competitive relationship, such a requirement is, by definition, innate to the concept of likelihood of confusion, on which Article 13 is based.[494] Other court judgments follow this later view on likelihood of confusion and conclude that similar company names are not infringing one another if they are used in different sectors and different types of business enterprises.[495]

499. Another issue on which Greek jurisprudence is not clear is whether it is possible to apply Article 6(1) of Directive 2008/95 in a situation of conflict among a company name and an earlier trademark. Article 6(1) is titled 'Limitation of the effects of a trade mark' and reads:

492. For a detailed discussion *see* Ch. Chrissanthis, *Conflicts among Company Names and Trademarks in the Jurisprudence of the Greek Courts and of the ECJ*, in *Studies in Honor of N.K. Rokas*, 1322, 1333 (Athens 2012 (in Greek)).
493. *See* AP 197/1989, *EEmpD* 1989, 496, CA of Athens 4543/1997, *DEE* 1997, 149.
494. Ch. Chrissanthis, *supra* n. 493 at 1333.
495. AP 1445/1997, *EEmpD* 1998, 378.

> The trade mark shall not entitle the proprietor to prohibit a third party from using, in the course of trade: (a) his own name or address; ... (c) the trade mark where it is necessary to indicate the intended purpose of a product or service, in particular as accessories or spare parts; provided he uses them in accordance with honest practices in industrial or commercial matters.

It is suggested that the limitation of trademark rights provided under Article 6.1 can apply in a conflict among a company name and a trademark, in the sense that a company name is not used as a trademark, i.e., it is not used to identify goods or services; instead, it is used in order to identify the business enterprise itself. So, what is suggested is that there is no likelihood of confusion, due to the different operation of a company name and a trademark, i.e., the former identifying the business entity itself and the latter the goods or services. This argument has been applied particularly in case that the 'own name' defence was applicable, i.e., in cases where the earlier trademark consisted of, or included, the name of a natural person and another person with the same name used his/her own name as a company name. Some court judgments have indeed reasoned that likelihood of confusion is avoided in such a situation, because of the different function of company names and trademarks and formulated this reasoning through limitation of trademark rights under Article 6(1) of Directive 2008/95.[496] Again, it is suggested that this reasoning is wrong and that the different function of company names and trademarks cannot, by itself, justify absence of likelihood of confusion in any case.[497] The 'own name' defence is a rather different issue and such matters usually result in the right of a person to use its own name in the course of trade, subject to an obligation to add a supplementary element that prohibits likelihood of confusion.

In an important recent case relating to conflicts among personal names and trademarks the Greek courts applied the 'own name defence'. The facts of the case are very interesting: In 1971 Mr P.G. Nikas founded the legal entity 'P.G. Nikas SA', a sausages and cold cuts manufacturer. He has been its controlling shareholders and general managers until about the end of 2003 when he sold his shares and left the company. By that time 'P.G. Nikas SA' had become a leader in the local market and the word mark 'NIKAS' had developed substantial reputation and fame. The legal entity had registered in its name a number of national and Community trademarks consisting in the personal name 'P.G. Nikas' and 'NIKAS'. The shares sale and purchase agreement provided that Mr Nikas would be able to continue carrying on a sausages and cold cuts business through another legal entity he controlled (Brelle SA), provided he would not cause any deception to consumers. As a matter of fact, Brelle SA, under the management and control of Mr Nikas carried on such business until about the end of 2012. At that time, Brelle was renamed to 'Lakoniki SA'. By the end of 2012 Mr Nikas entered into a licence agreement with 'Lakoniki SA' and granted it a licence to use his personal name in sausages and cold cuts produced under his personal supervision and with his own recipe. 'Lakoniki SA' introduced a new series of such sausages and cold cuts. The labels of the new products bore the

496. AP 1131/1995, *EEmpD* 1996, 169, CA of Athens, 866/2004, *EllDni* 2005, 644, AP 330/2007, *DEE* 2007, 913.

497. Ch. Chrissanthis, *supra* n. 493 at 1337.

marks 'Lakoniki', 'L' the initial letter of Lakoniki, as well a number of geographical terms, such as SPARTI, MISTRAS, TAIGETOS, PARORI, etc. The labels also bore certain drawings and other pictorial elements, as well as colours quite different than the red and white colours which were heavily used by 'P.G. Nikas SA'. At the bottom of the label, there appeared the slogan 'With recipe and care of Panagiotis Nikas' in special calligraphic lettering in italics and with fonts substantially smaller than the fonts of other word elements like 'Lakoniki' and the above-mentioned geographical terms. 'P.G. Nikas SA' objected to the use of the slogan 'With recipe and care of Panagiotis Nikas' and alleged infringement of its earlier trademarks and company name on the grounds of likelihood of confusion and unfair advantage from its fame and reputation and sought a cease-and-desist order, as well as damages. Mr Nikas intervened in the proceedings in favour of 'Lakoniki SA' and counter-argued that he enjoyed a legal right to personality, which entitled him to use his personal name and that such right should prevail over earlier trademarks and company names. He also argued that this was a case where it was appropriate to apply the limitation of trademark right, provided under Article 6(1) of Directive 2008/95 EC on the harmonization of the laws on trademarks and Article 12(1) CTMR 207/2009. According to this argumentation, the use of the slogan 'With recipe and care of Panagiotis Nikas' was essential to inform consumers about the person who was responsible for the quality and the production of the goods, an aspect which is of great interest to consumers in case of goods for human consumption. Moreover, he argued that such use was in accordance with good morals in the respective customs of trade, because in designing the labels of 'Lakoniki SA' all reasonable precautions to avoid likelihood of confusion were taken, that is, 'Lakoniki' and the terms SPARTI, MISTRAS, TAIGETOS, PARORI, etc. were dominant, rather than the challenged slogan and the colours used in the labels were quite different than those used by 'P.G. Nikas SA'. On its part, 'Lakoniki SA' argued that likelihood of confusion was absent because the dominant elements on its labels (i.e., its company name Lakoniki, its initial letter 'L', geographical terms like SPARTI, MISTRAS, etc., and other drawings and pictorial elements) were different than the earlier rights invoked by 'P.G. Nikas SA'. The court found in favour of the defendant and accepted that there was ground for limitation of the earlier rights arising from the registered trademark and company name of 'P.G. Nikas SA'. The first instance court of Athens[498] reasoned there is ground for limitation of earlier trademark rights, in case of a natural person using his personal name in products produced under his personal supervision and according to a recipe provided by him. The earlier rights consisted in a legal entity's earlier trademarks and company name, which comprised of the personal name of the above-mentioned natural person. The natural person was the founder of the legal entity and has been its manager for a long time, but he had sold his participation and carried on his own business through another legal entity controlled by him.

498. MMCFI of Athens 5246/2014.

500. The same issues have been dealt with by the ECJ in three cases, namely *Robeco/Robelco,*[499] *Budweiser,*[500] and *Celine.*[501] In the first case the court reasoned that the law of the EU has not specifically dealt with conflicts among trademarks and other distinctive signs and that, hence, the matter is open to be governed by the national law of the Member States. In the other two cases, the court reasoned that conflicts among trademarks and company names may possibly trigger limitation of trademark rights under Article 6(1) of the Directive, but this is subject to very substantial conditions that must be examined by courts in each case. Such conditions involve, above all, the matter whether use of a trademark as a company name is considered to be in compliance with honest practices, under the particular circumstances of each case. This greatly depends on the volume of reputation the earlier trademark enjoys; if it is about an earlier trademark with reputation, its use would inevitably confer an unfair advantage and due to this it would be difficult to be in accordance with honest practices. Moreover, a mark used as a company name, which at the same time appears on the packaging of products, as the case will usually be, is not used as a company name alone; when the company name appears on products also, it is used as a trademark as well, i.e., identifying the origin of the respective goods. Again, under such circumstances, use could difficultly be in accordance with honest practices. Finally, the court has reasoned that a use would not be in accordance with honest practices if it created the false impression of cooperation or other links among different enterprises. So, the jurisprudence of the ECJ is rather favourable to trademark owners on the issue of conflicts with company names.

499. C-23/01, 21 Nov. 2002.
500. C-245/02, 16 Nov. 2004.
501. C-17/06, 11 Sept. 2007.

Chapter 6. Industrial Designs

Ch. Chrissanthis

§1. Sources of Law

501. Industrial designs have been recognized in Greece as independent intellectual property rights by virtue of L. 2417/1996 and PD 259/1997. Before these legislative instruments, industrial designs were not recognized as such, and legal protection could be granted only under the law of unfair competition and possibly under copyright law, although copyright usually requires a higher level of originality, than that found in industrial designs.

502. Greece is party to the Paris Convention (implemented by virtue of L. 213/1975), which refers to industrial designs in Article 5(5). Greece has also implemented the Hague Convention for International Registration of Designs dated 6 November 1925 and its supplement dated 28 November 1960 (implemented by L. 2417/1996). In addition, Greece has implemented the Locarno Convention for the International Classification of Designs (implemented by L. 2697/1999). The EU Directive 98/71 on industrial designs has been implemented by virtue of PD 161/2002, while the EU Regulations 6/2002 and 245/2002 on community designs are also applicable in Greece.

§2. Basic Principles

503. Industrial designs are deemed to be of some aesthetic value. However, they are not registered and protected for their aesthetic value as such; instead, the reason that they are protected is that they may contribute to the merchantability of certain products. As a result, a material prerequisite for their registration is that they are capable of being applied to certain products.

504. The EU Directive 1998/71 on industrial designs does not refer to aesthetic value as a prerequisite for registration. This caused a very long discussion in legal literature whether shapes, drawings and other types of designs are capable of being registered, even if they are deprived of any aesthetic value. The prevailing opinion in Greece is that a very basic aesthetic value is necessary for registration, although not specifically mentioned as such in the legislation. Designs that are of a functional nature are not capable of being registered either.

505. A minimum degree of novelty and individual character is also necessary to achieve registration, although the test and the criteria applied to access these prerequisites are rather relaxed and not strict.

506. Component parts destined to be incorporated in larger complex products are capable of being registered, only if they remain visible after being affixed to such larger products. So, e.g., machinery spare parts that are placed inside larger machines and are not visible are not allowed for registration as industrial designs.

507. The designs system in Greece is really a filing and not a registration system. This means that the certificate of registration granted is not binding on civil courts. Each time the owner of a registered design applies to a civil court seeking protection, the court will examine whether all the prerequisites for registration are in place.

508. The level of civil protection of industrial designs before the Greek civil courts is rather limited. The courts are usually very suspicious of exclusive rights granted through the designs registration system. Unless there is evident novelty and strong individual character the courts will refuse to grant an injunction or a cease-and-desist order, or damages under ordinary proceedings.

509. It is questionable whether copyright law can also be used for the protection of industrial designs. Although it is true that in a limited number of cases Greek courts applied copyright law in cases of industrial designs, the prevailing opinion is that designs do not involve the necessary level of originality which is required under copyright protection. Another argument is that copyright law can be applied in those designs that do involve a high level of originality; this argument suggests that some designs may incorporate important artistic elements and that such artistic elements could be separated from the design and enjoy additional protection under copyright law. Again, the prevailing view is that the concept of design is destined to be applied to mass production articles and that, in principle, it is difficult to find in such mass production articles artistic elements with a high level of originality like that required for copyright protection. Unlike copyright law, the law of unfair competition can be invoked for the protection of industrial designs.

Chapter 7. Protection of Topographies of Semiconductor Products

D. Kallinikou

§1. Sources and Legislation

510. The legal framework on the protection of topographies of semiconductor products is based on PD 45/1991 harmonizing the Council Directive 87/54/EEC of 16 December 1986, as complemented by the Council Decisions 87/532/EEC and 88/311/EEC. PD 45/1991 was amended and supplemented by PD 415/1995 in compliance with the above-mentioned Directive and Council Decisions 90/510/EEC, 93/17/EEC, 95/237/EC, 94/700/EC, and 94/828/EC. Article 53(3) and (4) of L. 3966/2011 harmonizing the national law on industrial property with Directive 2004/48 modified certain provisions of PD 45/1991 and, in particular, Article 17(1) and (3) concerning infringement.

511. In Greece the system of protection of topographies of semiconductor products is based on the Council Directive 87/54/EEC and on the L. 1733/1987 concerning technology transfer, invention and technological innovation.[502] The protection of topographies of integrated circuits is also regulated in Articles 35–38 of the TRIPS Agreement.[503]

§2. Subject Matter and Conditions of Protection

512. The subject matter of protection is the 'topography of a semiconductor product'. Semiconductors, commonly known as silicon or microchips are used to operate electronic equipment.[504]

513. In accordance with Article 2(b) of PD 45/1991 a 'topography of a semiconductor product' is 'a series of related images, however fixed or encoded, (i) representing the three-dimensional pattern of the layers of which a semiconductor product is composed and (ii) in which series every image includes the pattern or part of the pattern of a surface of the semiconductor product at any stage of its manufacture'.

514. According to Article 2(a) of PD 45/1991 'semiconductor product' is the final or intermediate form of any product (i) consisting of a body of material that

502. For the protection of topographies of semiconductor products *see* M. Marinos, *The Protection of Semiconductor Products*, 35 et seq. (Athens-Komotini 1991 (in Greek)), A. Liakopoulos, *supra* n. 35 at 138 et seq., B. Antonopoulos, *supra* n. 218 at 852 et seq., N. Rokas, *supra* n. 25 at 58.

503. It is to be noted that the Washington Treaty on Intellectual Property in respect of Integrated Circuits (1989) was never entered into force but was partly incorporated into the arrangements of the TRIPS Agreement.

504. IPR Helpdesk *Legal Protection of Topographies of Semiconductor Products*, www.ipr-helpdesk.org.

contains a layer of semiconductor material, and (ii) having one or more layers composed of conducting, insulating or semiconducting material, the layers being arranged in accordance with a predetermined three-dimensional pattern, and (iii) intended to perform electronic functions, either exclusively or together with other functions.

515. The protected subject matter is the topographical design and not the product itself. The topography of a semiconductor product is protected if it is the result of its creator's intellectual effort and is not commonplace in the semiconductor industry.[505] Topographies which consist of elements that are commonplace in the semiconductor industry can be protected only if the combination of such elements, as a total, fulfils the above-mentioned conditions. The protection of topography covers the mode of expression and is not extended to the principles, procedures, systems, technique, or encrypted information that may be integrated into the topography.[506]

§3. Formalities and Procedure for Obtaining Protection

516. In Greece the legislator followed the formalities system for the recognition of the topography protection. The right to file an application for registration[507] with the OBI[508] and to protection of topography belongs to: (a) natural persons who are nationals of a Member State of the EU or have their habitual residence on the territory of a Member State or of a Member State of the European Free Trade Association (EFTA), with the exception of Switzerland; (b) companies or other legal persons which have a real and effective industrial or commercial establishment on the territory of a Member State or a Member State of the EFTA, with the exception of Switzerland. The right to file an application belongs also to natural persons who are nationals or usually reside in certain third countries and to legal persons of these countries to the condition of reciprocity regarding Greek companies.[509]

517. According to Article 4(2) of PD 45/1991 the person who first files an application for registration is considered to be the creator of the topography. The vindication of the topography is relative to that of the Patent Law.[510] Special regulations are provided for the joint ownership of the topography,[511] as well as for topographies created by employees.[512]

518. Articles 9–12 of PD 45/1991 regulate the registration procedure. According to Article 9 whoever wishes to register a topography must submit an application

505. Article 3(1) of PD 45/1991.
506. Article 3(4) of PD 45/1991.
507. Article 6 (1) and (2) of PD 45/1991, as amended by PD 415/1995.
508. OBI is the Athens based Industrial Property Organization (L. 1733/1987).
509. Article 6(3) (a) and (b) of PD 45/1991, as amended by PD 415/1995.
510. Article 8 of PD 45/1991. *See also* A. Liakopoulos, *supra* n. 35 at 139.
511. Article 5 of PD 45/1991.
512. Article 7 of PD 45/1991.

to OBI, which must contain the full name, nationality, place, or residence or head office, a description of the topography, a statement regarding the date of the first non-confidential commercial exploitation of the topography when this date is earlier than the date of the registration application, an application for registration of the topography accompanied by the receipt of the topography transmission, and registration fee. If the application satisfies all the necessary conditions, it is accepted for submission, it is considered regular and a submission date is recorded in the register.

519. The following documents must be attached to the application:[513] the drawings or images to which the description refers, the material that constitutes a representative sample of the topography, the applicant's documents of legalization in the case of a legal or natural person who is not the creator.

520. Within the next two years from the first commercial exploitation of a topography, the creator must submit to OBI the application for registration of the topography. Otherwise, the application is deemed overdue, no date of registration is granted, and there are no rights to exclusiveness.[514]

521. Article 10 of PD 45/1991 regulates the secrecy of a topography if the applicant declares that this is a case of commercial secrecy. Article 11 deals upon the additional items the applicant must submit within ten months of the orderly deposition. In accordance to this provision, if, on expiry of this time limit, the OBI establishes that not all of the items have been submitted, the application is considered as not filed.

522. If the topography registration is complete and proper, OBI grants a registration certificate[515] for the topography of semiconductor products, without any previous control of the conditions of protection, on the applicant's responsibility. Any third party can ask for information and copies of the application and additional items concerning the protected topography. Items of the application are published in the Special Industrial Property Bulletin.

§4. Ownership and Transfer

523. In accordance with Article 4(1) of PD 45/1991 the right to the protection of the topography is given to the creator or the right holder as well as to their successors.

513. Article 9(2) of PD 45/1991.
514. Article 9(4) of PD 45/1991.
515. Article 12 of PD 45/1991.

524. If more than one person have jointly created the topography and provided there is no other agreement, the right is granted to all of them jointly.[516] Every joint owner can freely transfer his/her share and procure for the protection of the joint topography.

525. When topographies are created during an employment relationship,[517] the right to protection is granted to the creator's employer, if there is no opposing contractual regulation between the employee and the employer. In the event that topographies are created on a contract which is not an employment contract, the right to protection is granted to the party who has the order for topography, if there is no opposing contractual regulation. In any case the creator's name is mentioned in the registration certificate and the creator has the right to demand protection from the applicant or his/her recognition as the creator from the holder of the certificate.

526. The right to register a topography and the rights to exclusiveness deriving from the protected topography can be transferred by a written agreement, or inherited.[518] The transfer takes place from the registration of the agreement or the inheritance certificate to the register of topographies and is published in the Special Industrial Property Bulletin. The compulsory licence of a topography is permitted according to Articles 13 and 14 of L. 1733/1987 applied *mutatis mutandis.*

§5. Scope of Exclusive Rights and Limitations of the Scope of Protection

527. The creator of a protected topography has the exclusive but time-limited right to permit or prohibit the reproduction of topographies and the commercial exploitation[519] or import of topography or of a semiconductor product manufactured by using the protected topography.[520]

528. The creator of the protected topography cannot prohibit the following actions: (a) the private reproduction or use of a topography for non-commercial purposes; (b) the reproduction of a topography for the purposes of analysing, evaluating, or teaching the principles, procedures, systems, or techniques that are integrated in the topographies or the topographies themselves.[521]

516. Article 5 of PD 45/1991.
517. For topographies created by employees *see* Art. 7 of PD 45/1991, as amended by Art. 3 of PD 415/1995.
518. Article 15 of PD 45/1991.
519. According to Art. 2(c) of PD 45/1991 'commercial exploitation' does not include exploitation under conditions of confidentiality to the extent that no further distribution to third parties occurs, unless the exploitation of a topography occurs under the conditions of confidentiality for the protection of the essential interests of State security which are connected with the production or trade of arms, munitions and war material in accordance with the provisions of Art. 223(1)(b) of the EEC Treaty.
520. Article 13(1) of PD 45/1991.
521. Article 13(2) of PD 45/1991.

529. The person who exploits commercially a semiconductor product or a topography and did not know or did not have reasonable grounds to believe that the product or the topography are protected by a right to exclusiveness is entitled to continue such commercial exploitation.[522] The right holder may claim a reasonable compensation against actions committed after the person exploiting the topography or the semiconductor product has become aware of the topography right.[523]

§6. Duration of Protection

530. The exclusive rights are limited in time. According to Article 14 of PD 45/1991 the exclusive right starts to apply on the day after that application for registration of the topography was properly submitted to OBI. Whenever the date of topography's first commercial exploitation follows the date mentioned above, the exclusive right applies on the date of the first commercial exploitation. The term of protection is ten years after the end of the calendar year in which the topography was first commercially exploited, anywhere in the world, or after the end of the calendar year in which the proper registration application was submitted to OBI. The exclusive rights come to an end if the topography has not been commercially exploited, anywhere in the world, within fifteen years from the date of the first fixation or encoding.

531. The exclusive right to topography ceases with its declaration as null[524] and void by court order if: (a) the holder of the certificate of the protected topography is not the creator or the transferee or the entitled person in accordance with Article 7 (topographies created by employees); (b) the topography is not entitled to protection under Article 3; (c) the application for registration of the topography is submitted after the expiry of the time limit set out in Article 9(4); (d) the depositor of the application for registration does not belong to the category of persons entitled to register the topography according to Article 6.

§7. Infringement and Remedies

532. Civil protection is relative to that granted of patents and in certain cases the provisions of L. 1733/1987 are accordingly applied.[525] According to Article 17(1) of PD 45/1991, as replaced by Article 53(3) of L. 3966/201, in case of infringement

522. Article 13(5) of PD 45/1991.
523. Article 13(6) of PD 45/1991.
524. Article 16 of PD 45/1991.
525. Article 17(3) of PD 45/1991, as replaced by Art. 53(4) of L. 3966/2011: The provisions of Art. 17(3), (4), (5), (6) and (7) of Art. 17 of L. 1733/1987, as well as Arts 17(A)–17(F) of this law as amended, are accordingly applied.

or threatened infringement of an exclusive right deriving from the protected topography, the right holder may request suspension of the infringement and the omission in the future. The right holder may also exercise these rights against intermediaries whose services are used by a third party to infringe the topography rights.

533. The suspension of the infringement may include, on application by the right holder, indicatively and not restrictively: (a) the recall of the goods that were found to be infringing a topography right and, as in appropriate cases, materials principally used in the creation or manufacture of these goods from the channels of the commerce; (b) the definitive removal of these goods from the channels of commerce; or (c) the destruction of these goods and materials. In considering the application of the previous clause, the need for proportionality between the seriousness of the infringement and the remedies ordered, as well as the interests of third parties, shall be taken into account. It is to be noted that the above-mentioned measures are carried out at the expenses of the infringer unless particular reasons are invoked for not doing so.

534. In case of intentional infringement, the plaintiff is entitled to demand the restitution of the damage or return of the benefit deriving from the illicit exploitation of the protected topography or payment of a sum corresponding to the value of the licence.[526] The rights set out in the above paragraph are also recognized in respect of any person who has reason to believe that the topography is protected if a third party reproduces, commercially exploits or imports it in bad faith.[527]

§8. Overlapping and Relation to Other Intellectual Property Laws

535. Protection of topographies according to other legal provisions is not excluded. However, protection of topographies under the terms of provisions concerning intellectual property does not apply in the case of topographies that have been created after the entry into force of PD 45/1991.[528] The provisions concerning the protection of topographies do not affect the implementation of any other provisions concerning industrial property.[529]

526. Article 17(2) of PD 45/1991.
527. Article 17(2) of PD 45/1991.
528. Article 18(2) of PD 45/1991.
529. Article 18(1) of PD 45/1991.

Chapter 8. Unfair Competition

Ch. Chrissanthis

536. Among the various fields of intellectual property law, the law of unfair competition is the less harmonized and more country-unique. Save for Article 10*bis* of the Paris Convention, there are no other provisions of any international treaty attempting to set uniform standards for the law of unfair competition.

§1. A Comparative Approach

537. There are countries, like France, where the law of unfair competition derives mainly from the general principles of civil law, while in other countries, like Germany, the law of unfair competition derives from specific legislation on this matter. In other countries, particularly in the UK, a more close equivalent of unfair competition law, the law of passing off, has been developed through the courts, irrespective of any legislative developments. The English law of passing off, however, has very little in common with the law of unfair competition, as the latter is developed in continental Europe. The former is mainly oriented towards protection of goodwill, associated with non-registered distinctive marks, while the latter has a broader scope of protection, which exceeds protection of non-registered distinctive signs. Even with respect to the protection of non-registered marks, what is protected under the English law of passing off are not the marks as such, but only the goodwill (the power to attract customers and generate sales) associated and attached to such marks; in addition, what triggers legal protection is deception. On the contrary, in continental Europe non-registered marks are protected as such under the law of unfair competition and what triggers protection is likelihood of confusion.

538. The Greek law of unfair competition is very much similar to German law. There is a specific law regarding unfair competition, L. 146/1914, one of the oldest laws in the country that are still applicable. It is noteworthy that this law has received only limited amendments and most of its provisions remain in force unchanged from the date they were enacted.

539. An issue that has been much discussed in legal literature is the justifying reason behind the law of unfair competition, or, in other words, what is the true subject matter of protection in this field of law. One view, which is the most traditional one, identifies the private interests of merchants as the subject matter of protection. It is merchants that the law of unfair competition is destined to protect against unfair and unethical practices employed by their competitors. Another view holds that consumers' interests are also among the subject matter of protection and that the provisions of this field of law should be interpreted in view of consumers' interests also. According to another approach, the purpose of unfair competition law is to secure freedom of competition; this view holds that the law of free competition and the law of unfair competition are not conflicting one another but are, instead, supplementary and that the law of unfair competition should be interpreted in view of the targets set by antitrust law. Although this last approach has received much support[530] in legal literature, it is the first view that remains the prevailing one in court jurisprudence.[531]

540. Another issue much discussed in legal literature with respect to unfair competition law is whether consumer associations should be allowed to invoke, or not, the provisions of unfair competition law. In Greece, consumer associations have not been granted such *locus standi* in unfair competition cases; however, merchants associations, like chambers of commerce, do enjoy such *locus standi* (Article 10 of L. 146/1914).

541. The law of unfair competition is part of the law of torts. There are, though, certain substantial peculiarities and deviations from the ordinary principles of the law of torts. For example, in unfair competition law, proof of actual damage is not necessary in order to seek for a cease-and-desist order; likelihood of damage would suffice, while proof of actual damage is necessary only in order to seek compensation. Similarly, at least with respect to protection of distinctive non-registered marks (under Article 13 of L. 146/1914), fault is not a prerequisite in order to seek for a cease-and-desist order and it is necessary only if the claimant wishes to claim damages.

§2. Basic Principles of Law 146/1914

542. Article 1 of L. 146/1914 contains a general clause (a general principle of law) prohibiting competitive acts in the course of trade that are contrary to good morals. Good morals stand for honest commercial practices. There are four prerequisites that must be fulfilled so that Article 1 comes into operation: (a) There must be an act which can objectively reinforce the competitive position of the defendant against his competitors (a competitive act); from this requirement it is derived that there must be some competitive relationship among the claimant and the defendant, that is, they must be competing against one another. (b) There must be intent on the part of the defendant; such intent has to be addressed towards enforcing his position in the market as a competitor. Intent should not necessarily be addressed towards causing damage to the claimant; it suffices that the purpose of the defendant is to be in a better position with respect to his competitors. (c) The act in question must be contrary to good commercial morals, that is, contrary to honest practices that are customary in the respective market. The test as to honest practices is an objective one. The concept of honest practices appears in Article 10*bis* of the Paris Convention, as well as in Article 6(1) of the Trademarks Harmonization Directive 89/104

530. Ch. Chrissanthis, *supra* n. 493 at. 233.
531. N. Rokas, *supra* n. 25 at 181.

EU, now 2008/95 EU, as well as in Article 12 of the Community Trademark Regulation 40/1994 EU, now 207/2009 EU. (d) Finally, the act in question must be committed in the course of trade. Although this requirement initially restricted unfair competition law to merchants only,[532] the view that professionals like accountants, lawyers, artists, physicians, architects, etc., are also covered has progressively become the prevailing one.[533]

543. Article 3 of L. 146/1914 contains a general clause against misleading advertising and misleading representations in the course of trade. This article has been supplemented by the EU legislation on misleading advertising, i.e., Directives 2006/114 EU and 2005/29 EU. It is worth mentioning that Directive 2006/114 EU applies to business to business relationships and deals with misleading and comparative advertising while Directive 2005/29 EU on unfair trade practices applies to business to consumers relationships and deals with many practices that are considered to be contrary to good morals, including misleading, unfair, and aggressive advertising.

544. Article 13 of L. 146/1914 deals with non-registered distinctive signs and is the legal provision granting protection to marks that are not registered as trademarks. Unlike Article 1, it does not require intent of any form. It is not required that the claimant and the defendant be competitors either, although it requires likelihood of confusion and in assessing likelihood of confusion one has to take into account whether the respective goods or services are directly or indirectly competing against one another, although this is a materially different issue than establishing a competitive relationship between the claimant and the defendant. Article 13 grants exclusive rights over distinctive marks that have been used in the course of trade. Marks that are not inherently distinctive can only be protected if they have developed a secondary meaning through acquired distinctiveness; this would require evidence of a greater level of use and advertisement in the course of trade.

545. Much of the law on unfair competition has been developed through legal literature and the courts on a case by case basis. In particular, legal commentators and the courts have identified many different forms of unfair commercial practices by assessing good morals and honest practices, such as:

(a) Exploitation of another's reputation (i.e., unauthorized use of famous marks).
(b) Misappropriation of another's work, achievement, methods, and system of organization (including slavish imitation of products/achievements not protected by specific intellectual property law provisions, know-how, etc.).
(c) Destructing business reputation (i.e., defamation).
(d) Deceptive advertising, emotional advertising, excessively aggressive and annoying advertising.
(e) Intrusion into another's business activity, i.e., by way of soliciting employees, or clients, or threatening to sue, etc.

532. SMCFI of Athens 8011/1992, *EEmpD* 1992, 670.
533. CA of Larisa 730/2008, *EllDni* 2009, 1443.

(f) Violation of laws and contractual obligations.
(g) Intrusion with trade secrets of competitors.

546. The first two types, i.e., exploitation of another's reputation and misappropriation of another's work, require, on the one hand, confusion as to origin (hence, confusion as to products/achievements as such is usually not actionable) and, on the other, a certain level of either distinctiveness or originality. It is worth mentioning that it is easier to establish exploitation of reputation (unfair resemblance to a famous mark, where dilution due to loss of licensing opportunities can easily be argued), while it is more difficult to establish misappropriation (slavish imitation) of products, where confusion must be not only as to the products themselves but as to origin (source).

§3. Remedies and Defences

547. The basic remedy is a cease-and-desist order. This can be obtained through ordinary proceedings or through summary proceedings for an injunction. Damages can also be claimed if the specific volume can be substantiated, which involves great difficulties as to evidence. The law does not provide any criteria for the quantification of damages as in other fields of law, i.e., in case of copyright infringement. Due to the difficulties of proof as to the volume of damages, a claim for psychological (moral) damages is usually raised. Its volume is assessed by the court on discretion, however, taking into account the financial condition of the parties, the type of fault involved in the case, i.e., intent or negligence, the volume of the frustration caused, the impact on consumers and competition, as well as all other surrounding circumstances. In court practice the volume of psychological damages awarded usually varies from EUR 10,000 to EUR 30,000. Certain acts of unfair competition may also result in criminal sanctions.

548. There are certain time limitations with respect to civil claims for unfair competition. These are set by Article 19 of L. 146/1914. The time bar for a cease-and-desist order is eighteen months as from the date the claimant became aware of the infringing act and of the party behind it; however, a cease-and-desist order cannot be sought if five years from the act have lapsed. For a claim in damages the limitation period is five years as from the date that damage arose. The most common problem in court practice in relation to time limitation of actions is that the acts of unfair competition are usually repeated, i.e., they are not momentous but lasting. So, the legal issue that arises is whether the time limitation period commences when the first or the last infringing act took place. The prevailing view in court jurisprudence is that it is the first infringing act that is material in terms of time bars;[534] in legal literature, though, the opposite view is much supported.[535]

534. AP 700/1977, *NoV* 1978, 371, 12670/1989, *EEmpD* 1990, 720, 1285/2005, *EEmpD* 2005, 818.
535. N. Rokas, *supra* n. 25 at 229.

549. The claimant in an unfair competition legal action (or application for injunction) must carry on business in Greece (Article 23 of L. 146/1914). Due to this requirement, foreign entities without a local operation may be hindered from invoking unfair competition law.

§4. Endorsing and Merchandising

550. Endorsing of products by celebrities in the context of advertisement and character merchandising are among the more controversial issues regarding the applicability of the law of unfair competition. Celebrity endorsement refers to the idea that certain persons or entities, usually celebrities enjoying reputation either for their likeness (i.e., athletes, singers, actors), or for their assumed expertise in certain matters (i.e., a well know scientist), are supporting, or are somehow associated with certain goods or services. Endorsing, in this sense, is a form of advertisement. Character merchandising refers to the idea that certain fictional characters that are well-known from the cinema, etc. (e.g., cartoons like Mickey Mouse) are used in advertisements to promote products or services. The idea is that the likeness and consumer awareness attached to certain fictitious characters is used to promote certain goods or services.

551. There is a difference in the way celebrity endorsement and character merchandising cases are treated by the courts. Character merchandising cases can prove more difficult for the claimants when the defendant uses only the name of a famous fictional character and not the picture of the character. The picture of the character will usually be copyrighted, and when copyright is available it will easier to establish an infringement. However, when only the name is used, if such name has not been registered as a trademark it is questionable whether the name itself deserves legal protection under the law of unfair competition. The reason is that the name of a fictional character cannot function as an indication of origin since it does not refer to the manufacturer of the product or the creator of the fictional character. So, it will be extremely difficult to establish likelihood of confusion as this is basically understood as confusion as to origin, and the name of a fictional character used as an advertising support does not refer to any source of origin.

552. With respect to celebrity endorsement, it is worth mentioning that under Greek law there is a separate absolute right to personality. This is of great assistance in establishing a valid claim against unauthorized use of a celebrity's name or picture in advertising. In this context, under Greek law, the reputation accompanying a celebrity can enjoy legal protection even in the absence of goodwill and even in the absence of a competitive relationship with the infringer. However, celebrities may encounter difficulties to prove that they have suffered damages due to unauthorized use of their name or picture by a manufacturer of products in the context of advertisement; such damages will usually consist of loss of profits, or loss of licensing opportunities, or dilution. Moreover, they will encounter difficulties to establish a competitive relationship with the defendant manufacturer. Courts, however, are becoming increasingly cognizant of modern endorsing and merchandising techniques and, in most cases, will use the right to personality to overcome such difficulties raised by the traditional theory of unfair competition law. There is, though, a concern that protection of reputation alone may be superfluous and unnecessary in certain cases and may lead to excessive restraints of free competition; for example, an abuse of the absolute right to personality may result in a celebrity being able to prohibit any use of his or her name by anybody in any context, even irrespective to any advertising and marketing promotion, and even in the context of private use, or parody, or public commenting.

553. Another problem relating to damages in celebrity endorsement and character merchandising cases is that the amount of damages awarded are usually equal to a licence fee that would otherwise have been agreed on, had the defendant asked for the claimant's licence. This means that the defendant has no real motive to seek the authorization of the claimant and to avoid litigation, in the sense that he/she can make an attempt to use the reputation of the claimant without his authorization and in case of litigation he/she will pay the licence fee which he/she would have paid in any case; so he/she has no motive to risk being involved in litigation.

554. In a pure unfair competition context (i.e., irrespective of the right to personality), establishing a valid claim in connection to unauthorized celebrity endorsing or character merchandising would require either an act contrary to honest commercial practices under Article 1 or a misleading representation under Article 3, or likelihood of confusion due to unauthorized use of a name under Article 13, provided, however, that in the latter case such name has been used in the course of trade and has become a distinctive sign as well. In all these cases, what is usually necessary is to prove a misrepresentation associated with the unauthorized use of the name, or the picture of a celebrity or a fiction character. Such misrepresentation may consist in falsely implying that the sponsor supports or recommends the defendant's products with his expertise, likeness, reputation, or just with the glamour accompanying him/her. In case of character merchandising the misrepresentation may consist in that the defendant falsely purports to offer another's copyrighted work under a licence, while he/she truly provides his/her own work which is a different thing.

555. Another approach to celebrity endorsement and character merchandising in the context of unfair competition law is that unauthorized use of the name or the picture of a celebrity or a fictitious character qualifies as an unfair exploitation of another's reputation. In this context, the unauthorized use of a third party's reputation and likeliness is contrary to honest commercial practices. Still, though a major problem is that confusion as to origin must be established and not any type of confusion with reference to any matter.

§5. 'Look Alike' Products, Products Get-Up and Trade Dress

556. The law of unfair competition is usually employed to obtain legal protection in connection with the product's overall appearance (get-up, trade dress), its colour combinations, its design, etc. A legal action based on unfair competition in such cases is useful particularly when the overall appearance of the product is not protected under any specific intellectual property laws, i.e., when the packaging has not been registered as a trademark, or when the artistic elements of the packaging (e.g., colour combinations and designs) are not covered by copyright. If there are such specific intellectual property rights in connection to the product get-up, legal protection can be obtained on this basis. However, in the absence of such specific rights, a legal action based on unfair competition is the only available remedy.

557. The idea that imitating the overall appearance of another product is based on the idea that this is contrary to honest commercial practices and that it qualifies either as exploitation of another's reputation or as misappropriation of another's work and achievement. In connection to the former approach, it is worth mentioning that Article 13 of L. 146/1914 expressly states that the product get-up (product trade dress and overall appearance) may constitute a distinctive sign.

558. One problem usually associated with such 'look alike' cases is that the claimant has to establish that the product and packaging get-up elements that are copied are distinctive to him/her only. This means that the claimant has to prove that such elements are distinctive as such, or that they have become distinctive through use in the course of trade and in addition to this that they are distinctive of his own products only, i.e., that they are not used by other competitors. In connection with these issues one has to point out that artistic elements, such as colour combinations, designs, etc., are not necessary and are not always distinctive. In most cases such artistic elements are not characteristic of the respective product, i.e., it is not such elements that identifies the product to consumers; instead, the product is identified by way of its trademark or brand name. So, artistic elements are distinctive only if they function as indications of origin, or quality, or if they have an advertising power. Furthermore, in many cases artistic elements, such as colour combinations, drawing, designs, etc., are characteristic of a whole class of products and not of specific products; for example, household appliances usually come in white colour while whisky usually come in light brown colour.

559. The jurisprudence of the Greek courts on the matter should not be regarded as reliable as it lacks predictability and judgments are sometimes conflicting to one another. This is mainly because such cases have been decided on the basis of the 'overall impression doctrine' and on the basis of their respective facts, which are always particular to each case. Below is a brief discussion of some indicative cases which provide a general idea of the attitude and approach of the Greek courts on product get-up and trade dress problems.

560. The 'Petro gas' liquid gas case: The subject matter of this case was whether legal protection could be granted in connection with the colour of the product's packaging (i.e., liquid gas cylinders for home use in blue colour). There seems to be no positive precedent from Greek civil courts in favour of protection of colour as such (i.e., colour alone, not taking into account other figurative and pictorial elements or words) under either trademark or unfair competition law. On the contrary, the only case that seems to have dealt with this issue has been decided against the protection of colour alone. This was the case of 'Petro gas' liquid gas for home use, which was traded in blue collared cylinders and whose colour was copied by 'Vitom gas'. The plaintiff's legal action was rejected in both the first instance and the appeal court. The cassation court[536] reasoned that copying of colour should be assessed in the context of the 'overall impression' doctrine; in other words, the other figurative or word elements, as well as the overall packaging and appearance should also be taken into account in order to determine whether there is any likelihood of confusion or association, unfair resemblance or dilution. The court, however, noted that copying of the colour alone could suffice to establish likelihood of confusion if, on the evidence, it was found that it is the colour which is the prevailing element of the whole packaging and appearance of the product and if it could be proved that copying of the colour alone could attract the attention of consumers.

561. The slice toast bread case: This case was about the colour combinations of the packaging of a product. In this case the court found that one of the main elements copied by the defendant was the basic overall colour of the packaging. The court found that the basic overall colour was prevailing in the overall impression of the packaging. However, in this case, the defendant had also copied the colour combination as well as other figurative and word elements used by the plaintiff, and this may reasonably have had an impact on the final ruling of the court.[537]

562. Camper Twins Shoes case: In this case the court[538] granted trade dress protection under unfair competition law to the red packaging and design of 'Camper twins shoes'. It is important that the court emphasized that the red packaging of the shoes was characteristic for 'Camper twin shoes' and was, therefore, protected as such. Another important point in this judgment was that the court found that the red Camper packaging had become distinctive, due to intense advertisement, although it circulated in the market only for a short period of time (two years). However, in this case, again, the defendant had copied the Camper shoes design as well, and this may reasonably have had an impact on the final court's judgment.

563. The Toblerone case: This case related mainly to the shape of the product. Protection was granted to Toblerone's chocolate shape and packaging.[539] Although the word elements were different in the products compared and although certain pictorial elements were different as well, the court found that likelihood of confusion was established mainly due to the copying of the triangle shape of the product, which was found to be characteristic for Toblerone chocolate.

---

536. AP 399/1989, *EEmpD* 1990, 144.
537. SMCFI of Athens 1265/2005, *EEmpD* 2005, 628.
538. MMCFI of Athens 6778/2004, *EEmpD* 2005, 634.
539. MMCFI of Athens 1478/2005, unreported. For a similar judgment granting protection to the cylinder shape of delicatessen products on the grounds that it was the shape that was characteristic of the product *see* SMCFI of Volos 53/1984, *EEmpD* 1984, 357.

564. The Nescafe Classic case: Finally, Greek courts have granted legal protection to the NESCAFE CLASSIC overall packaging and colour combination that were copied by a competitor with a different word element (Golden Coffee).[540]

§6. Trademarks and Unfair Competition

565. The traditional view was that the law of unfair competition is not applicable to registered trademarks and that the latter are protected exclusively by the trademark legislation alone; the law on trademarks is more specific on the matter and excludes the application of the law on unfair competition.[541] This view has been abandoned, however, and the approach currently prevailing in court practice is that the law on unfair competition is supplementary to trademark law, since both fields of law serve the same needs and support the same interests. So, a claimant trademark owner can invoke both trademark legislation and the law on unfair competition.[542]

566. There are, though, certain material differences among trademark law and the law on unfair competition that are worth mentioning. The most basic difference is that in a legal action based on trademark law, likelihood of confusion is assessed on the basis of the trademark filed, irrespective of how it is used in practice and irrespective of additional elements that might accompany the trademark in the packaging of the product; on the contrary, in a legal action based on unfair competition law, likelihood of confusion is assessed on the basis of the overall appearance of the respective products, that is, all the word and pictorial elements of the product and its packaging need to be taken into account. This means that, depending on the circumstances of each case, an action on trademark law may be preferable to the trademark owner instead of an action for unfair competition and vice versa. Usually, trademark law allows manufacturers to isolate specific word or pictorial elements and seek legal protection for such elements as such.

567. Moreover, an action for unfair competition requires proof of use in the course of trade, while an action based on trademark law requires only to produce to the court a certificate of registration.

568. Finally, foreign claimants without a business presence in Greece may find it more convenient to file a legal action based in trademark law since a legal action for unfair competition is inadmissible, unless the claimant has a business operation within the jurisdiction.

540. CA of Athens 1687/2004, *EEmpD* 2005, 623.
541. AP 608/1953, *EEN* vol. KA, 165.
542. AP 1254/1994, *DEE* 1995, 389.

Selected Bibliography

Antonopoulos, B. *Industrial Property*. Athens-Thessaloniki, 2005 (in Greek).
Argyriadis, A. *Patent*. Athens, 1985 (in Greek).
Chrissanthis, Ch. *Exhaustion of Intellectual Property Rights and Parallel Imports*. Athens, 2012 (in Greek).
Kallinikou, K. *Copyright and Related Rights*. Athens, 2008 (in Greek).
Kotsiris, L. *Greek Copyright Law*. IUS, 2012.
Kotsiris, L. *Copyright Law and Acquis Communautaire*. Athens-Komotini, 2017 (in Greek).
Koumantos, G. *Copyright Law*. Athens-Komotini, 2002 (in Greek).
Liakopoulos, A. *Intellectual Property Law in Greece*. Kluwer Law International-Sakkoulas, 1999.
Liakopoulos, A. *Industrial Property*. Athens, 2000 (in Greek).
Lymperopoulos, K. *Patent Law*. Athens, 2010 (in Greek).
Marinos, M. *The Protection of Semiconductor Products*. Athens-Komotini, 1991 (in Greek).
Marinos, M. *Trademark Law*. Athens, 2007 (in Greek).
Mikroulea, Al. *Utility Models*. Athens, 1999 (in Greek).
Rokas, N. *Trademarks Law*. Athens, 1978 (in Greek).
Rokas, N. *Industrial Property*. Athens, 2011 (in Greek).
Simitis, K. *The Invention Right*. Athens, 1967 (in Greek).
Tzouganatos, D. *Competition Law*. Athens, 2013 (in Greek).

Selected Bibliography

Index

The numbers here refer to paragraph numbers.

Index

Index

Made in the USA
Monee, IL
18 October 2026

66037576R10122